ALL·NEW X·MEN

HELL HATH
SO MUCH FURY

COLLECTION EDITOR: **JENNIFER GRÜNWALD**
ASSISTANT EDITOR: **CAITLIN O'CONNELL**
ASSOCIATE MANAGING EDITOR: **KATERI WOODY**
EDITOR, SPECIAL PROJECTS: **MARK D. BEAZLEY**
VP PRODUCTION & SPECIAL PROJECTS: **JEFF YOUNGQUIST**
SVP PRINT, SALES & MARKETING: **DAVID GABRIEL**
BOOK DESIGNER: **JAY BOWEN**

EDITOR IN CHIEF: **AXEL ALONSO**
CHIEF CREATIVE OFFICER: **JOE QUESADA**
PUBLISHER: **DAN BUCKLEY**
EXECUTIVE PRODUCER: **ALAN FINE**

ALL-NEW X-MEN: INEVITABLE VOL. 3 — HELL HATH SO MUCH FURY. Contains material originally published in magazine form as ALL-NEW X-MEN #12-16. First printing 2017. ISBN# 978-1-302-90291-9. Published by MARVEL WORLDWIDE, INC., a subsidiary of MARVEL ENTERTAINMENT, LLC. OFFICE OF PUBLICATION: 135 West 50th Street, New York, NY 10020. Copyright © 2017 MARVEL No similarity between any of the names, characters, persons, and/or institutions in this magazine with those of any living or dead person or institution is intended, and any such similarity which may exist is purely coincidental. **Printed in Canada.** ALAN FINE, President, Marvel Entertainment; DAN BUCKLEY, President, TV, Publishing & Brand Management; JOE QUESADA, Chief Creative Officer; TOM BREVOORT, SVP of Publishing; DAVID BOGART, SVP of Business Affairs & Operations, Publishing & Partnership; C.B. CEBULSKI, VP of Brand Management & Development, Asia; DAVID GABRIEL. SVP of Sales & Marketing, Publishing; JEFF YOUNGQUIST, VP of Production & Special Projects; DAN CARR, Executive Director of Publishing Technology; ALEX MORALES, Director of Publishing Operations; SUSAN CRESPI, Production Manager; STAN LEE, Chairman Emeritus. For information regarding advertising in Marvel Comics or on Marvel.com, please contact Vit DeBellis, Integrated Sales Manager, at vdebellis@marvel.com. For Marvel subscription inquiries, please call 888-511-5480. **Manufactured between 12/30/2016 and 2/6/2017 by SOLISCO PRINTERS, SCOTT, QC, CANADA.**

10 9 8 7 6 5 4 3 2 1

ALL·NEW X·MEN

HELL HATH SO MUCH FURY

DENNIS HOPELESS
WRITER

MARK BAGLEY
PENCILER

ANDREW HENNESSY
INKER

NOLAN WOODARD
COLORIST

VC's CORY PETIT
LETTERER

COVER ART: **MARK BAGLEY, ANDREW HENNESSY & NOLAN WOODARD**

CHRIS ROBINSON
ASSISTANT EDITOR

DANIEL KETCHUM
EDITOR

MARK PANICCIA
X-MEN GROUP EDITOR

X-MEN CREATED BY **STAN LEE** & **JACK KIRBY**

ALL·NEW X·MEN

THE **ALL-NEW X-MEN** HAVE LEARNED THE HARD WAY THAT IT WILL TAKE MORE THAN YOUTHFUL IDEALISM TO STEP OUT OF THE SHADOWS OF THEIR PREDECESSORS. AFTER A RUN-IN WITH THE BLOB, ANGEL AND WOLVERINE FIND THEIR RELATIONSHIP IN DIRE STRAITS. BEAST HAS SUFFERED YET ANOTHER FAILED ATTEMPT AT RETURNING THE TEAM TO THEIR RIGHTFUL TIME, DEMORALIZING EVAN IN THE PROCESS. AND AFTER BARELY ESCAPING A LIFE-THREATENING ASSAULT BY TOAD, CYCLOPS CONTINUES TO HEAL.

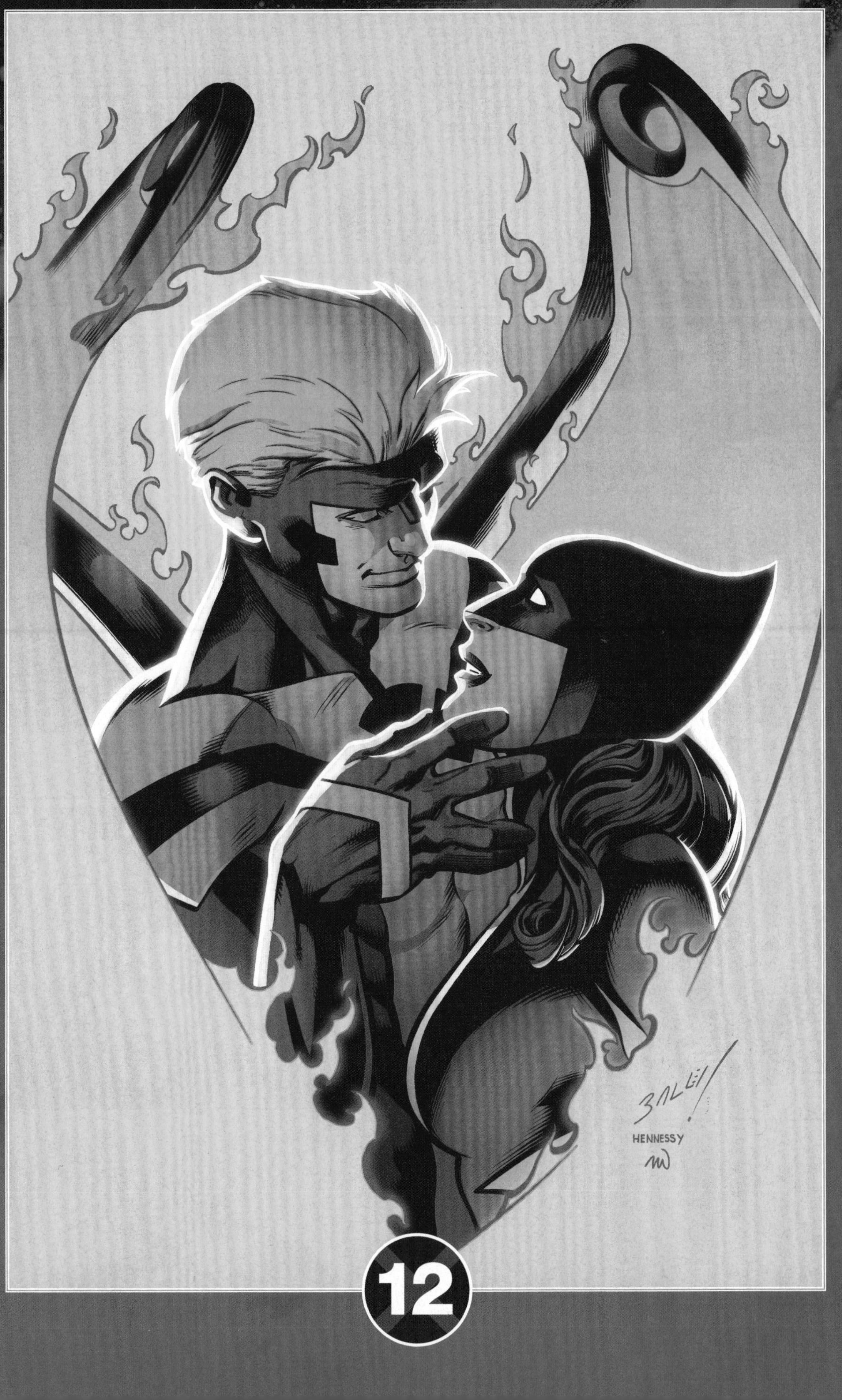
HENNESSY
12

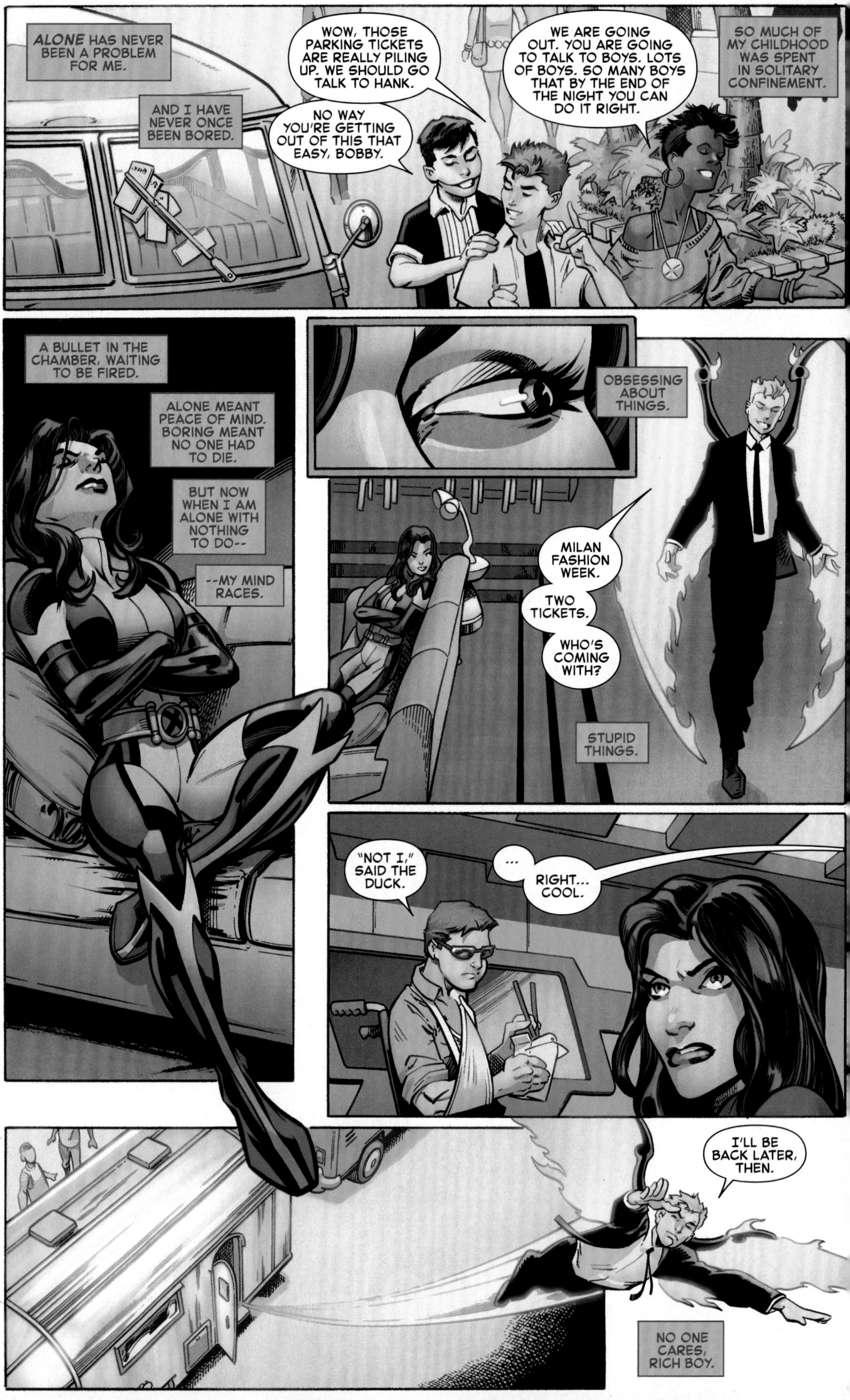

ALONE HAS NEVER BEEN A PROBLEM FOR ME.
AND I HAVE NEVER ONCE BEEN BORED.
WOW, THOSE PARKING TICKETS ARE REALLY PILING UP. WE SHOULD GO TALK TO HANK.
NO WAY YOU'RE GETTING OUT OF THIS THAT EASY, BOBBY.
WE ARE GOING OUT. YOU ARE GOING TO TALK TO BOYS. LOTS OF BOYS. SO MANY BOYS THAT BY THE END OF THE NIGHT YOU CAN DO IT RIGHT.
SO MUCH OF MY CHILDHOOD WAS SPENT IN SOLITARY CONFINEMENT.
A BULLET IN THE CHAMBER, WAITING TO BE FIRED.
ALONE MEANT PEACE OF MIND. BORING MEANT NO ONE HAD TO DIE.
BUT NOW WHEN I AM ALONE WITH NOTHING TO DO--
--MY MIND RACES.
OBSESSING ABOUT THINGS.
MILAN FASHION WEEK.
TWO TICKETS.
WHO'S COMING WITH?
STUPID THINGS.
"NOT I," SAID THE DUCK.
...
RIGHT... COOL.
I'LL BE BACK LATER, THEN.
NO ONE CARES, RICH BOY.

IT'S TAKING EVERY OUNCE OF SELF-CONTROL NOT TO KNOCK HIS PRETTY BLOCK OFF, HUH?

WHAT?

IT'S COOL, LAURA. I WON'T MAKE YOU ADMIT IT.

I'M PERCEPTIVE. I NOTICE THINGS.

YOU'RE CLEARLY GOING STIR-CRAZY ON HANK'S LITTLE FORCED X-CATION.

AND WARREN'S JUST MAKING IT WORSE WITH HIS BLONDING.

I DON'T KNOW WHAT THAT MEANS.

BUT YES.

WELL, AS LUCK WOULD HAVE IT, YOU LIVE WITH AN OCD LIST MAKER WHO'S BEEN TRAPPED IN A WHEELCHAIR FOR FIVE WEEKS.

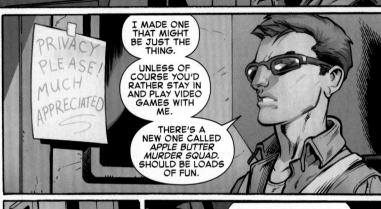

PRIVACY PLEASE! MUCH APPRECIATED

I MADE ONE THAT MIGHT BE JUST THE THING.

UNLESS OF COURSE YOU'D RATHER STAY IN AND PLAY VIDEO GAMES WITH ME.

THERE'S A NEW ONE CALLED APPLE BUTTER MURDER SQUAD. SHOULD BE LOADS OF FUN.

UM...

THAT WAS A JOKE, LAURA.

IT WON'T BE FUN AT ALL.

SO, I'VE BEEN MESSING AROUND WITH THE SETTINGS ON HANK'S THREAT TRACKER.

IT'S KIND OF FUN. YOU CAN TWEAK THE PROBABILITY SETTINGS AND FILTER OUT STUFF YOU DON'T WANT TO MESS WITH.

ANYWAY, I MADE THIS LIST OF FUN SOLO MISSIONS.

THEY'RE ALL TIME-SENSITIVE AND I'M IN NO SHAPE TO GO ON PATROL MYSELF--

--BUT I WAS THINKING YOU MIGHT WANT TO GIVE THEM A WHIRL.

MAPS. DOSSIERS. THREAT ASSESSMENT ANALYTICS.

HE HAS EVEN MARKED DOWN ALL OF THE POTENTIAL BLIND SPOTS.

JUST WHEN I THINK NO ONE SPEAKS MY LANGUAGE.

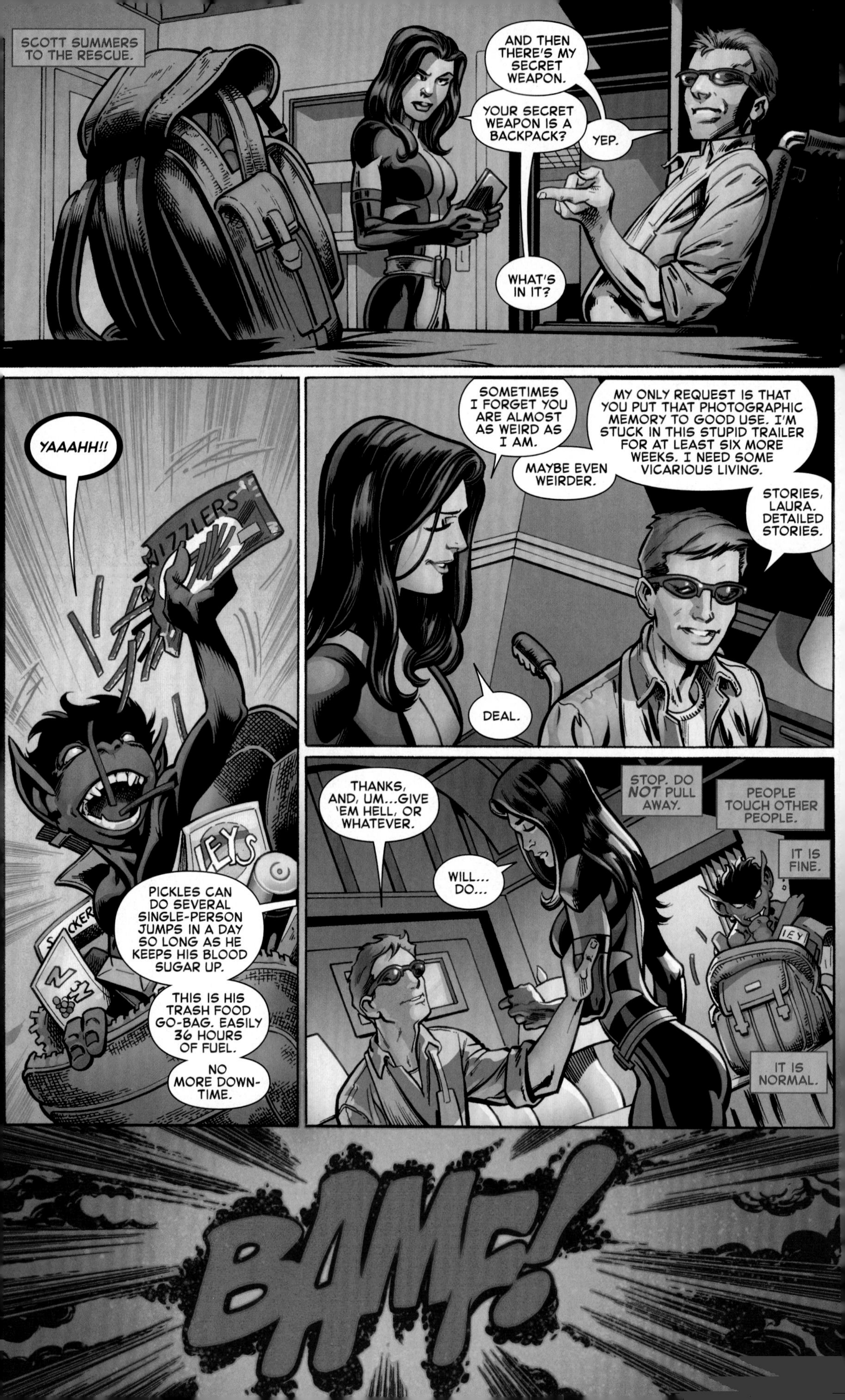
SCOTT SUMMERS TO THE RESCUE.
AND THEN THERE'S MY SECRET WEAPON.
YOUR SECRET WEAPON IS A BACKPACK?
YEP.
WHAT'S IN IT?
YAAAHH!!
SIZZLERS
PICKLES CAN DO SEVERAL SINGLE-PERSON JUMPS IN A DAY SO LONG AS HE KEEPS HIS BLOOD SUGAR UP.
THIS IS HIS TRASH FOOD GO-BAG. EASILY 36 HOURS OF FUEL.
NO MORE DOWN-TIME.
SOMETIMES I FORGET YOU ARE ALMOST AS WEIRD AS I AM.
MAYBE EVEN WEIRDER.
MY ONLY REQUEST IS THAT YOU PUT THAT PHOTOGRAPHIC MEMORY TO GOOD USE. I'M STUCK IN THIS STUPID TRAILER FOR AT LEAST SIX MORE WEEKS. I NEED SOME VICARIOUS LIVING.
STORIES, LAURA. DETAILED STORIES.
DEAL.
THANKS, AND, UM...GIVE 'EM HELL, OR WHATEVER.
WILL... DO...
STOP. DO NOT PULL AWAY.
PEOPLE TOUCH OTHER PEOPLE.
IT IS FINE.
IT IS NORMAL.
BAMF!

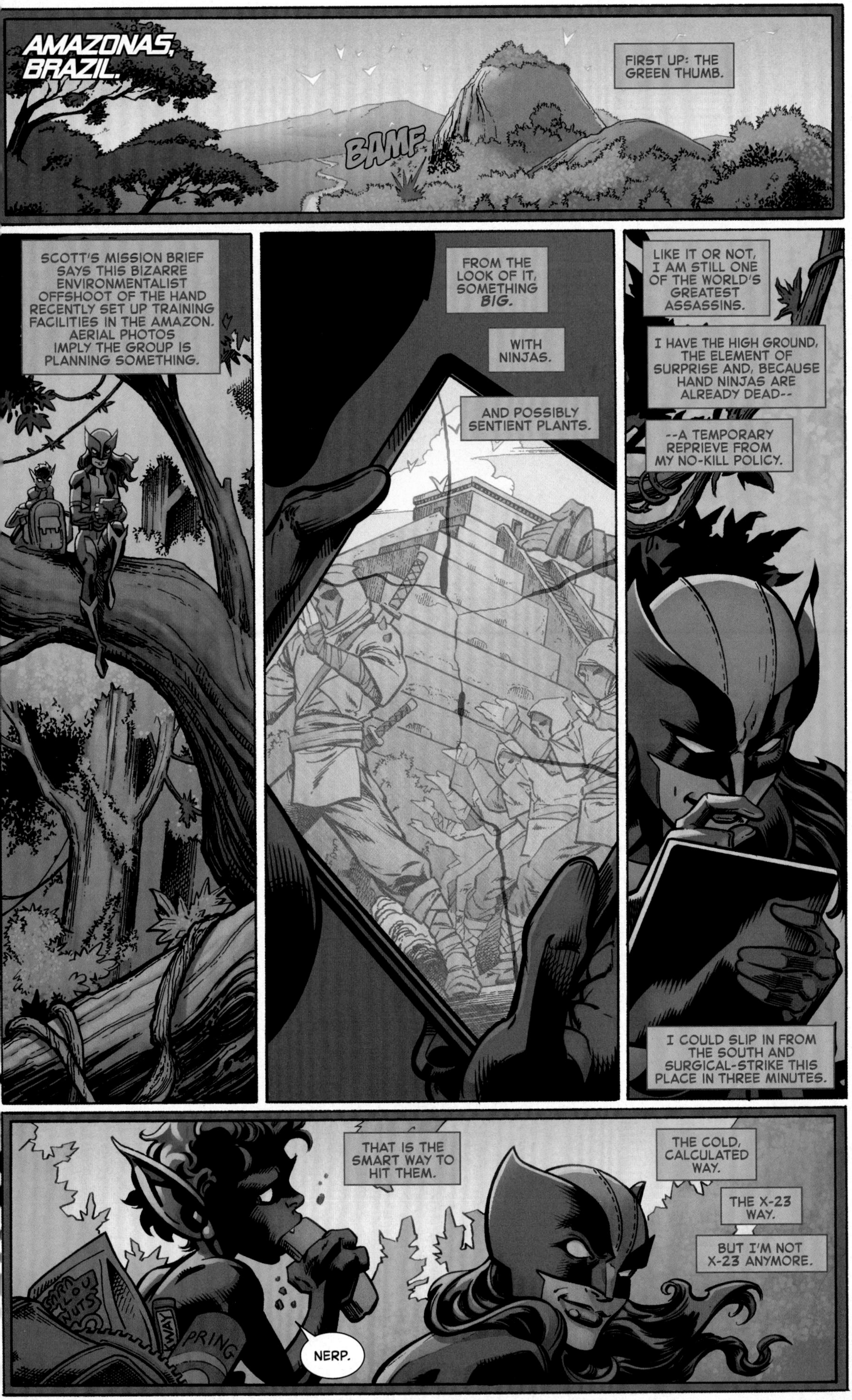
AMAZONAS, BRAZIL.
FIRST UP: THE GREEN THUMB.
BAMF
SCOTT'S MISSION BRIEF SAYS THIS BIZARRE ENVIRONMENTALIST OFFSHOOT OF THE HAND RECENTLY SET UP TRAINING FACILITIES IN THE AMAZON. AERIAL PHOTOS IMPLY THE GROUP IS PLANNING SOMETHING.
FROM THE LOOK OF IT, SOMETHING BIG.
WITH NINJAS.
AND POSSIBLY SENTIENT PLANTS.
LIKE IT OR NOT, I AM STILL ONE OF THE WORLD'S GREATEST ASSASSINS.
I HAVE THE HIGH GROUND, THE ELEMENT OF SURPRISE AND, BECAUSE HAND NINJAS ARE ALREADY DEAD--
--A TEMPORARY REPRIEVE FROM MY NO-KILL POLICY.
I COULD SLIP IN FROM THE SOUTH AND SURGICAL-STRIKE THIS PLACE IN THREE MINUTES.
THAT IS THE SMART WAY TO HIT THEM.
THE COLD, CALCULATED WAY.
THE X-23 WAY.
BUT I'M NOT X-23 ANYMORE.
NERP.

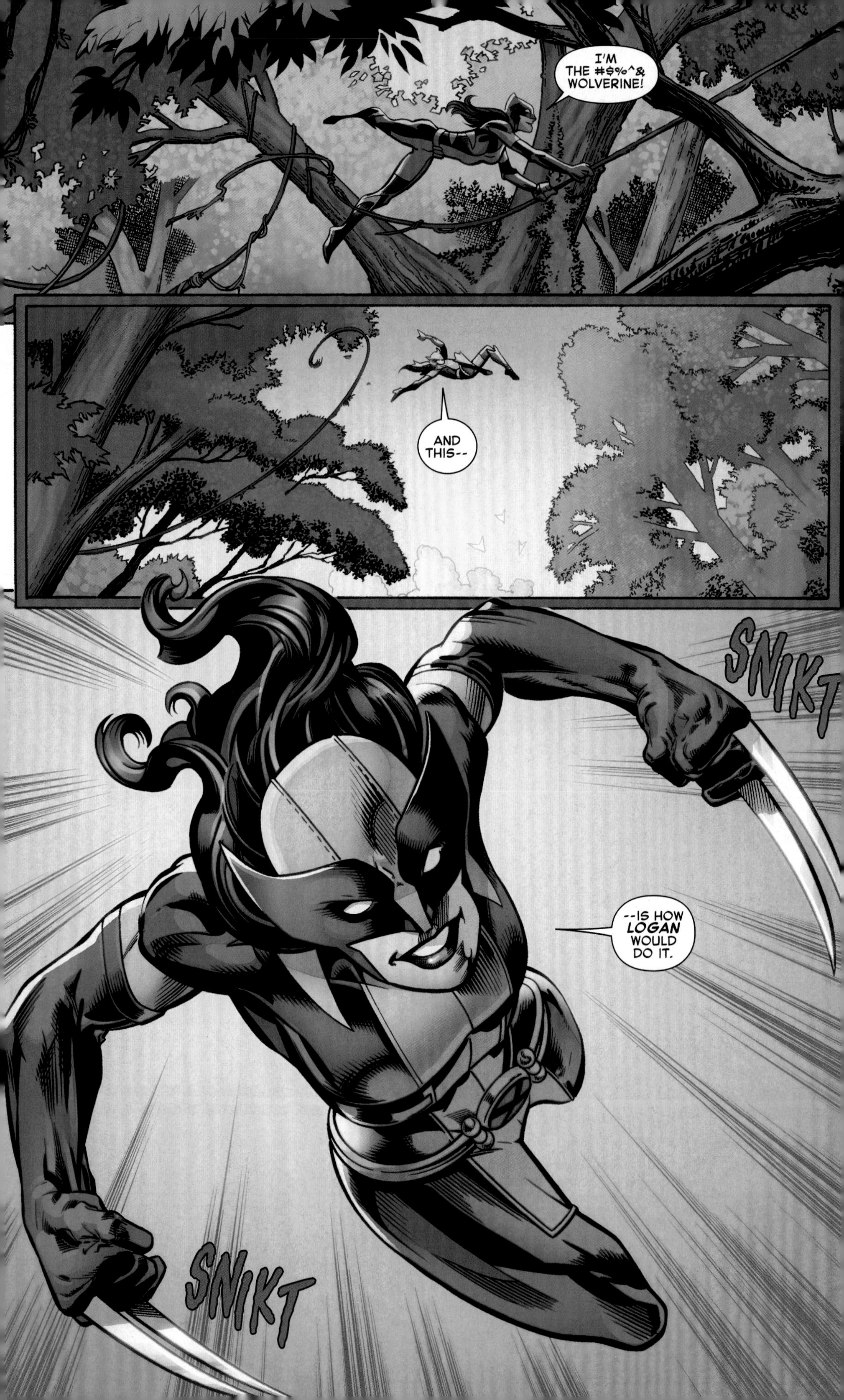
I'M THE #$%^& WOLVERINE!
AND THIS--
SNIKT
--IS HOW LOGAN WOULD DO IT.
SNIKT

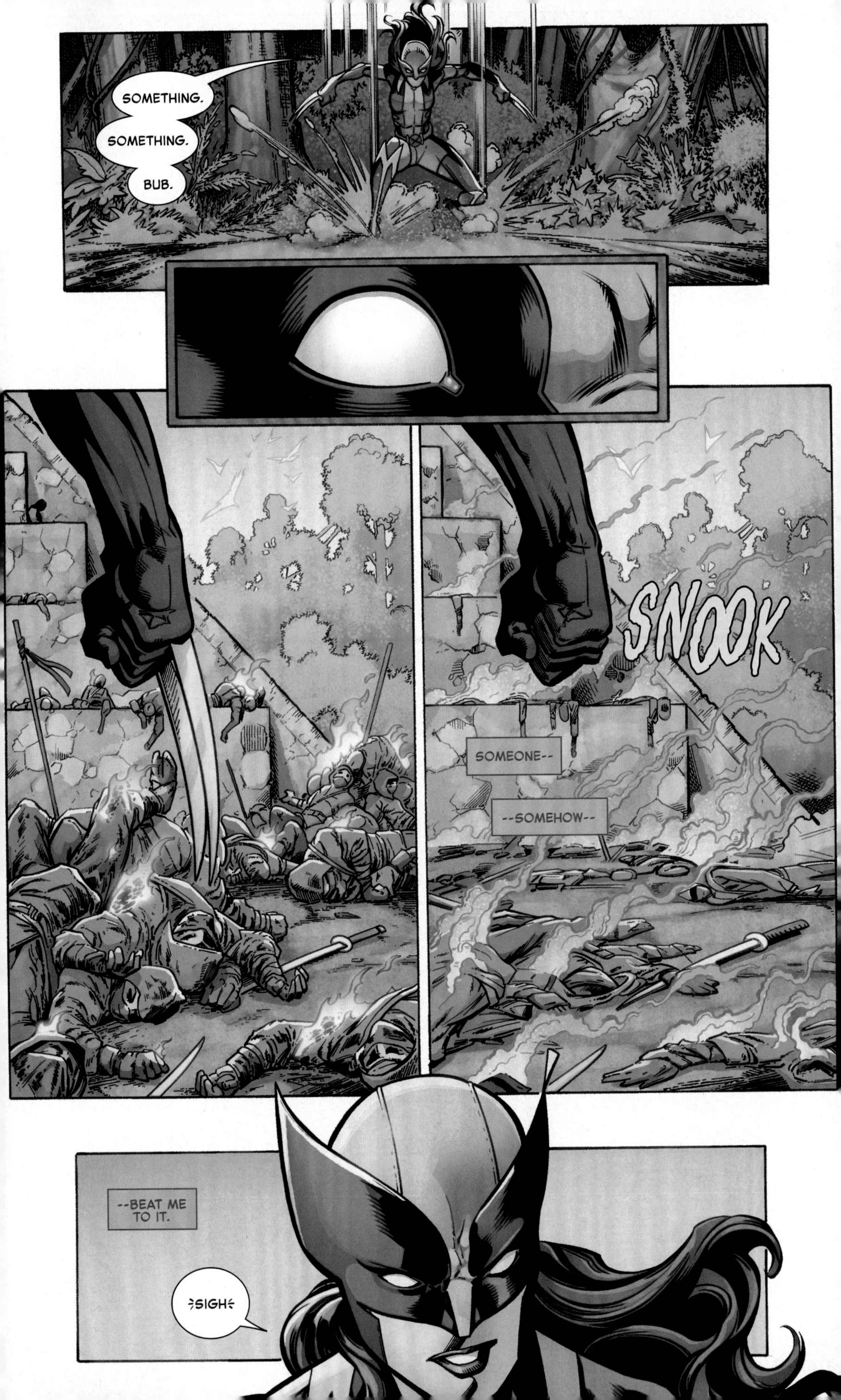
SOMETHING.
SOMETHING.
BUB.
SNOOK
SOMEONE--
--SOMEHOW--
--BEAT ME TO IT.
⁼SIGH⁼

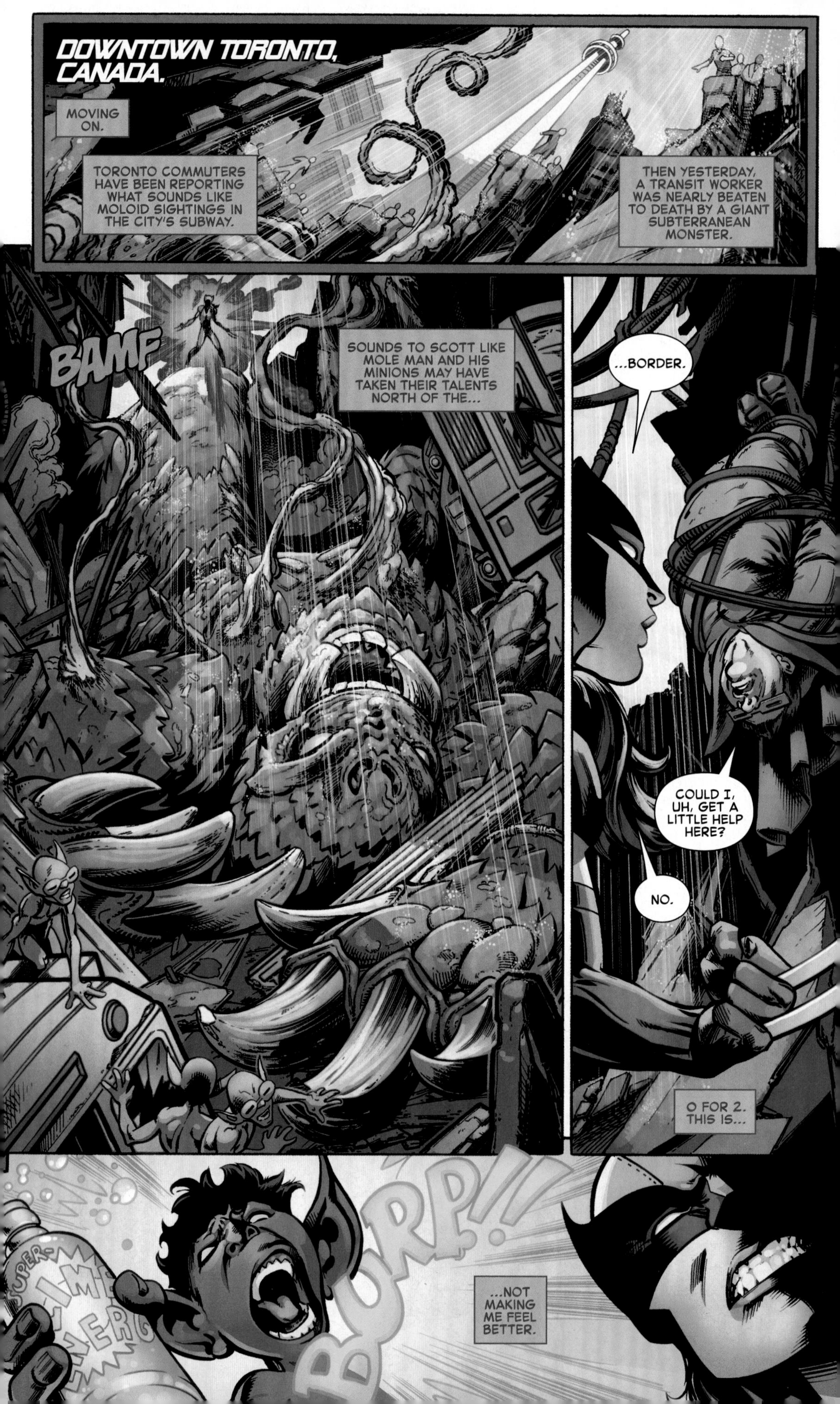
DOWNTOWN TORONTO, CANADA.
MOVING ON.
TORONTO COMMUTERS HAVE BEEN REPORTING WHAT SOUNDS LIKE MOLOID SIGHTINGS IN THE CITY'S SUBWAY.
THEN YESTERDAY, A TRANSIT WORKER WAS NEARLY BEATEN TO DEATH BY A GIANT SUBTERRANEAN MONSTER.
BAMF
SOUNDS TO SCOTT LIKE MOLE MAN AND HIS MINIONS MAY HAVE TAKEN THEIR TALENTS NORTH OF THE...
...BORDER.
COULD I, UH, GET A LITTLE HELP HERE?
NO.
0 FOR 2. THIS IS...
BURP!!
...NOT MAKING ME FEEL BETTER.

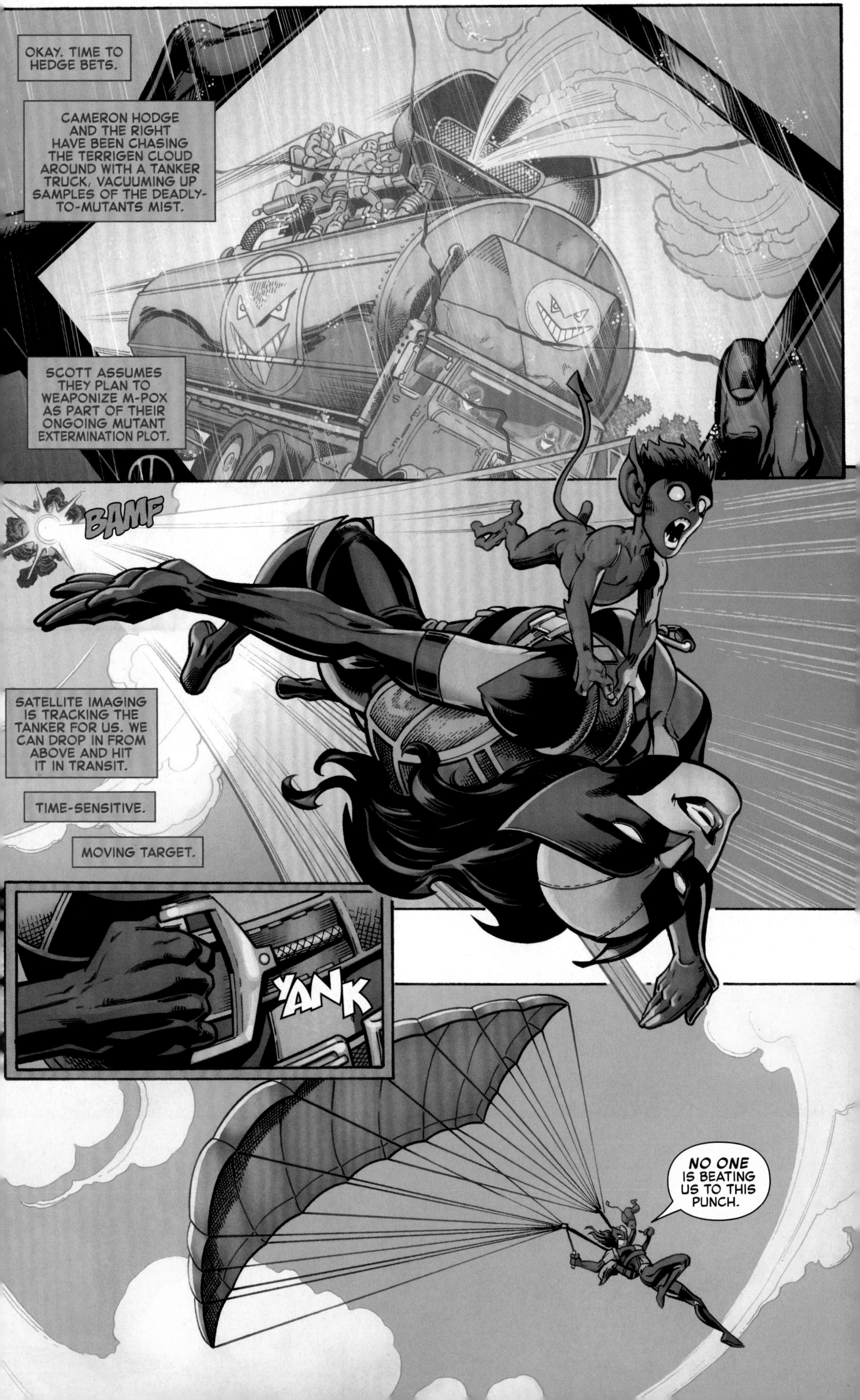
OKAY. TIME TO HEDGE BETS.
CAMERON HODGE AND THE RIGHT HAVE BEEN CHASING THE TERRIGEN CLOUD AROUND WITH A TANKER TRUCK, VACUUMING UP SAMPLES OF THE DEADLY-TO-MUTANTS MIST.
SCOTT ASSUMES THEY PLAN TO WEAPONIZE M-POX AS PART OF THEIR ONGOING MUTANT EXTERMINATION PLOT.
BAMF
SATELLITE IMAGING IS TRACKING THE TANKER FOR US. WE CAN DROP IN FROM ABOVE AND HIT IT IN TRANSIT.
TIME-SENSITIVE.
MOVING TARGET.
YANK
NO ONE IS BEATING US TO THIS PUNCH.

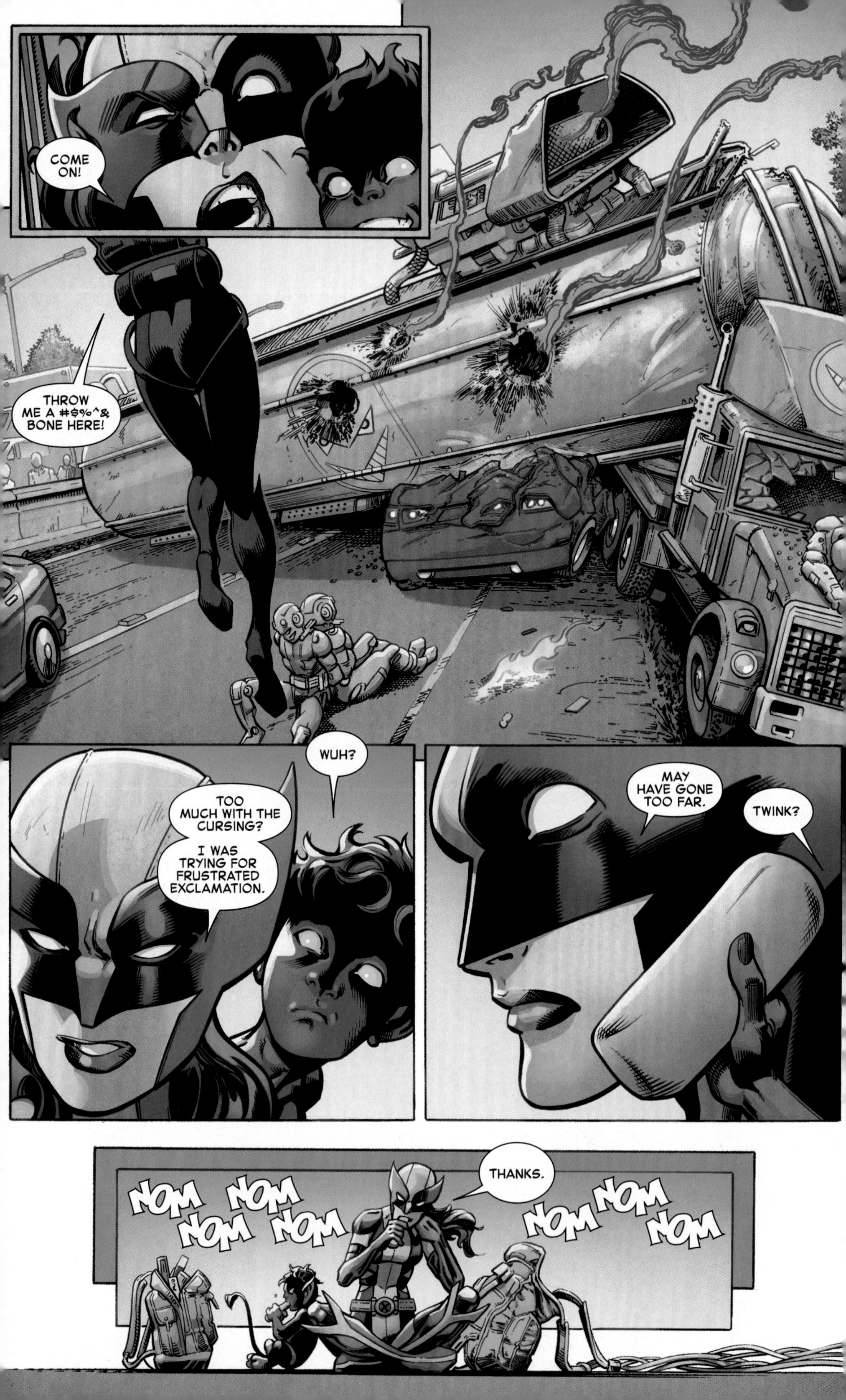
COME ON!
THROW ME A #$%^& BONE HERE!
TOO MUCH WITH THE CURSING?
I WAS TRYING FOR FRUSTRATED EXCLAMATION.
WUH?
MAY HAVE GONE TOO FAR.
TWINK?
NOM NOM NOM NOM
THANKS.
NOM NOM NOM NOM

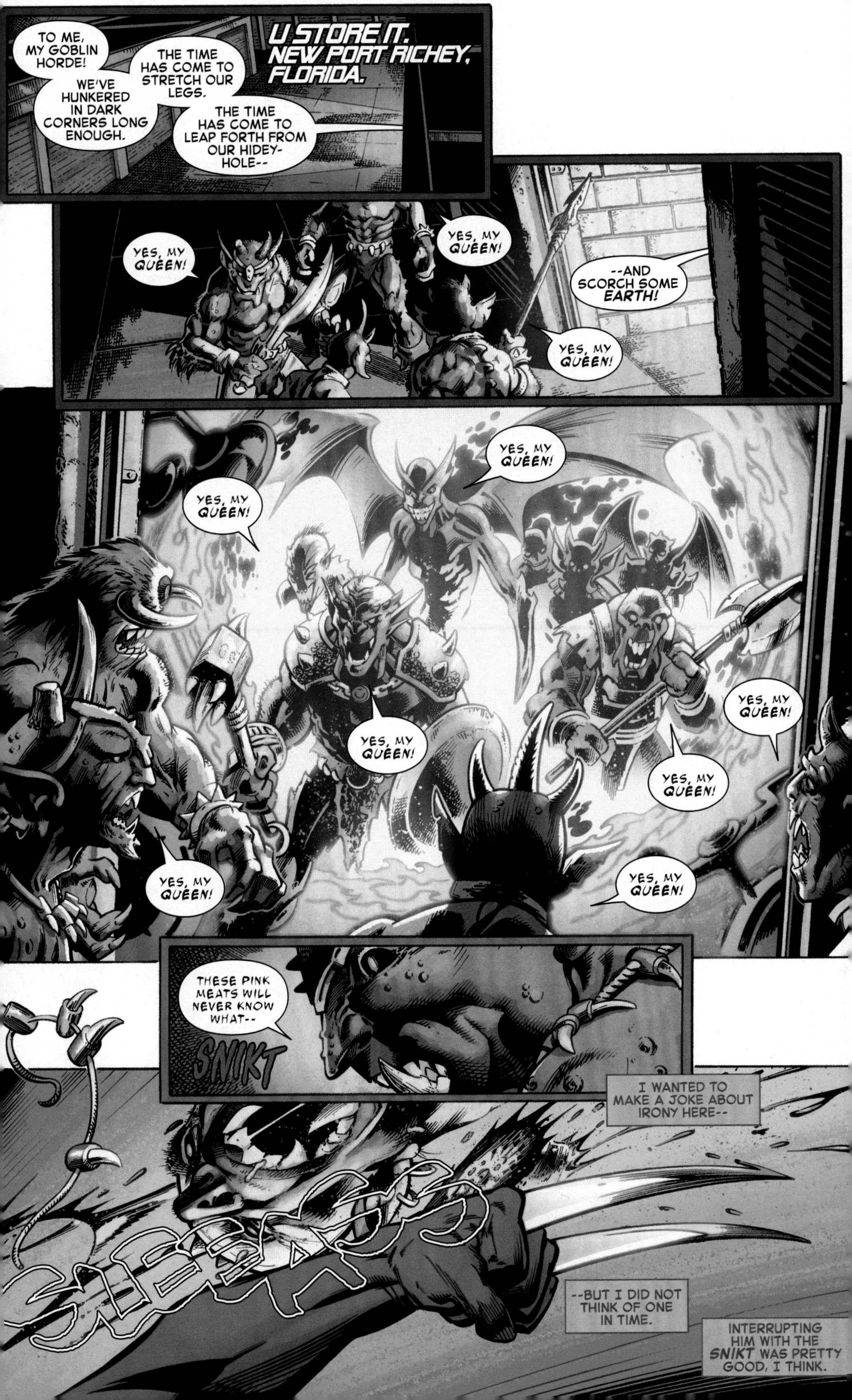

TO ME, MY GOBLIN HORDE!
WE'VE HUNKERED IN DARK CORNERS LONG ENOUGH.
THE TIME HAS COME TO STRETCH OUR LEGS.
THE TIME HAS COME TO LEAP FORTH FROM OUR HIDEY-HOLE--
U STORE IT. NEW PORT RICHEY, FLORIDA.
YES, MY QUEEN!
YES, MY QUEEN!
--AND SCORCH SOME EARTH!
YES, MY QUEEN!
YES, MY QUEEN!
YES, MY QUEEN!
YES, MY QUEEN!
YES, MY QUEEN!
YES, MY QUEEN!
YES, MY QUEEN!
YES, MY QUEEN!
THESE PINK MEATS WILL NEVER KNOW WHAT--
SNIKT
I WANTED TO MAKE A JOKE ABOUT IRONY HERE--
--BUT I DID NOT THINK OF ONE IN TIME.
INTERRUPTING HIM WITH THE SNIKT WAS PRETTY GOOD, I THINK.

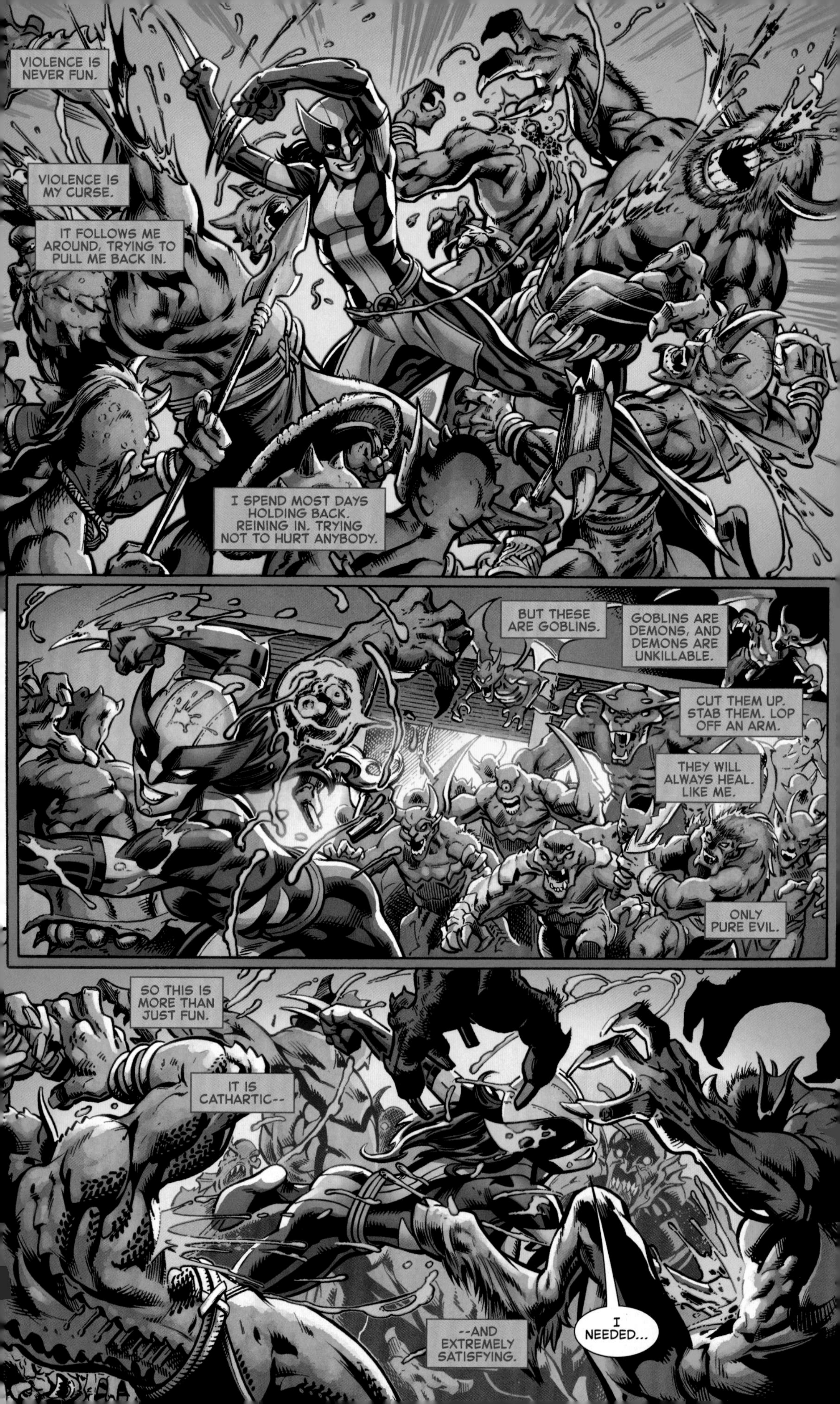
VIOLENCE IS NEVER FUN.
VIOLENCE IS MY CURSE.
IT FOLLOWS ME AROUND, TRYING TO PULL ME BACK IN.
I SPEND MOST DAYS HOLDING BACK. REINING IN. TRYING NOT TO HURT ANYBODY.
BUT THESE ARE GOBLINS.
GOBLINS ARE DEMONS, AND DEMONS ARE UNKILLABLE.
CUT THEM UP. STAB THEM. LOP OFF AN ARM.
THEY WILL ALWAYS HEAL. LIKE ME.
ONLY PURE EVIL.
SO THIS IS MORE THAN JUST FUN.
IT IS CATHARTIC--
--AND EXTREMELY SATISFYING.
I NEEDED...

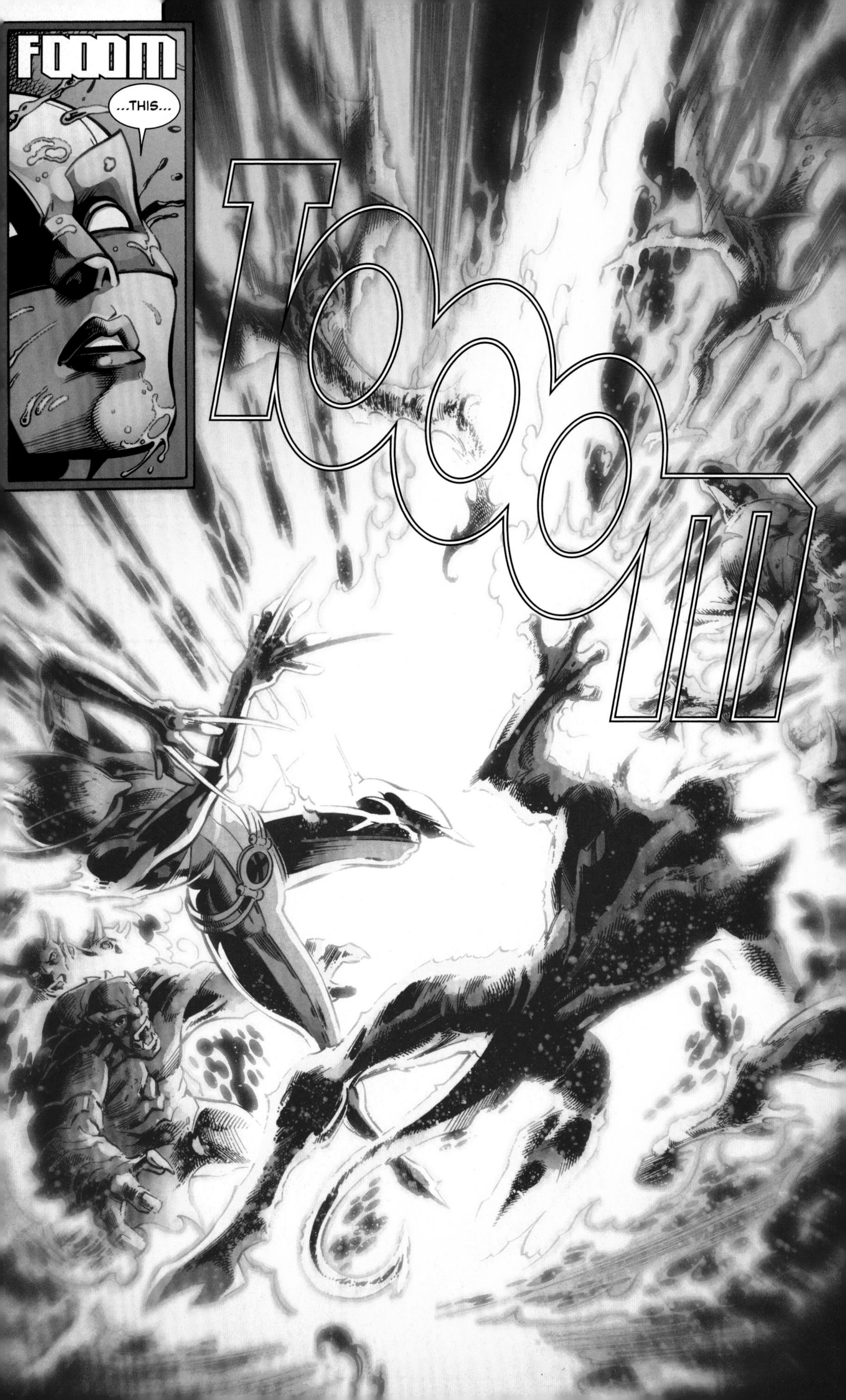
FOOOM
...THIS...
TOOOOM

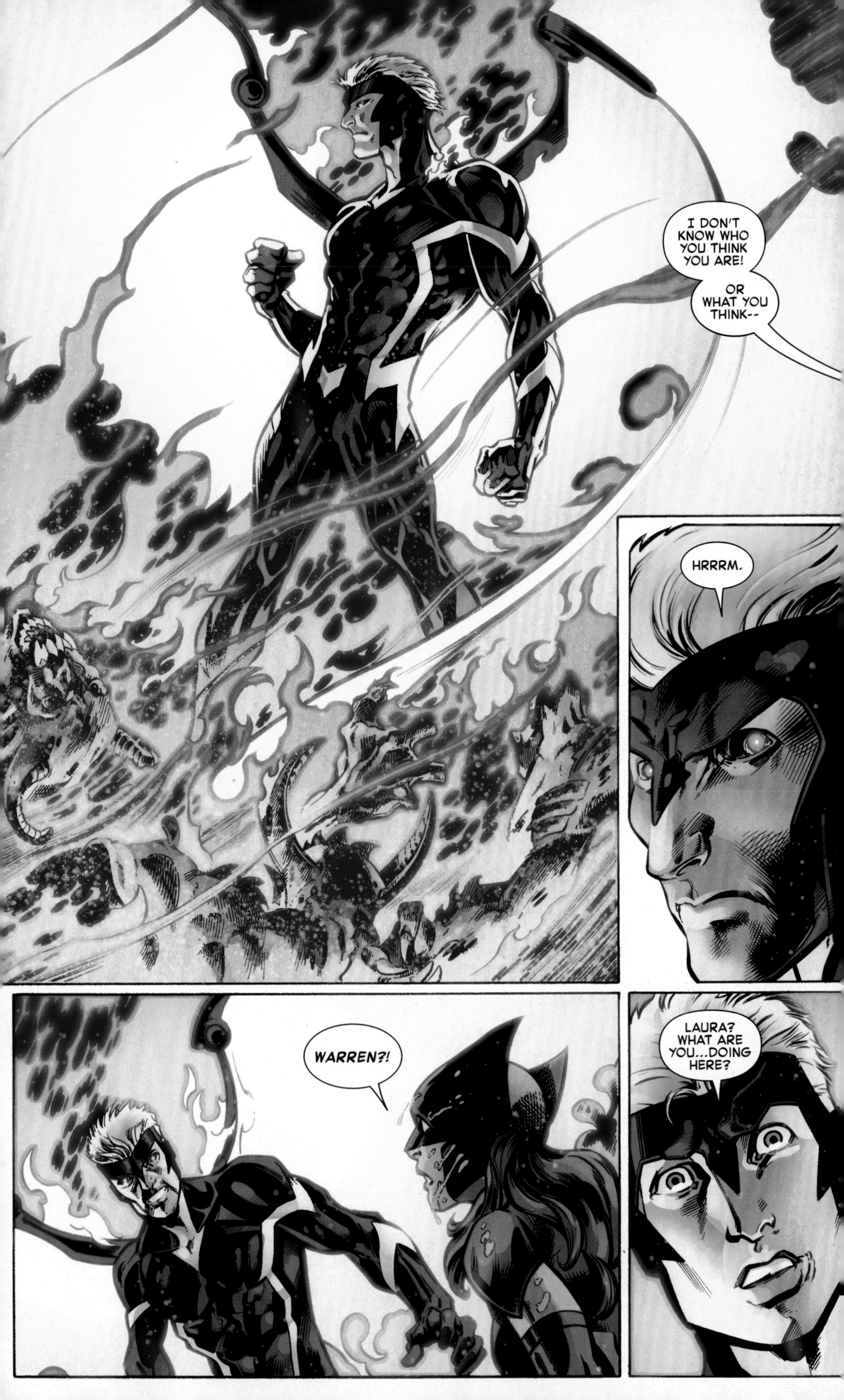

I DON'T KNOW WHO YOU THINK YOU ARE!
OR WHAT YOU THINK--
HRRRM.
WARREN?!
LAURA? WHAT ARE YOU...DOING HERE?

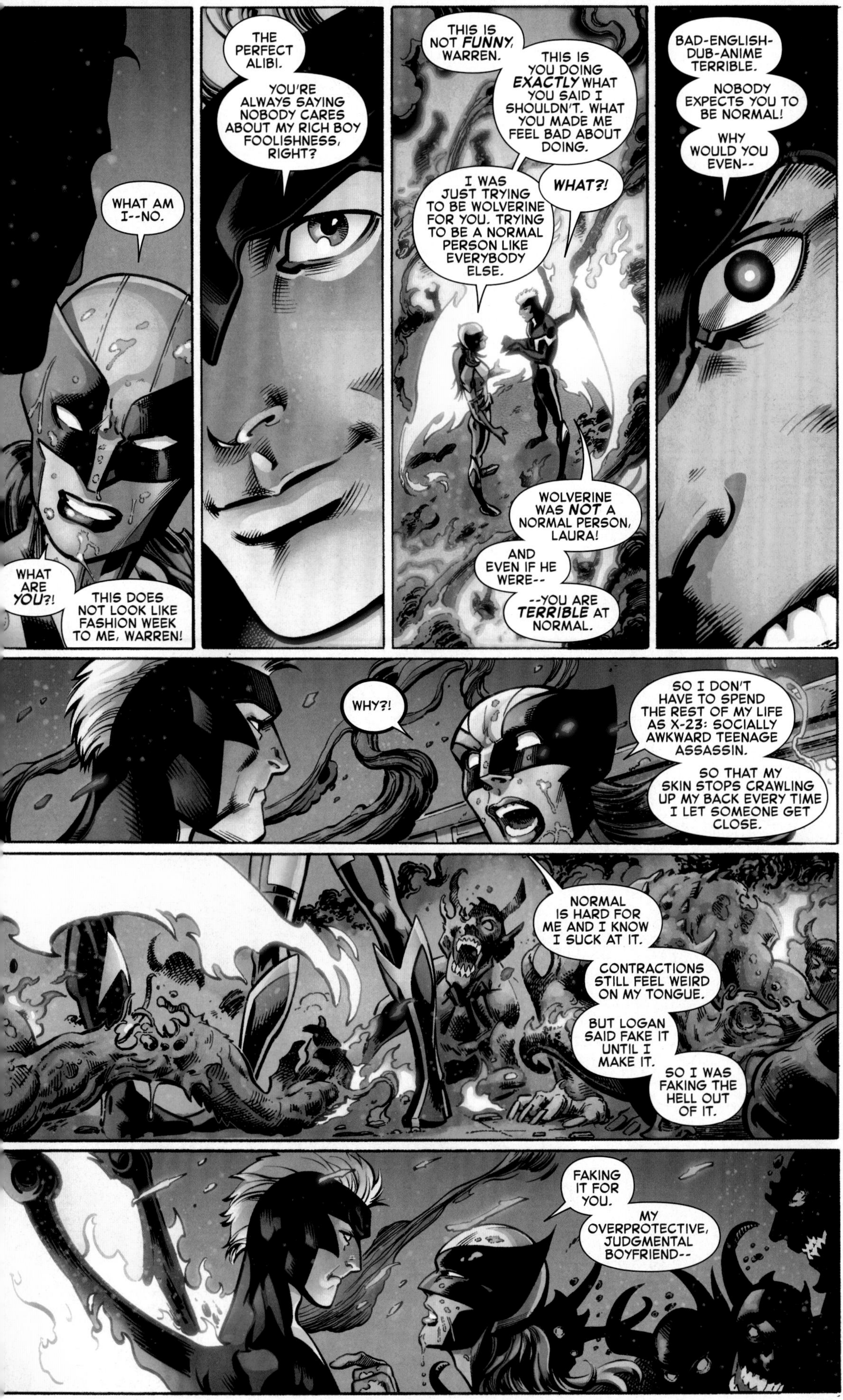

WHAT AM I--NO.
WHAT ARE YOU?!
THIS DOES NOT LOOK LIKE FASHION WEEK TO ME, WARREN!
THE PERFECT ALIBI.
YOU'RE ALWAYS SAYING NOBODY CARES ABOUT MY RICH BOY FOOLISHNESS, RIGHT?
THIS IS NOT FUNNY, WARREN.
THIS IS YOU DOING EXACTLY WHAT YOU SAID I SHOULDN'T. WHAT YOU MADE ME FEEL BAD ABOUT DOING.
I WAS JUST TRYING TO BE WOLVERINE FOR YOU. TRYING TO BE A NORMAL PERSON LIKE EVERYBODY ELSE.
WHAT?!
WOLVERINE WAS NOT A NORMAL PERSON, LAURA!
AND EVEN IF HE WERE--
--YOU ARE TERRIBLE AT NORMAL.
BAD-ENGLISH-DUB-ANIME TERRIBLE.
NOBODY EXPECTS YOU TO BE NORMAL!
WHY WOULD YOU EVEN--
WHY?!
SO I DON'T HAVE TO SPEND THE REST OF MY LIFE AS X-23: SOCIALLY AWKWARD TEENAGE ASSASSIN.
SO THAT MY SKIN STOPS CRAWLING UP MY BACK EVERY TIME I LET SOMEONE GET CLOSE.
NORMAL IS HARD FOR ME AND I KNOW I SUCK AT IT.
CONTRACTIONS STILL FEEL WEIRD ON MY TONGUE.
BUT LOGAN SAID FAKE IT UNTIL I MAKE IT.
SO I WAS FAKING THE HELL OUT OF IT.
FAKING IT FOR YOU.
MY OVERPROTECTIVE, JUDGMENTAL BOYFRIEND--

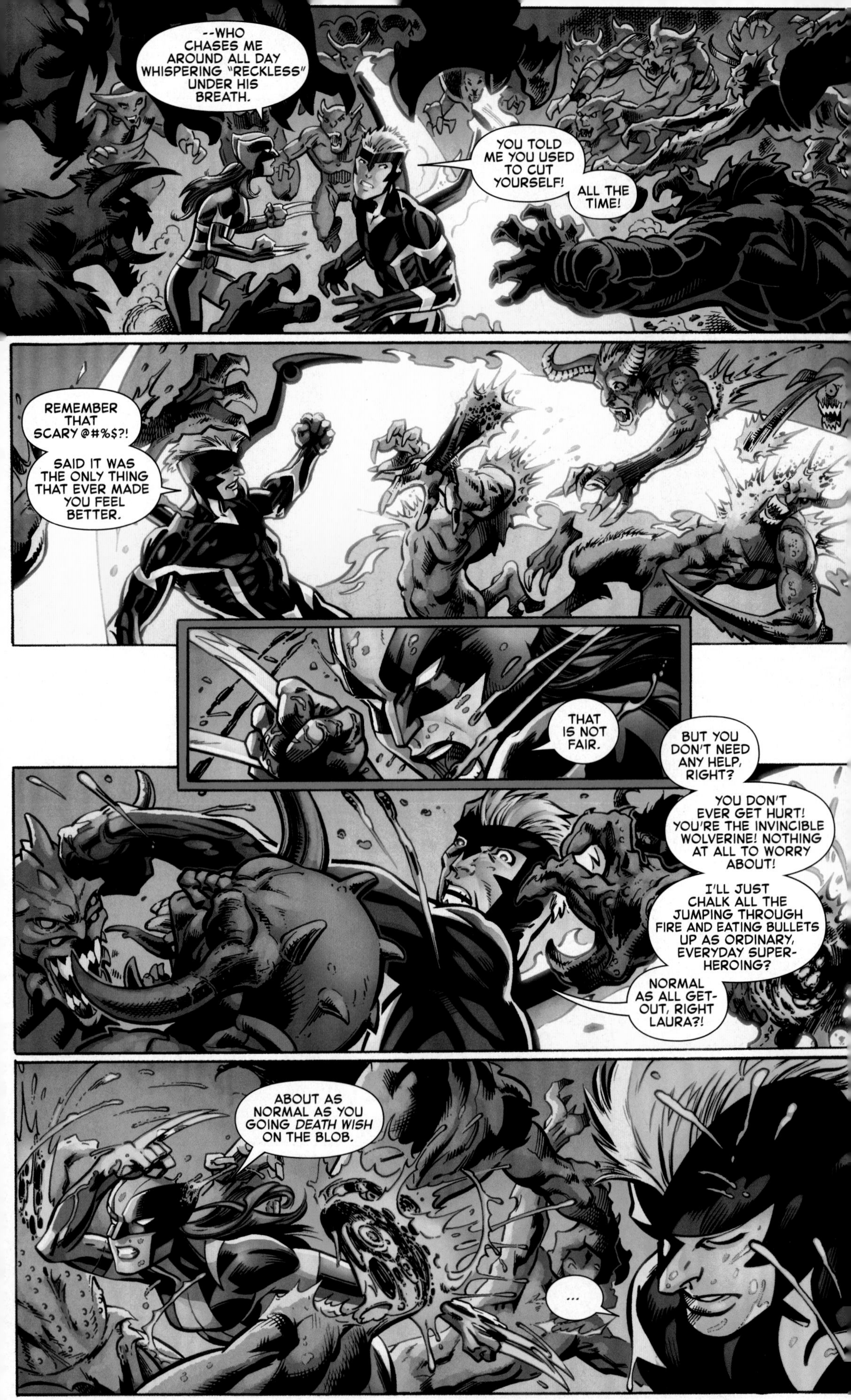
--WHO CHASES ME AROUND ALL DAY WHISPERING "RECKLESS" UNDER HIS BREATH.
YOU TOLD ME YOU USED TO CUT YOURSELF!
ALL THE TIME!
REMEMBER THAT SCARY @#%$?!
SAID IT WAS THE ONLY THING THAT EVER MADE YOU FEEL BETTER.
THAT IS NOT FAIR.
BUT YOU DON'T NEED ANY HELP, RIGHT?
YOU DON'T EVER GET HURT! YOU'RE THE INVINCIBLE WOLVERINE! NOTHING AT ALL TO WORRY ABOUT!
I'LL JUST CHALK ALL THE JUMPING THROUGH FIRE AND EATING BULLETS UP AS ORDINARY, EVERYDAY SUPER-HEROING?
NORMAL AS ALL GET-OUT, RIGHT LAURA?!
ABOUT AS NORMAL AS YOU GOING *DEATH WISH* ON THE BLOB.
...

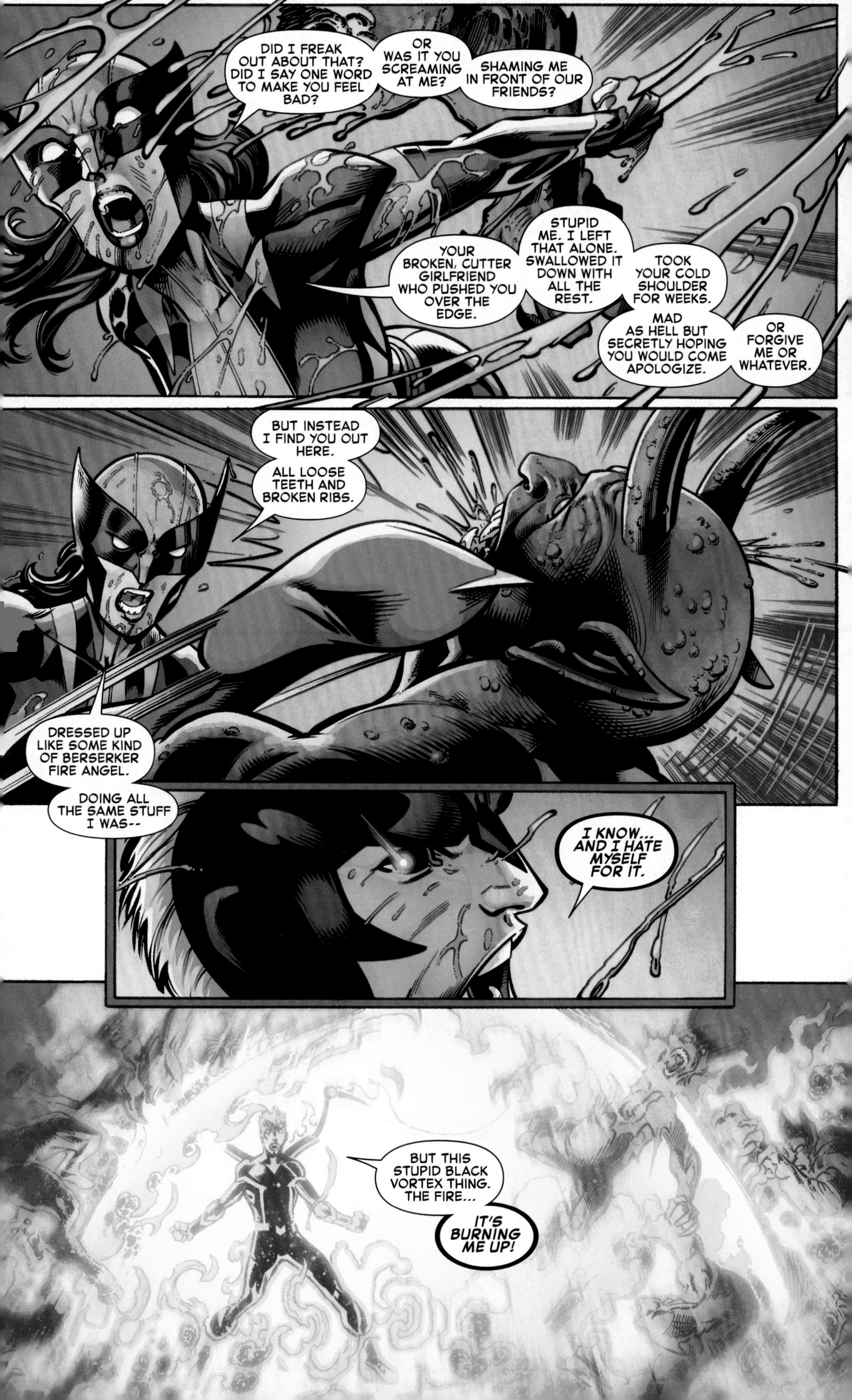
DID I FREAK OUT ABOUT THAT? DID I SAY ONE WORD TO MAKE YOU FEEL BAD?
OR WAS IT YOU SCREAMING AT ME?
SHAMING ME IN FRONT OF OUR FRIENDS?
YOUR BROKEN, CUTTER GIRLFRIEND WHO PUSHED YOU OVER THE EDGE.
STUPID ME. I LEFT THAT ALONE. SWALLOWED IT DOWN WITH ALL THE REST.
TOOK YOUR COLD SHOULDER FOR WEEKS.
MAD AS HELL BUT SECRETLY HOPING YOU WOULD COME APOLOGIZE.
OR FORGIVE ME OR WHATEVER.
BUT INSTEAD I FIND YOU OUT HERE.
ALL LOOSE TEETH AND BROKEN RIBS.
DRESSED UP LIKE SOME KIND OF BERSERKER FIRE ANGEL.
DOING ALL THE SAME STUFF I WAS--
I KNOW... AND I HATE MYSELF FOR IT.
BUT THIS STUPID BLACK VORTEX THING. THE FIRE...
IT'S BURNING ME UP!

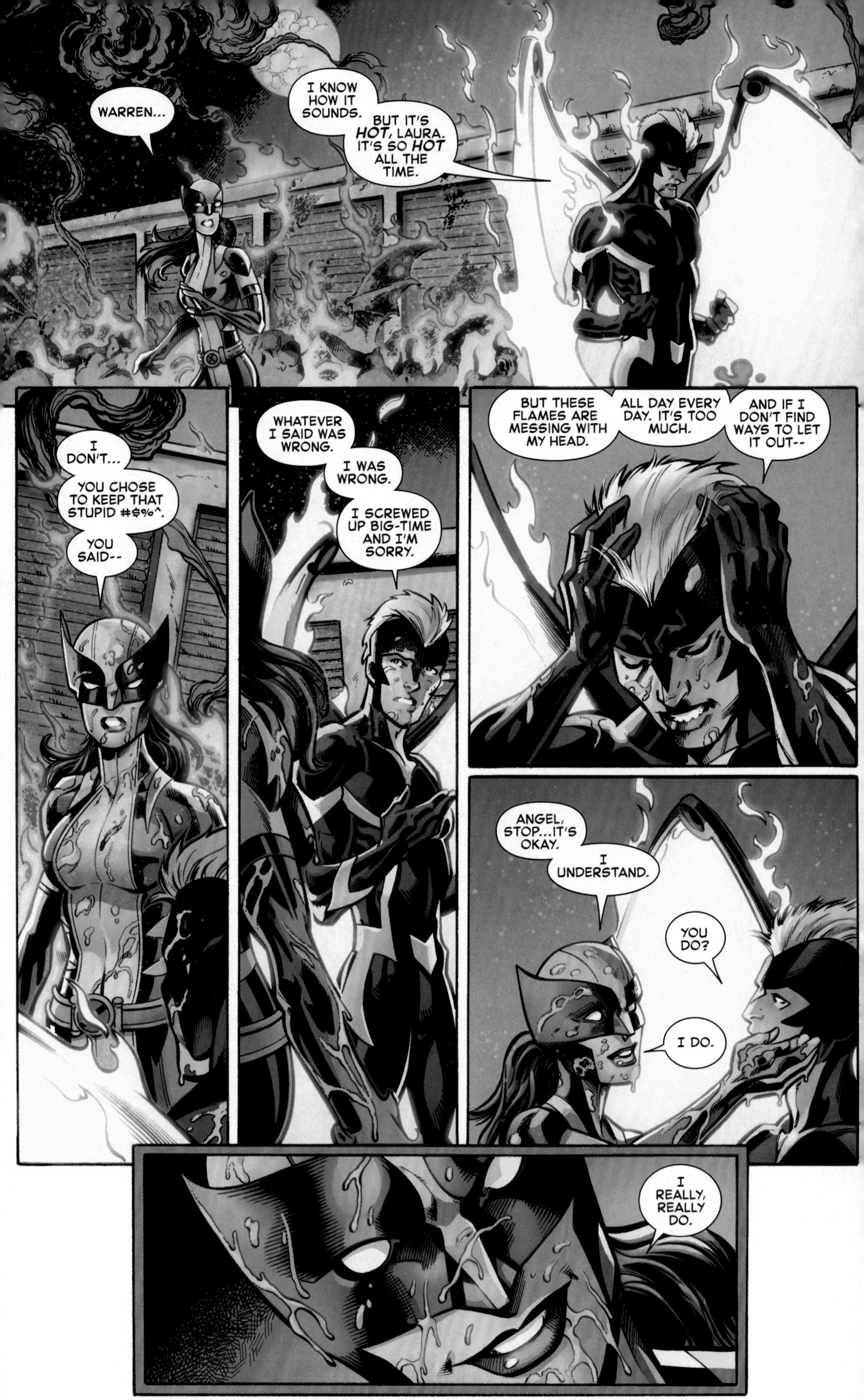
WARREN...
I KNOW HOW IT SOUNDS.
BUT IT'S HOT, LAURA. IT'S SO HOT ALL THE TIME.
I DON'T...
YOU CHOSE TO KEEP THAT STUPID #$%^.
YOU SAID--
WHATEVER I SAID WAS WRONG.
I WAS WRONG.
I SCREWED UP BIG-TIME AND I'M SORRY.
BUT THESE FLAMES ARE MESSING WITH MY HEAD.
ALL DAY EVERY DAY. IT'S TOO MUCH.
AND IF I DON'T FIND WAYS TO LET IT OUT--
ANGEL, STOP...IT'S OKAY.
I UNDERSTAND.
YOU DO?
I DO.
I REALLY, REALLY DO.

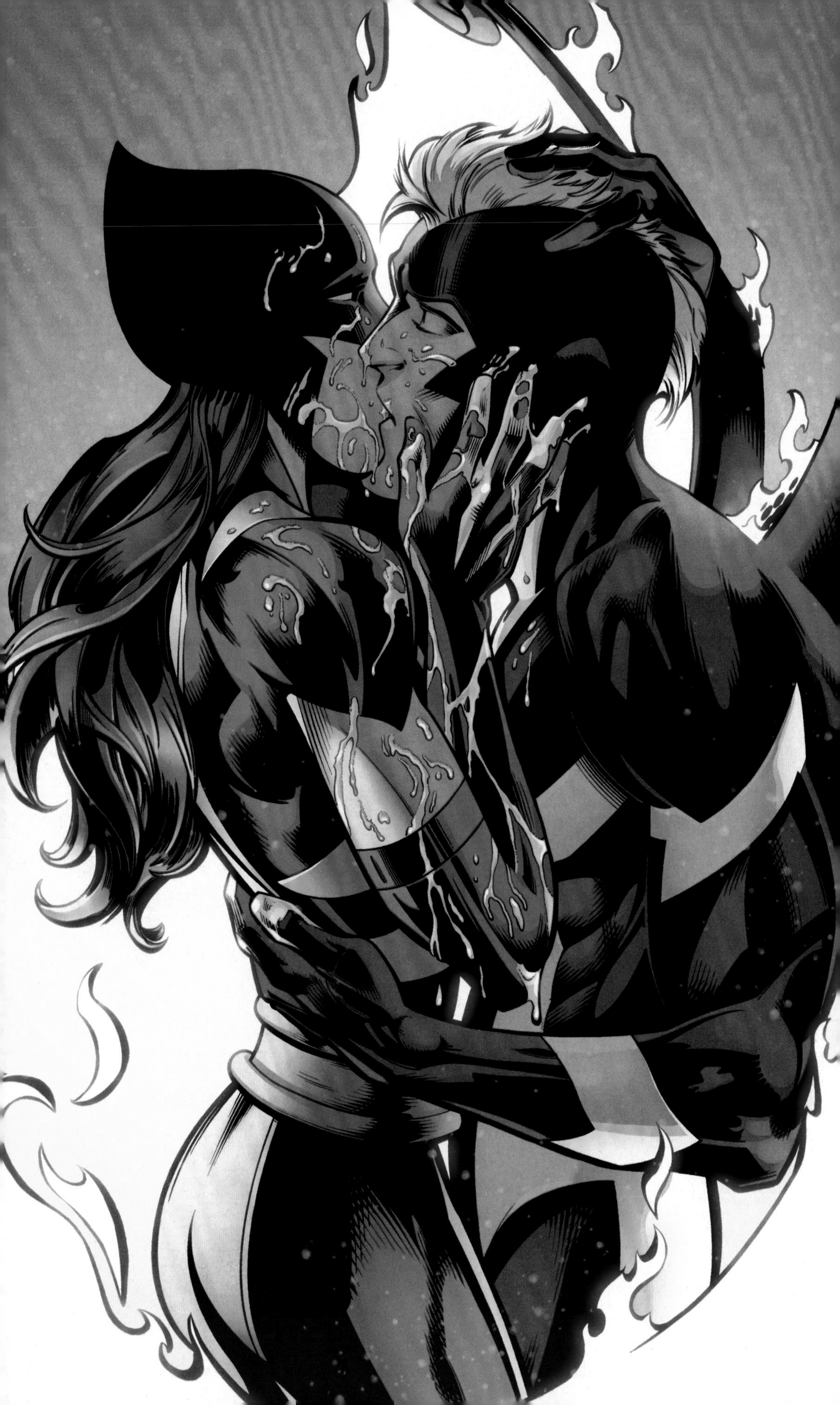

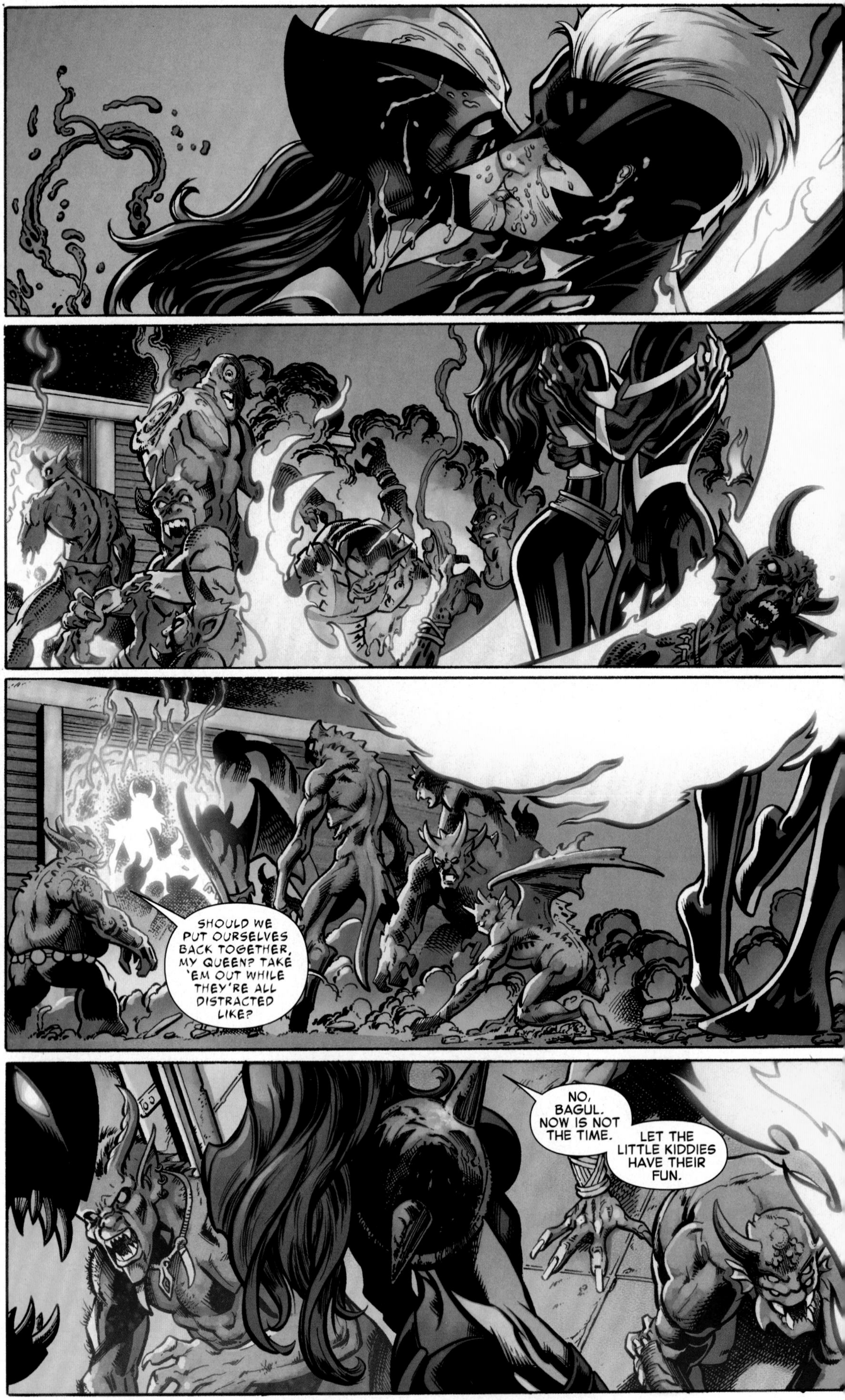
SHOULD WE PUT OURSELVES BACK TOGETHER, MY QUEEN? TAKE 'EM OUT WHILE THEY'RE ALL DISTRACTED LIKE?
NO, BAGUL. NOW IS NOT THE TIME.
LET THE LITTLE KIDDIES HAVE THEIR FUN.

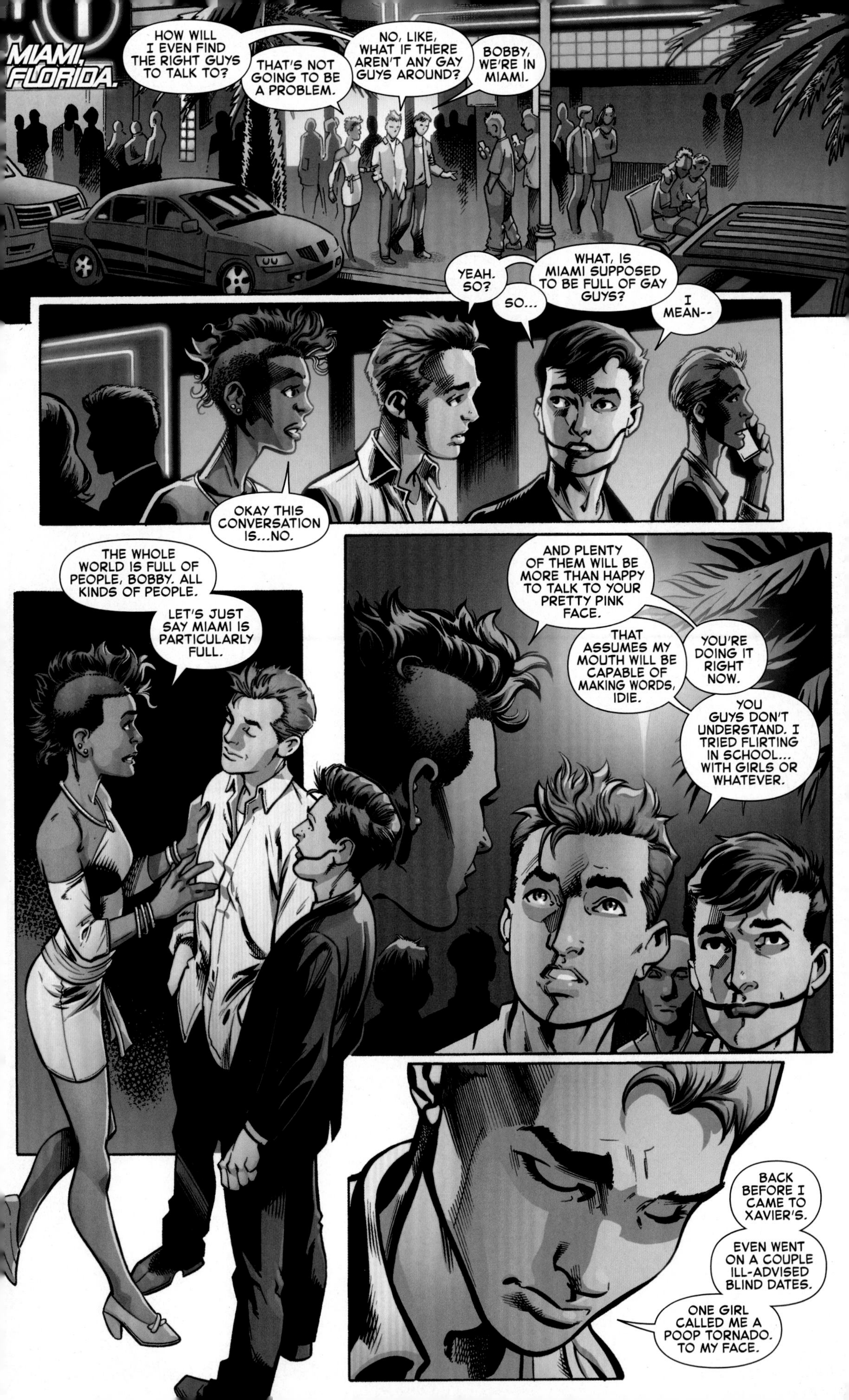
MIAMI, FLORIDA.
HOW WILL I EVEN FIND THE RIGHT GUYS TO TALK TO?
THAT'S NOT GOING TO BE A PROBLEM.
NO, LIKE, WHAT IF THERE AREN'T ANY GAY GUYS AROUND?
BOBBY, WE'RE IN MIAMI.
YEAH. SO?
SO...
WHAT, IS MIAMI SUPPOSED TO BE FULL OF GAY GUYS?
I MEAN--
OKAY THIS CONVERSATION IS...NO.
THE WHOLE WORLD IS FULL OF PEOPLE, BOBBY. ALL KINDS OF PEOPLE.
LET'S JUST SAY MIAMI IS PARTICULARLY FULL.
AND PLENTY OF THEM WILL BE MORE THAN HAPPY TO TALK TO YOUR PRETTY PINK FACE.
THAT ASSUMES MY MOUTH WILL BE CAPABLE OF MAKING WORDS, IDIE.
YOU'RE DOING IT RIGHT NOW.
YOU GUYS DON'T UNDERSTAND. I TRIED FLIRTING IN SCHOOL... WITH GIRLS OR WHATEVER.
BACK BEFORE I CAME TO XAVIER'S.
EVEN WENT ON A COUPLE ILL-ADVISED BLIND DATES.
ONE GIRL CALLED ME A POOP TORNADO. TO MY FACE.

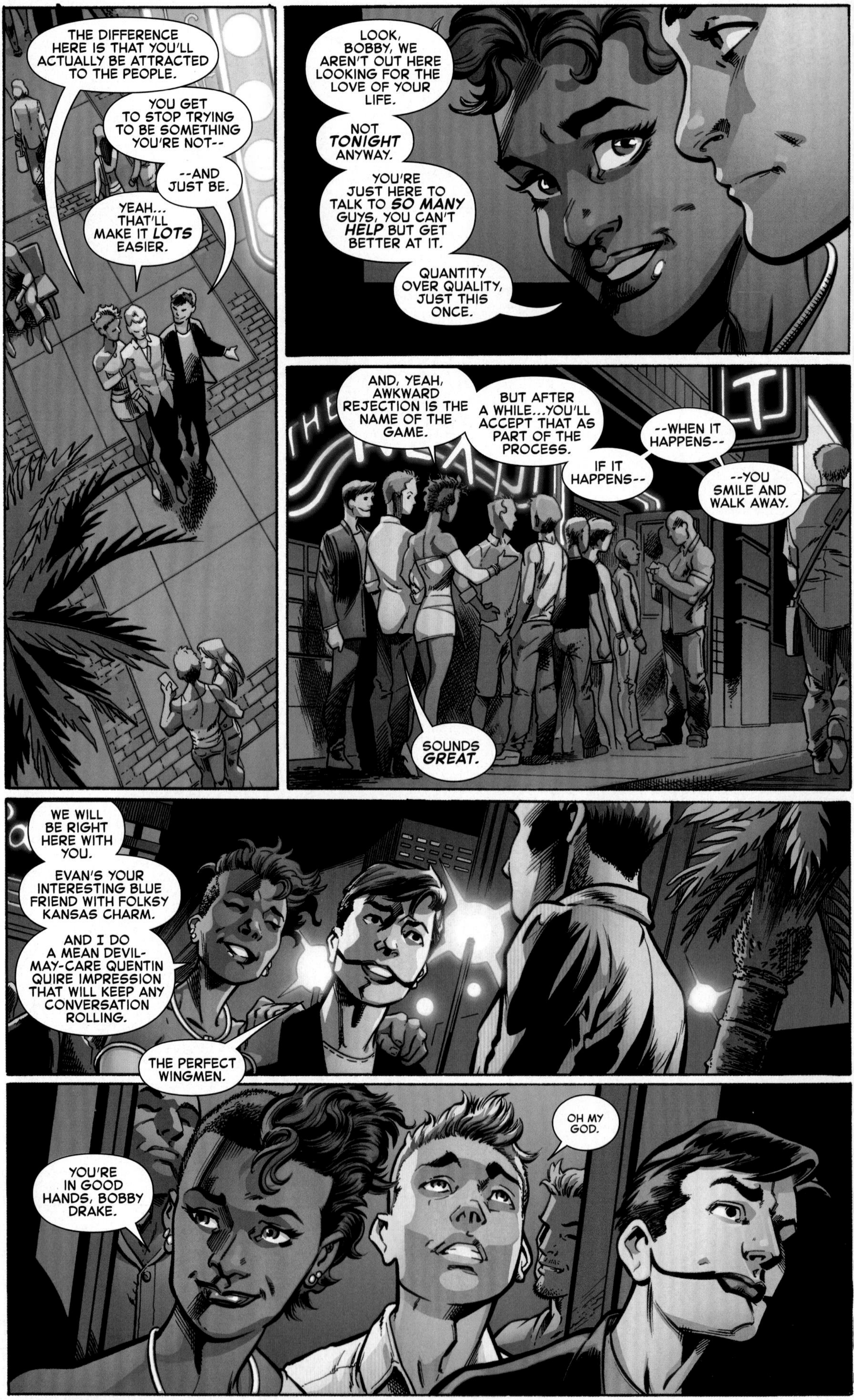

THE DIFFERENCE HERE IS THAT YOU'LL ACTUALLY BE ATTRACTED TO THE PEOPLE.
YOU GET TO STOP TRYING TO BE SOMETHING YOU'RE NOT--
--AND JUST BE.
YEAH... THAT'LL MAKE IT LOTS EASIER.
LOOK, BOBBY, WE AREN'T OUT HERE LOOKING FOR THE LOVE OF YOUR LIFE.
NOT TONIGHT ANYWAY.
YOU'RE JUST HERE TO TALK TO SO MANY GUYS, YOU CAN'T HELP BUT GET BETTER AT IT.
QUANTITY OVER QUALITY, JUST THIS ONCE.
AND, YEAH, AWKWARD REJECTION IS THE NAME OF THE GAME.
BUT AFTER A WHILE...YOU'LL ACCEPT THAT AS PART OF THE PROCESS.
IF IT HAPPENS--
--WHEN IT HAPPENS--
--YOU SMILE AND WALK AWAY.
SOUNDS GREAT.
WE WILL BE RIGHT HERE WITH YOU.
EVAN'S YOUR INTERESTING BLUE FRIEND WITH FOLKSY KANSAS CHARM.
AND I DO A MEAN DEVIL-MAY-CARE QUENTIN QUIRE IMPRESSION THAT WILL KEEP ANY CONVERSATION ROLLING.
THE PERFECT WINGMEN.
YOU'RE IN GOOD HANDS, BOBBY DRAKE.
OH MY GOD.

GO TIME.

JUST BE YOURSELF.

UMM...

I... I...

I LIKE TURTLES.

WHAT, MAN?

I, UM...DIDN'T THINK ABOUT WHAT TO SAY BEFORE I GOT UP HERE AND THEN...

UH-OH.

ABORT. ABORT.

DEAR GOD... WHY WOULD I EVER...

MY FAULT. TOTALLY MY FAULT. WE THREW YOU INTO THE DEEP END.

BUT NO, IT'S GOOD. NOW WE GOT SUPER AWKWARD OUT OF THE WAY, HAS TO BE EASY FROM HERE.

JUST...LET ME DO THE HEAVY LIFTING THIS TIME.

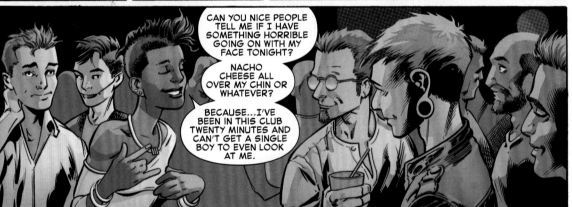

CAN YOU NICE PEOPLE TELL ME IF I HAVE SOMETHING HORRIBLE GOING ON WITH MY FACE TONIGHT?

NACHO CHEESE ALL OVER MY CHIN OR WHATEVER?

BECAUSE...I'VE BEEN IN THIS CLUB TWENTY MINUTES AND CAN'T GET A SINGLE BOY TO EVEN LOOK AT ME.

WRONG CLUB, SWEETHEART.

SO YOU'RE SAYING I MIGHT HAVE TO BUY MY OWN RED BULLS TONIGHT?

YES MA'AM. AFRAID SO.

I SUPPOSE I CAN LIVE WITH THAT...

...BUT WHICH ONE OF YOU IS FOOTING THE BILL FOR MY FRIEND BOB--

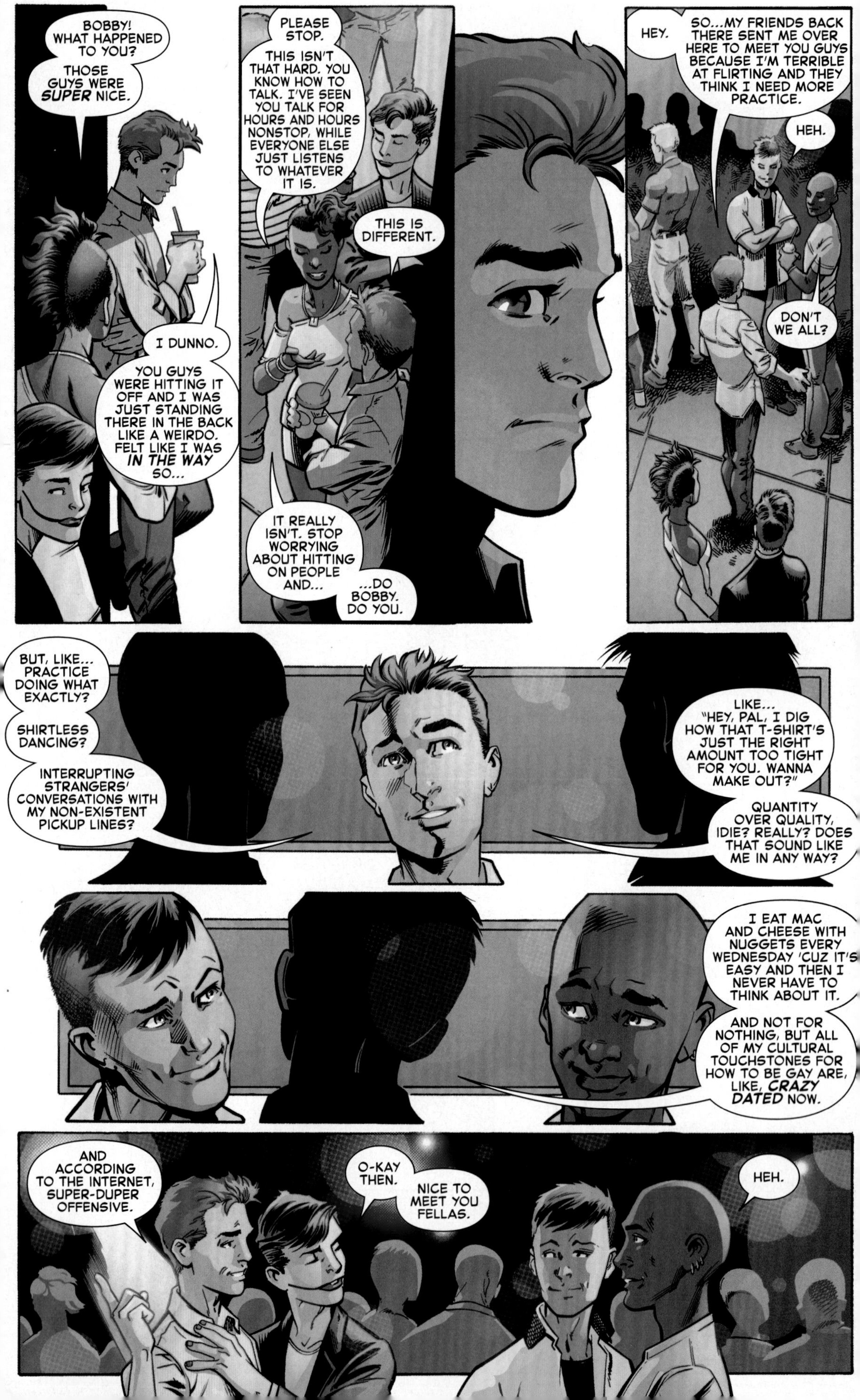

BOBBY! WHAT HAPPENED TO YOU?
THOSE GUYS WERE SUPER NICE.
I DUNNO.
YOU GUYS WERE HITTING IT OFF AND I WAS JUST STANDING THERE IN THE BACK LIKE A WEIRDO. FELT LIKE I WAS IN THE WAY SO...
PLEASE STOP.
THIS ISN'T THAT HARD. YOU KNOW HOW TO TALK. I'VE SEEN YOU TALK FOR HOURS AND HOURS NONSTOP, WHILE EVERYONE ELSE JUST LISTENS TO WHATEVER IT IS.
THIS IS DIFFERENT.
IT REALLY ISN'T. STOP WORRYING ABOUT HITTING ON PEOPLE AND...
...DO BOBBY. DO YOU.
HEY.
SO...MY FRIENDS BACK THERE SENT ME OVER HERE TO MEET YOU GUYS BECAUSE I'M TERRIBLE AT FLIRTING AND THEY THINK I NEED MORE PRACTICE.
HEH.
DON'T WE ALL?
BUT, LIKE... PRACTICE DOING WHAT EXACTLY?
SHIRTLESS DANCING?
INTERRUPTING STRANGERS' CONVERSATIONS WITH MY NON-EXISTENT PICKUP LINES?
LIKE... "HEY, PAL, I DIG HOW THAT T-SHIRT'S JUST THE RIGHT AMOUNT TOO TIGHT FOR YOU. WANNA MAKE OUT?"
QUANTITY OVER QUALITY, IDIE? REALLY? DOES THAT SOUND LIKE ME IN ANY WAY?
I EAT MAC AND CHEESE WITH NUGGETS EVERY WEDNESDAY 'CUZ IT'S EASY AND THEN I NEVER HAVE TO THINK ABOUT IT.
AND NOT FOR NOTHING, BUT ALL OF MY CULTURAL TOUCHSTONES FOR HOW TO BE GAY ARE, LIKE, CRAZY DATED NOW.
AND ACCORDING TO THE INTERNET, SUPER-DUPER OFFENSIVE.
O-KAY THEN.
NICE TO MEET YOU FELLAS.
HEH.

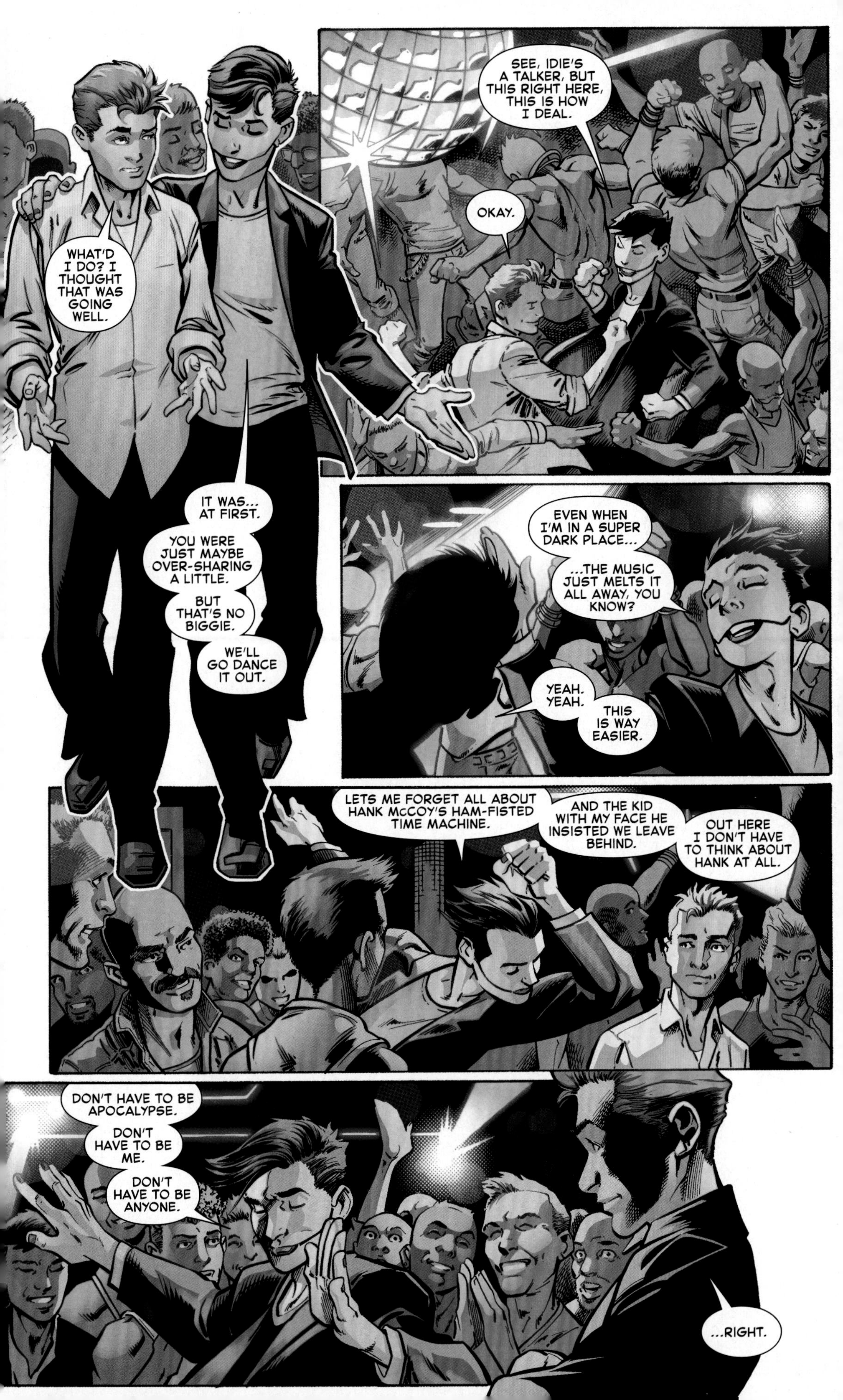
WHAT'D I DO? I THOUGHT THAT WAS GOING WELL.
SEE, IDIE'S A TALKER, BUT THIS RIGHT HERE, THIS IS HOW I DEAL.
OKAY.
IT WAS... AT FIRST.
YOU WERE JUST MAYBE OVER-SHARING A LITTLE.
BUT THAT'S NO BIGGIE.
WE'LL GO DANCE IT OUT.
EVEN WHEN I'M IN A SUPER DARK PLACE...
...THE MUSIC JUST MELTS IT ALL AWAY, YOU KNOW?
YEAH. YEAH.
THIS IS WAY EASIER.
LETS ME FORGET ALL ABOUT HANK McCOY'S HAM-FISTED TIME MACHINE.
AND THE KID WITH MY FACE HE INSISTED WE LEAVE BEHIND.
OUT HERE I DON'T HAVE TO THINK ABOUT HANK AT ALL.
DON'T HAVE TO BE APOCALYPSE.
DON'T HAVE TO BE ME.
DON'T HAVE TO BE ANYONE.
...RIGHT.

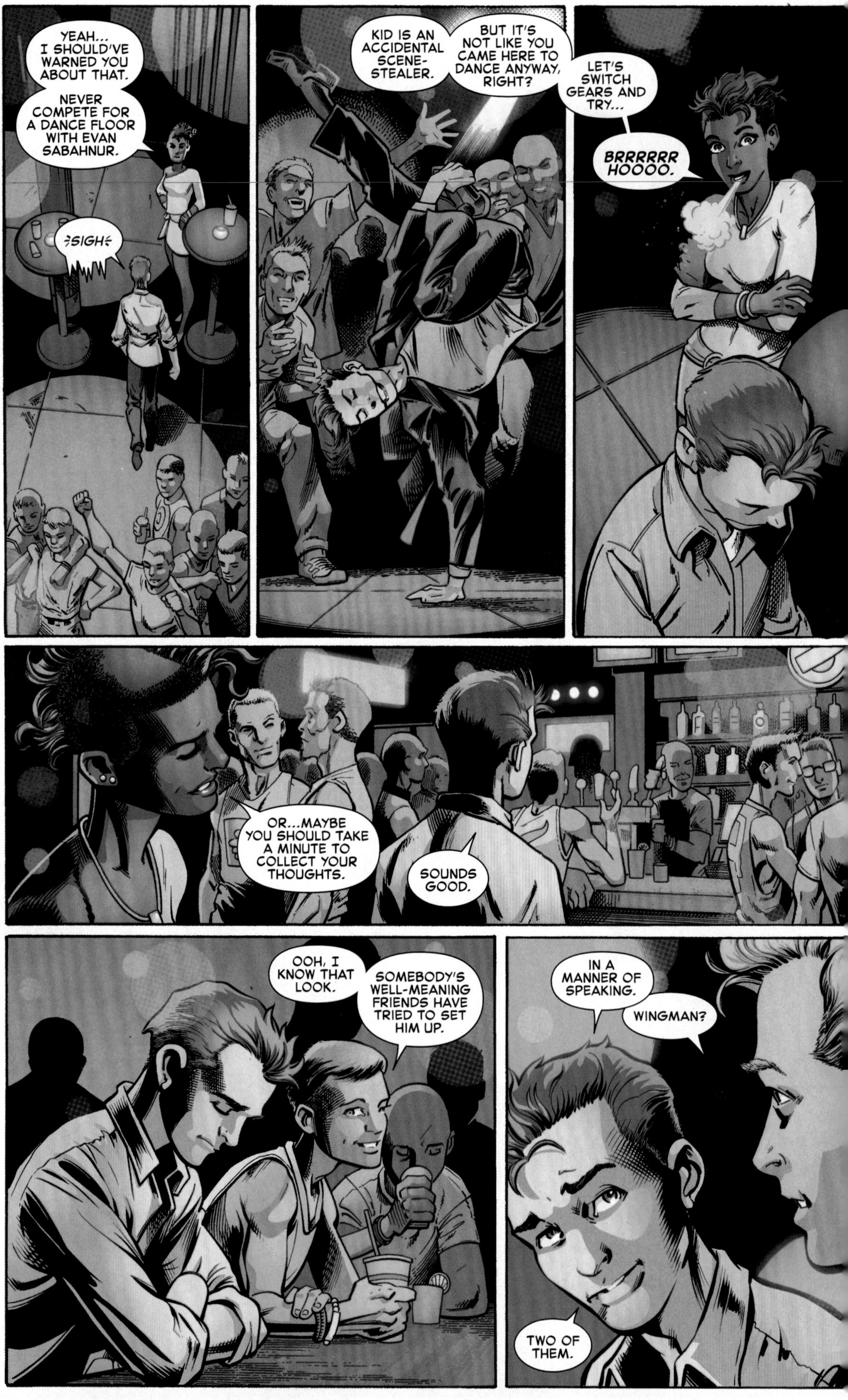
YEAH... I SHOULD'VE WARNED YOU ABOUT THAT.
NEVER COMPETE FOR A DANCE FLOOR WITH EVAN SABAHNUR.
SIGH
KID IS AN ACCIDENTAL SCENE-STEALER.
BUT IT'S NOT LIKE YOU CAME HERE TO DANCE ANYWAY, RIGHT?
LET'S SWITCH GEARS AND TRY...
BRRRRRR HOOOO.
OR...MAYBE YOU SHOULD TAKE A MINUTE TO COLLECT YOUR THOUGHTS.
SOUNDS GOOD.
OOH, I KNOW THAT LOOK.
SOMEBODY'S WELL-MEANING FRIENDS HAVE TRIED TO SET HIM UP.
IN A MANNER OF SPEAKING.
WINGMAN?
TWO OF THEM.

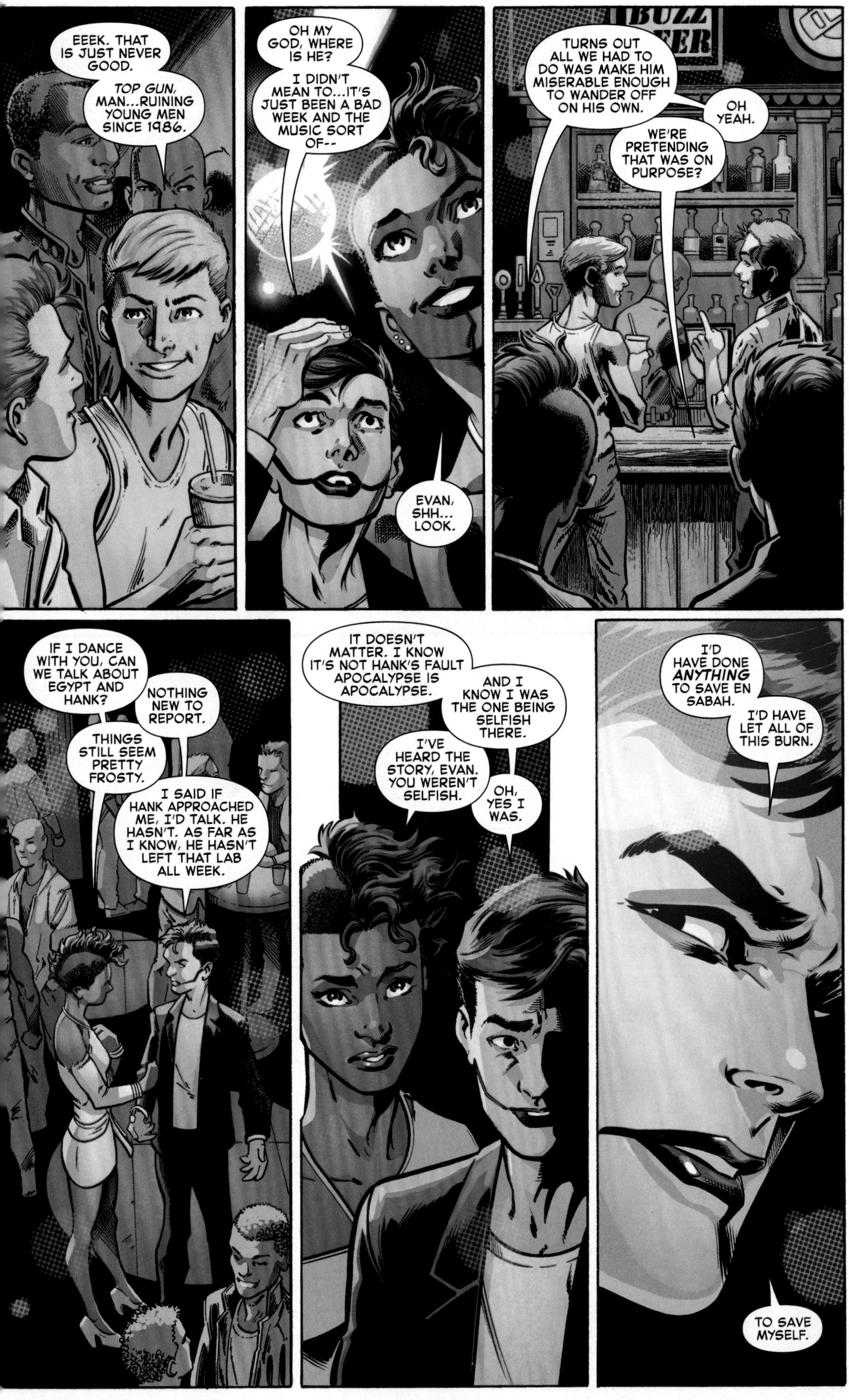

EEEK. THAT IS JUST NEVER GOOD.
TOP GUN, MAN...RUINING YOUNG MEN SINCE 1986.
OH MY GOD, WHERE IS HE?
I DIDN'T MEAN TO...IT'S JUST BEEN A BAD WEEK AND THE MUSIC SORT OF--
EVAN, SHH... LOOK.
BUZZ
TURNS OUT ALL WE HAD TO DO WAS MAKE HIM MISERABLE ENOUGH TO WANDER OFF ON HIS OWN.
OH YEAH.
WE'RE PRETENDING THAT WAS ON PURPOSE?
IF I DANCE WITH YOU, CAN WE TALK ABOUT EGYPT AND HANK?
NOTHING NEW TO REPORT.
THINGS STILL SEEM PRETTY FROSTY.
I SAID IF HANK APPROACHED ME, I'D TALK. HE HASN'T. AS FAR AS I KNOW, HE HASN'T LEFT THAT LAB ALL WEEK.
IT DOESN'T MATTER. I KNOW IT'S NOT HANK'S FAULT APOCALYPSE IS APOCALYPSE.
AND I KNOW I WAS THE ONE BEING SELFISH THERE.
I'VE HEARD THE STORY, EVAN. YOU WEREN'T SELFISH.
OH, YES I WAS.
I'D HAVE DONE ***ANYTHING*** TO SAVE EN SABAH.
I'D HAVE LET ALL OF THIS BURN.
TO SAVE MYSELF.

BUT BEAST'S LASER THING DOESN'T LIKE KNOCK UNUS OUT OR WHATEVER.

IT MAKES HIS UNTOUCHABLE POWERS CRAZY STRONG. NOW HE CAN'T TOUCH *ANYTHING.*

SO UNUS IS CHASING THIS PIECE OF PIE AROUND THE ROOM, FREAKING THE EFF OUT.

GHAHAHAHA!

YOU GUYS BEAT UNUS THE UNTOUCHABLE WITH PIE?

WELL, THE LACK OF PIE.

BUT YEAH, WE TOTALLY DID.

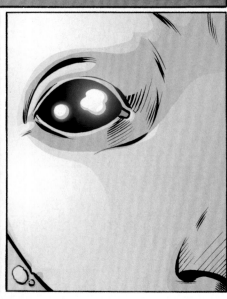

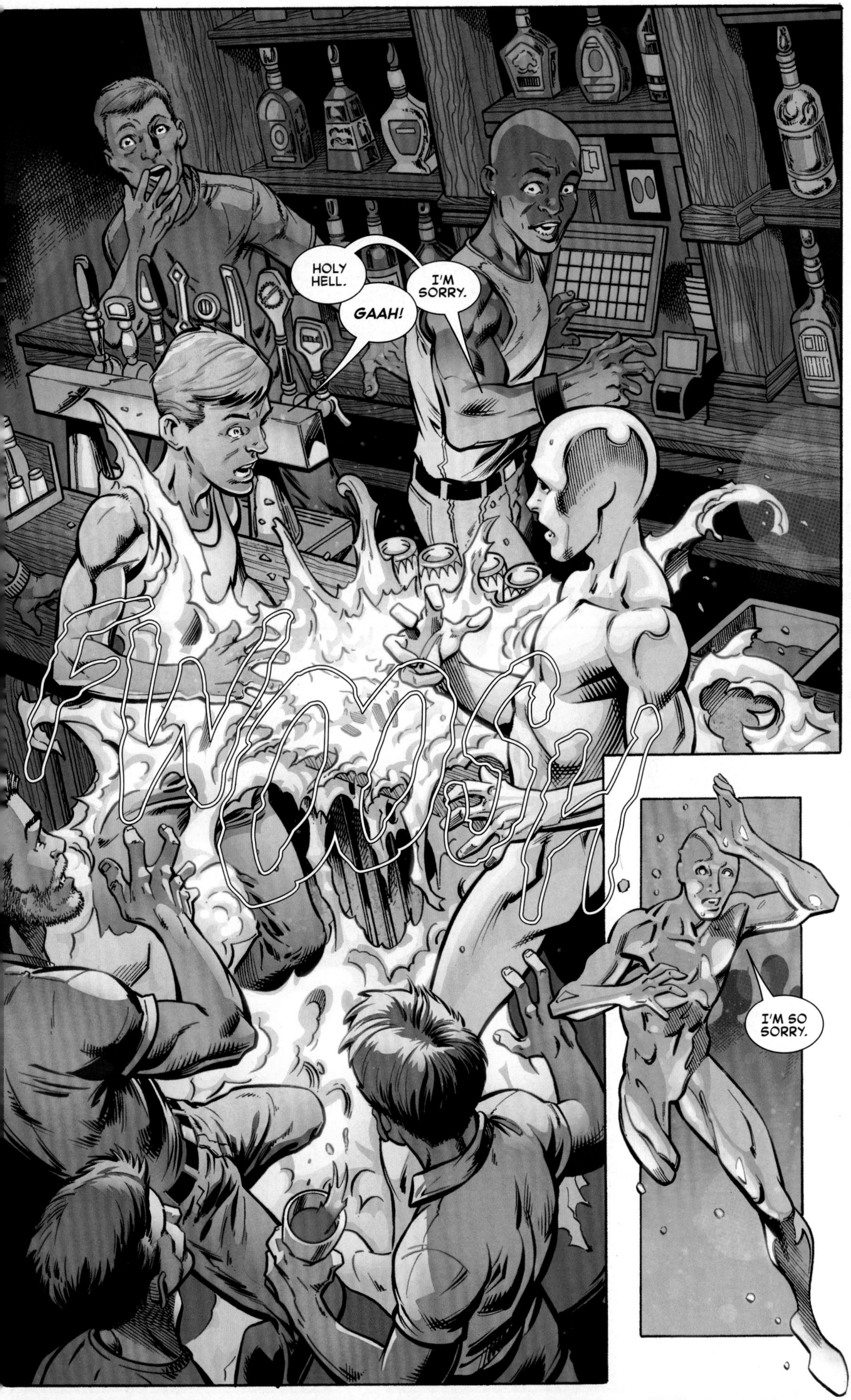
HOLY HELL.
GAAH!
I'M SORRY.
SWOOSH
I'M SO SORRY.

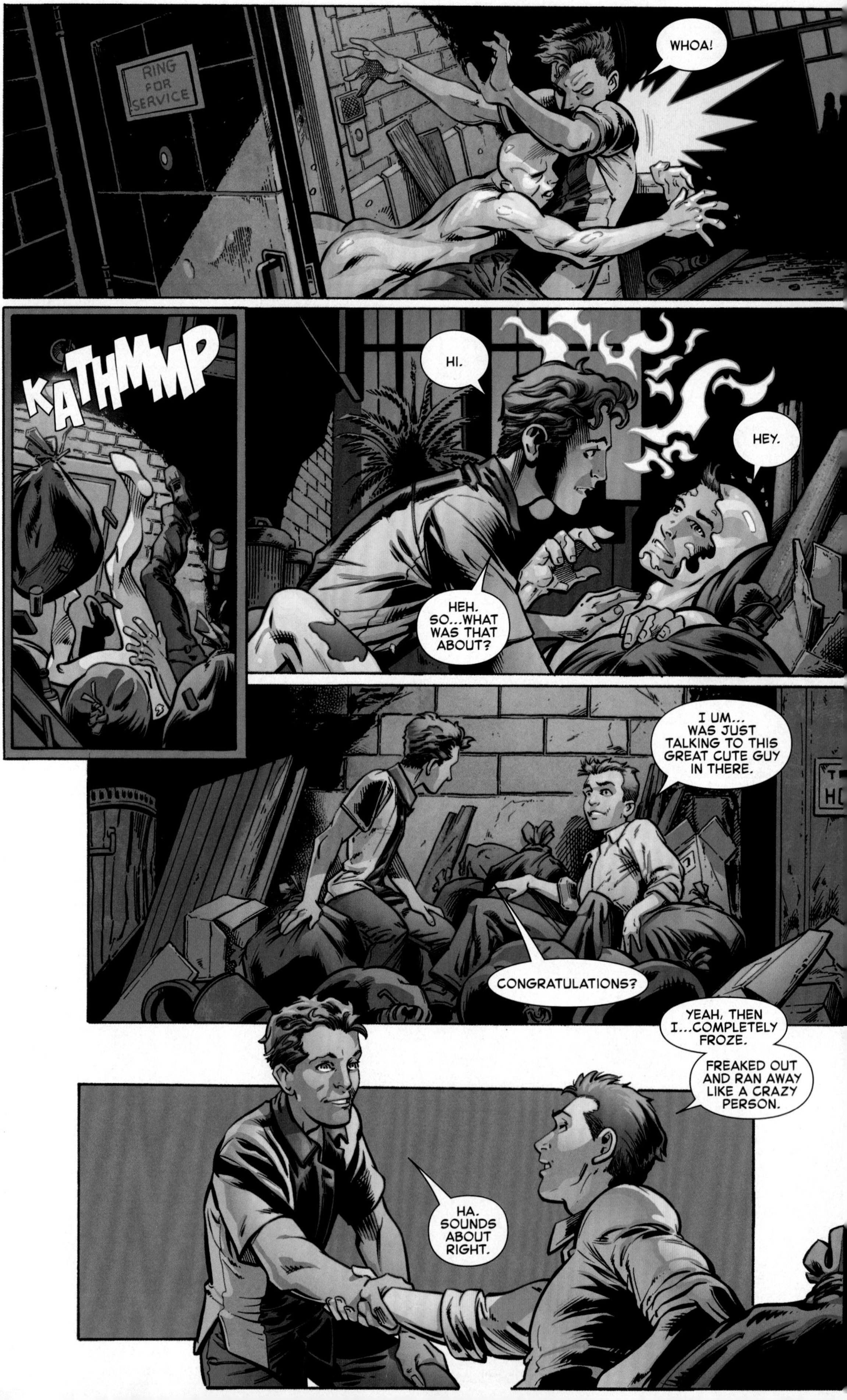
RING FOR SERVICE
WHOA!
KATHMMP
HI.
HEY.
HEH. SO...WHAT WAS THAT ABOUT?
I UM... WAS JUST TALKING TO THIS GREAT CUTE GUY IN THERE.
CONGRATULATIONS?
YEAH, THEN I...COMPLETELY FROZE.
FREAKED OUT AND RAN AWAY LIKE A CRAZY PERSON.
HA. SOUNDS ABOUT RIGHT.

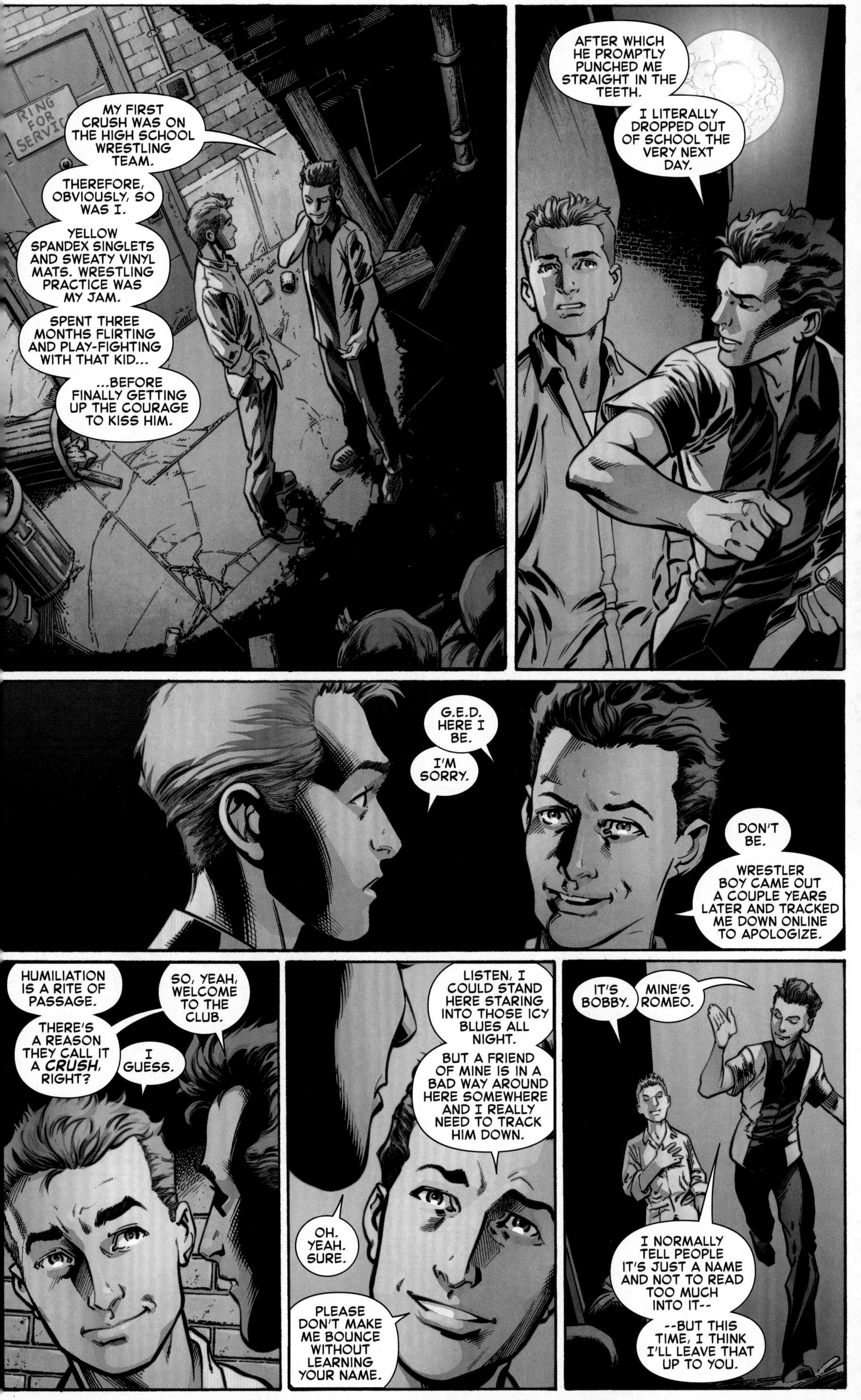
RING FOR SERVICE
MY FIRST CRUSH WAS ON THE HIGH SCHOOL WRESTLING TEAM.
THEREFORE, OBVIOUSLY, SO WAS I.
YELLOW SPANDEX SINGLETS AND SWEATY VINYL MATS. WRESTLING PRACTICE WAS MY JAM.
SPENT THREE MONTHS FLIRTING AND PLAY-FIGHTING WITH THAT KID...
...BEFORE FINALLY GETTING UP THE COURAGE TO KISS HIM.
AFTER WHICH HE PROMPTLY PUNCHED ME STRAIGHT IN THE TEETH.
I LITERALLY DROPPED OUT OF SCHOOL THE VERY NEXT DAY.
G.E.D. HERE I BE.
I'M SORRY.
DON'T BE.
WRESTLER BOY CAME OUT A COUPLE YEARS LATER AND TRACKED ME DOWN ONLINE TO APOLOGIZE.
HUMILIATION IS A RITE OF PASSAGE.
THERE'S A REASON THEY CALL IT A *CRUSH*, RIGHT?
I GUESS.
SO, YEAH, WELCOME TO THE CLUB.
LISTEN, I COULD STAND HERE STARING INTO THOSE ICY BLUES ALL NIGHT.
BUT A FRIEND OF MINE IS IN A BAD WAY AROUND HERE SOMEWHERE AND I REALLY NEED TO TRACK HIM DOWN.
OH. YEAH. SURE.
PLEASE DON'T MAKE ME BOUNCE WITHOUT LEARNING YOUR NAME.
IT'S BOBBY.
MINE'S ROMEO.
I NORMALLY TELL PEOPLE IT'S JUST A NAME AND NOT TO READ TOO MUCH INTO IT--
--BUT THIS TIME, I THINK I'LL LEAVE THAT UP TO YOU.

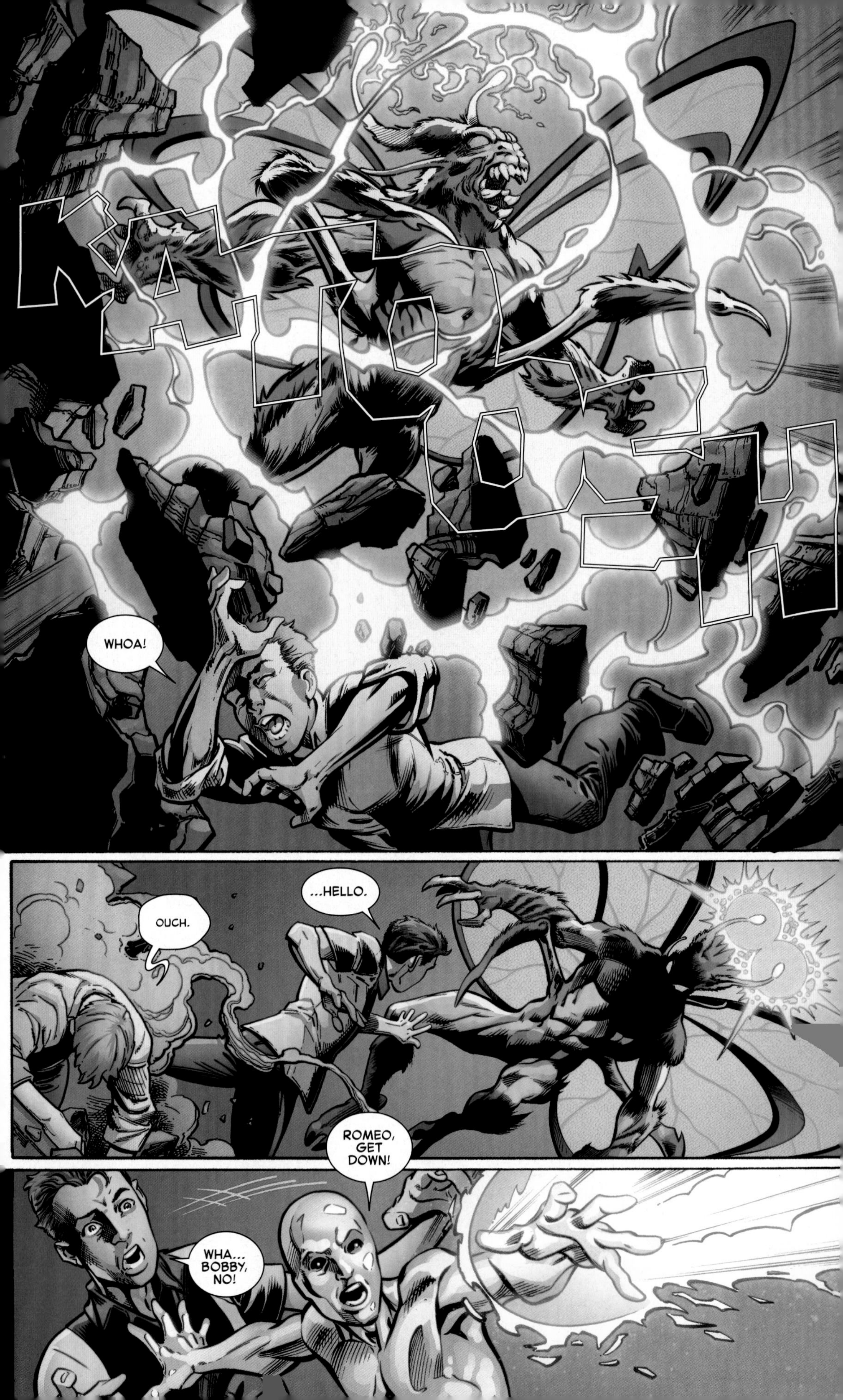

KATHOOOSH
WHOA!
OUCH.
...HELLO.
ROMEO, GET DOWN!
WHA... BOBBY, NO!

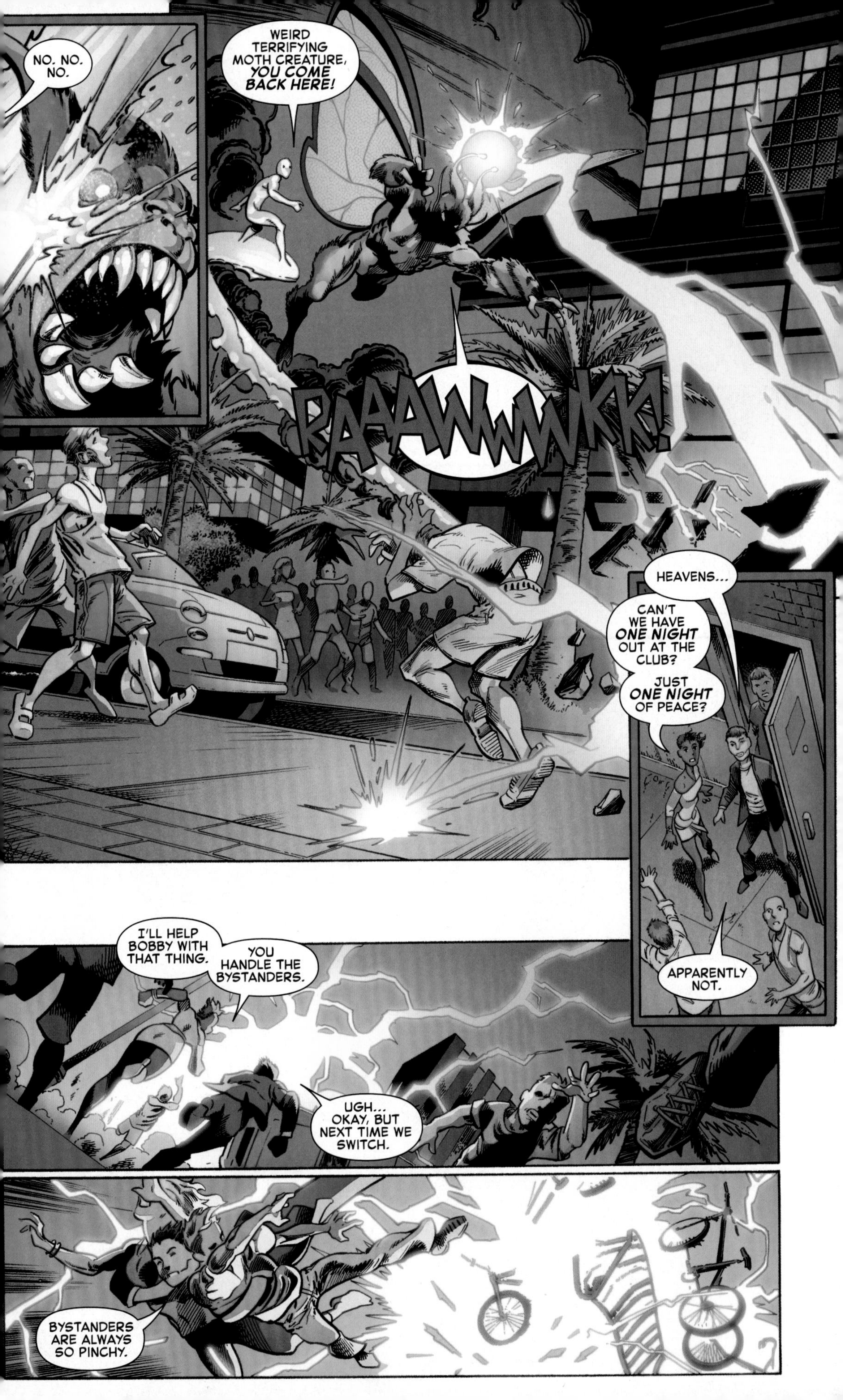
NO. NO. NO.
WEIRD TERRIFYING MOTH CREATURE, *YOU COME BACK HERE!*
RAAAWWWKK!
HEAVENS...
CAN'T WE HAVE *ONE NIGHT* OUT AT THE CLUB?
JUST *ONE NIGHT* OF PEACE?
APPARENTLY NOT.
I'LL HELP BOBBY WITH THAT THING.
YOU HANDLE THE BYSTANDERS.
UGH... OKAY, BUT NEXT TIME WE SWITCH.
BYSTANDERS ARE ALWAYS SO PINCHY.

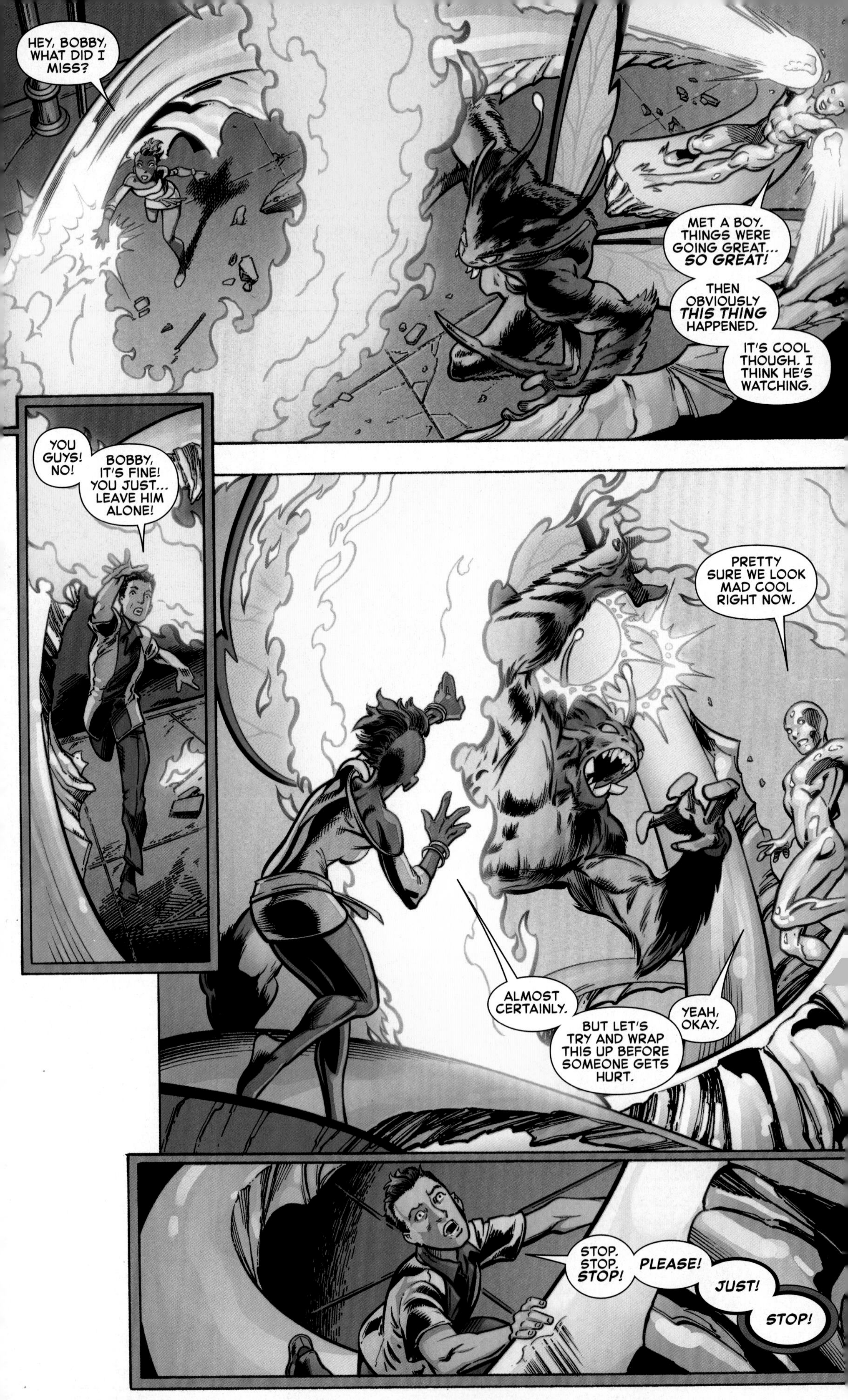
HEY, BOBBY, WHAT DID I MISS?
MET A BOY. THINGS WERE GOING GREAT... SO GREAT!
THEN OBVIOUSLY THIS THING HAPPENED.
IT'S COOL THOUGH. I THINK HE'S WATCHING.
YOU GUYS! NO!
BOBBY, IT'S FINE! YOU JUST... LEAVE HIM ALONE!
PRETTY SURE WE LOOK MAD COOL RIGHT NOW.
ALMOST CERTAINLY.
BUT LET'S TRY AND WRAP THIS UP BEFORE SOMEONE GETS HURT.
YEAH, OKAY.
STOP. STOP. STOP!
PLEASE!
JUST!
STOP!

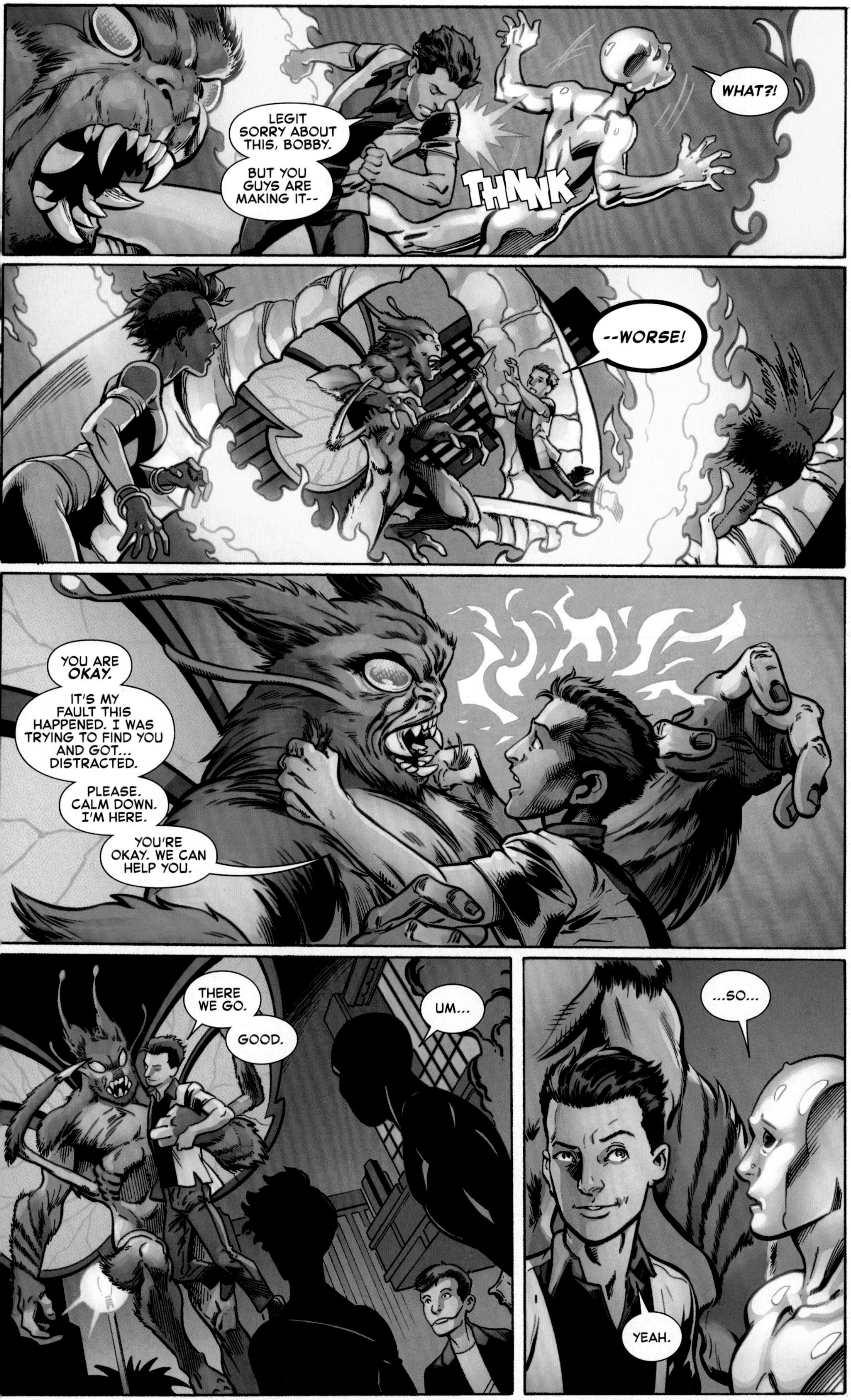
LEGIT SORRY ABOUT THIS, BOBBY.
BUT YOU GUYS ARE MAKING IT--
THNNK
WHAT?!
--WORSE!
YOU ARE OKAY.
IT'S MY FAULT THIS HAPPENED. I WAS TRYING TO FIND YOU AND GOT... DISTRACTED.
PLEASE. CALM DOWN. I'M HERE.
YOU'RE OKAY. WE CAN HELP YOU.
THERE WE GO.
GOOD.
UM...
...SO...
YEAH.

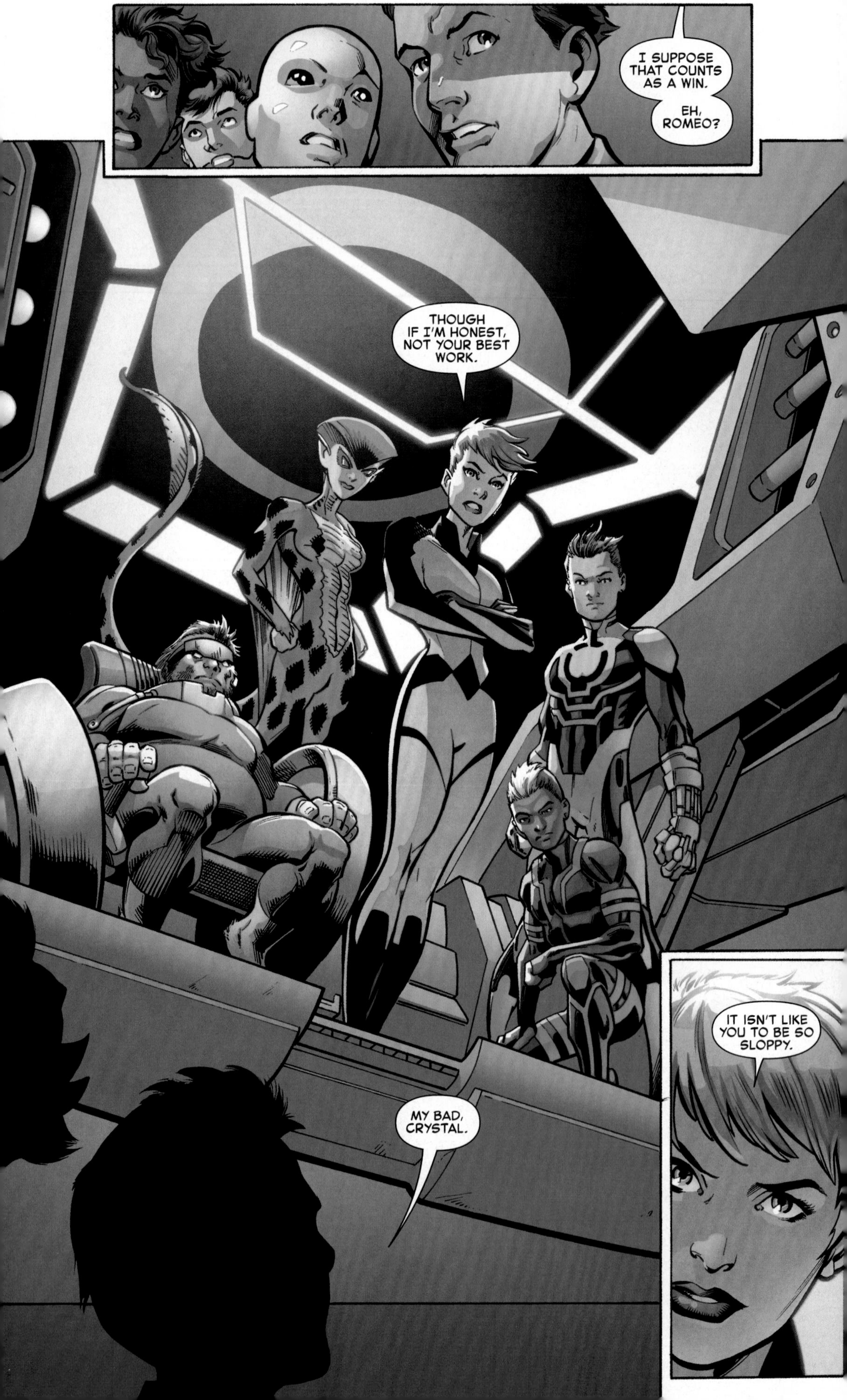
I SUPPOSE THAT COUNTS AS A WIN.
EH, ROMEO?
THOUGH IF I'M HONEST, NOT YOUR BEST WORK.
IT ISN'T LIKE YOU TO BE SO SLOPPY.
MY BAD, CRYSTAL.

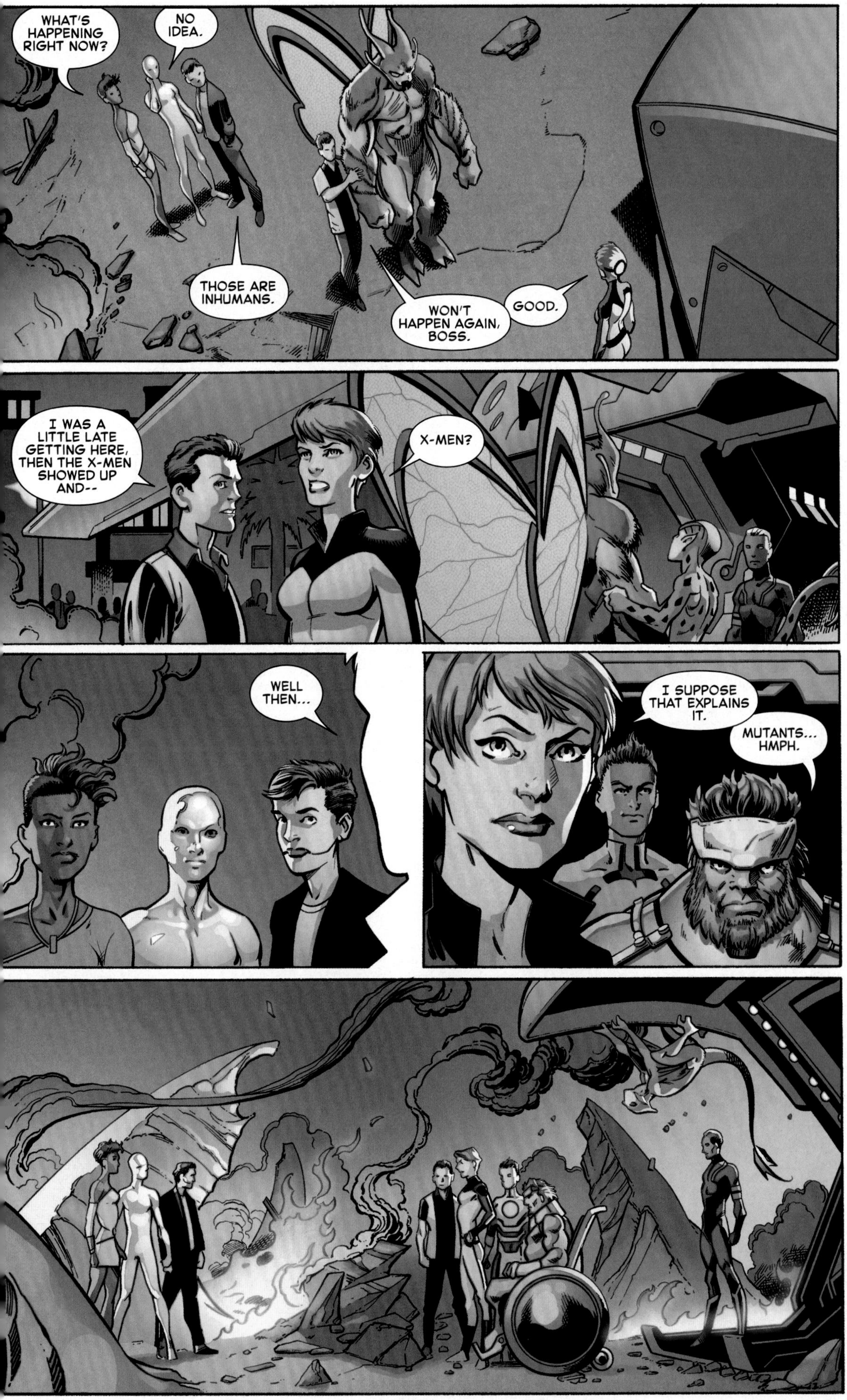

WHAT'S HAPPENING RIGHT NOW?
NO IDEA.
THOSE ARE INHUMANS.
WON'T HAPPEN AGAIN, BOSS.
GOOD.
I WAS A LITTLE LATE GETTING HERE, THEN THE X-MEN SHOWED UP AND--
X-MEN?
WELL THEN...
I SUPPOSE THAT EXPLAINS IT.
MUTANTS... HMPH.

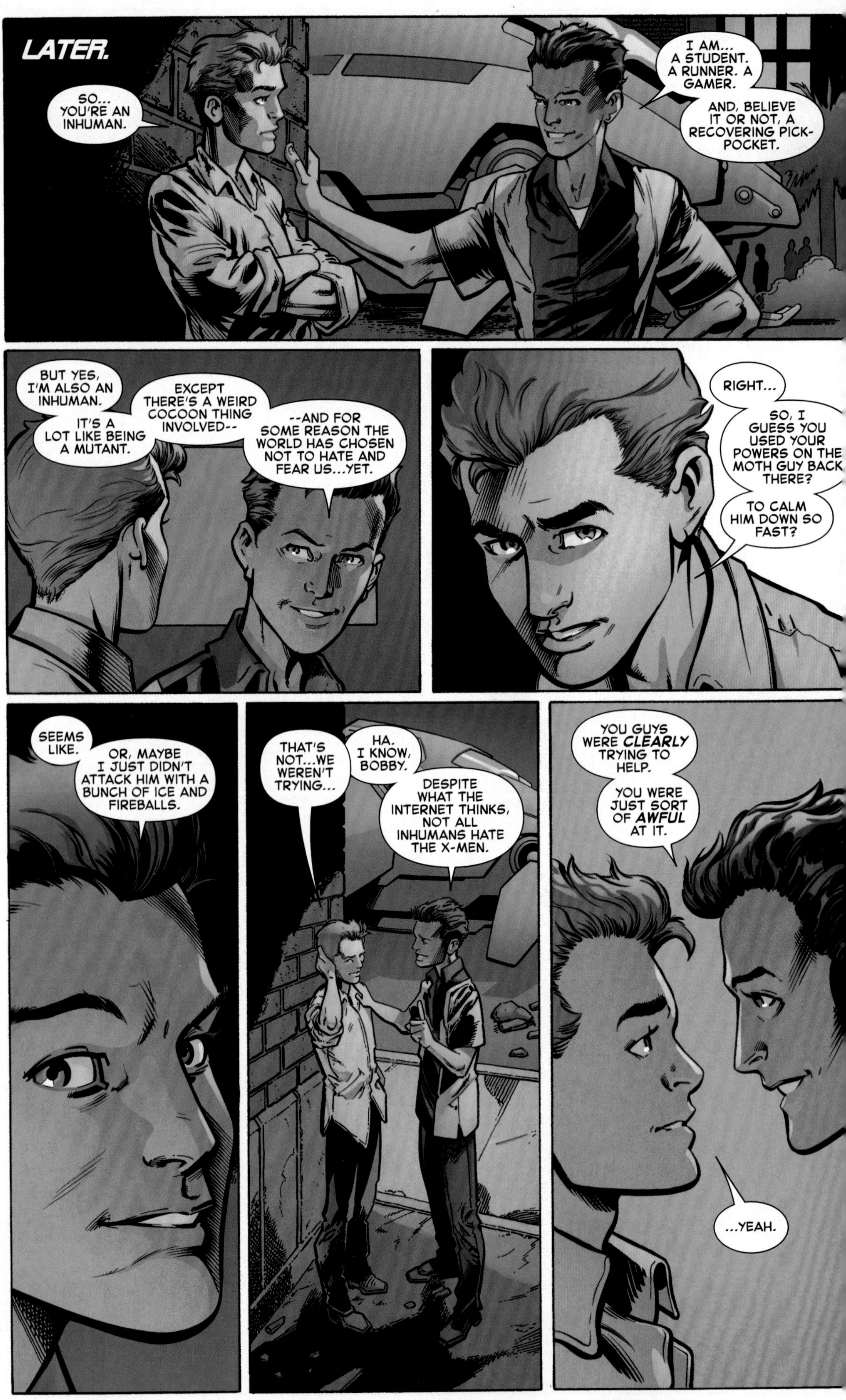
LATER.
SO... YOU'RE AN INHUMAN.
I AM... A STUDENT. A RUNNER. A GAMER.
AND, BELIEVE IT OR NOT, A RECOVERING PICK-POCKET.
BUT YES, I'M ALSO AN INHUMAN.
IT'S A LOT LIKE BEING A MUTANT.
EXCEPT THERE'S A WEIRD COCOON THING INVOLVED--
--AND FOR SOME REASON THE WORLD HAS CHOSEN NOT TO HATE AND FEAR US...YET.
RIGHT...
SO, I GUESS YOU USED YOUR POWERS ON THE MOTH GUY BACK THERE?
TO CALM HIM DOWN SO FAST?
SEEMS LIKE.
OR, MAYBE I JUST DIDN'T ATTACK HIM WITH A BUNCH OF ICE AND FIREBALLS.
THAT'S NOT...WE WEREN'T TRYING...
HA. I KNOW, BOBBY.
DESPITE WHAT THE INTERNET THINKS, NOT ALL INHUMANS HATE THE X-MEN.
YOU GUYS WERE CLEARLY TRYING TO HELP.
YOU WERE JUST SORT OF AWFUL AT IT.
...YEAH.

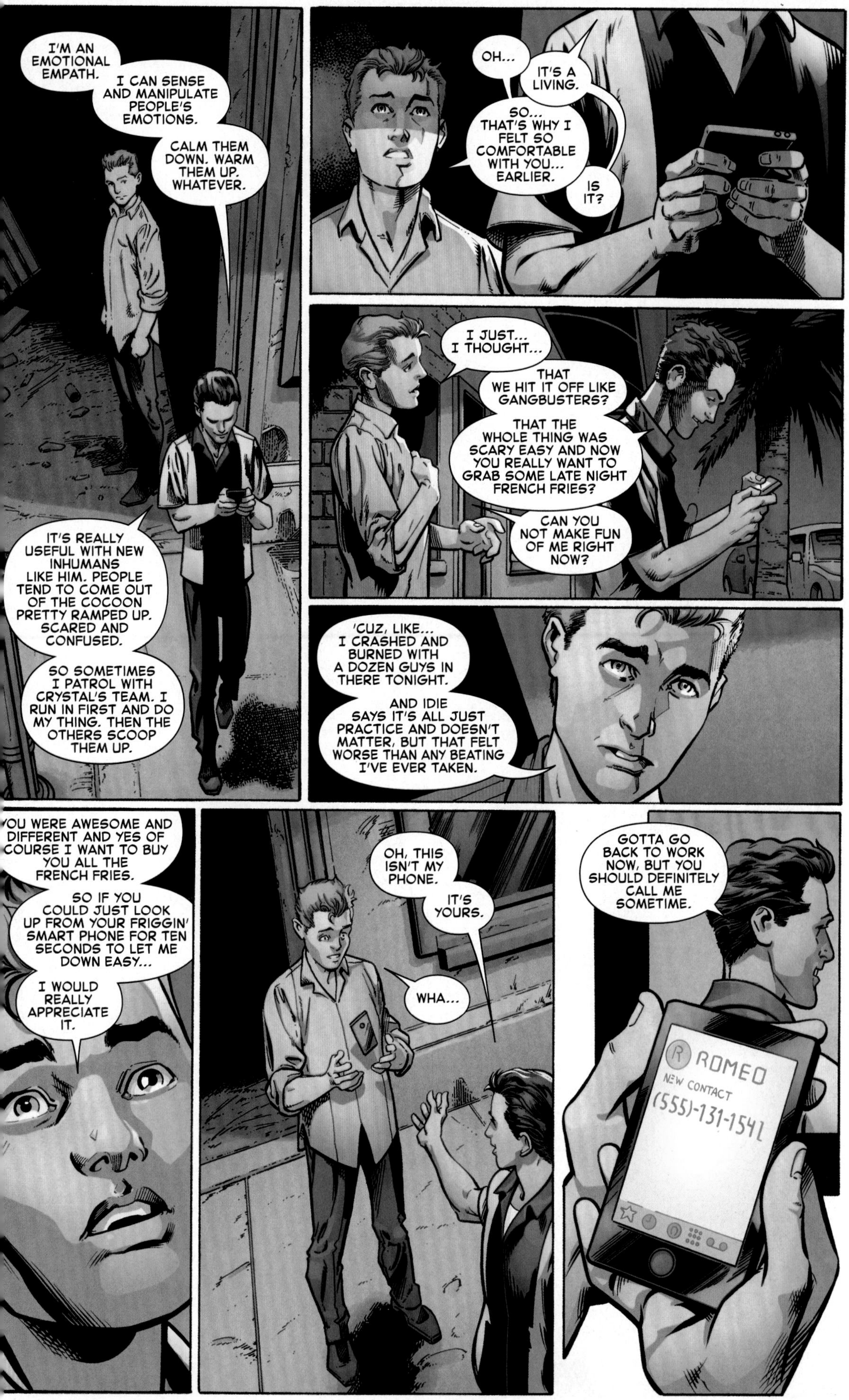

I'M AN EMOTIONAL EMPATH.
I CAN SENSE AND MANIPULATE PEOPLE'S EMOTIONS.
CALM THEM DOWN. WARM THEM UP. WHATEVER.
IT'S REALLY USEFUL WITH NEW INHUMANS LIKE HIM. PEOPLE TEND TO COME OUT OF THE COCOON PRETTY RAMPED UP. SCARED AND CONFUSED.
SO SOMETIMES I PATROL WITH CRYSTAL'S TEAM. I RUN IN FIRST AND DO MY THING. THEN THE OTHERS SCOOP THEM UP.
OH...
IT'S A LIVING.
SO... THAT'S WHY I FELT SO COMFORTABLE WITH YOU... EARLIER.
IS IT?
I JUST... I THOUGHT...
THAT WE HIT IT OFF LIKE GANGBUSTERS?
THAT THE WHOLE THING WAS SCARY EASY AND NOW YOU REALLY WANT TO GRAB SOME LATE NIGHT FRENCH FRIES?
CAN YOU NOT MAKE FUN OF ME RIGHT NOW?
'CUZ, LIKE... I CRASHED AND BURNED WITH A DOZEN GUYS IN THERE TONIGHT.
AND IDIE SAYS IT'S ALL JUST PRACTICE AND DOESN'T MATTER, BUT THAT FELT WORSE THAN ANY BEATING I'VE EVER TAKEN.
YOU WERE AWESOME AND DIFFERENT AND YES OF COURSE I WANT TO BUY YOU ALL THE FRENCH FRIES.
SO IF YOU COULD JUST LOOK UP FROM YOUR FRIGGIN' SMART PHONE FOR TEN SECONDS TO LET ME DOWN EASY...
I WOULD REALLY APPRECIATE IT.
OH, THIS ISN'T MY PHONE.
IT'S YOURS.
WHA...
GOTTA GO BACK TO WORK NOW, BUT YOU SHOULD DEFINITELY CALL ME SOMETIME.
ROMEO
NEW CONTACT
(555)-131-1541

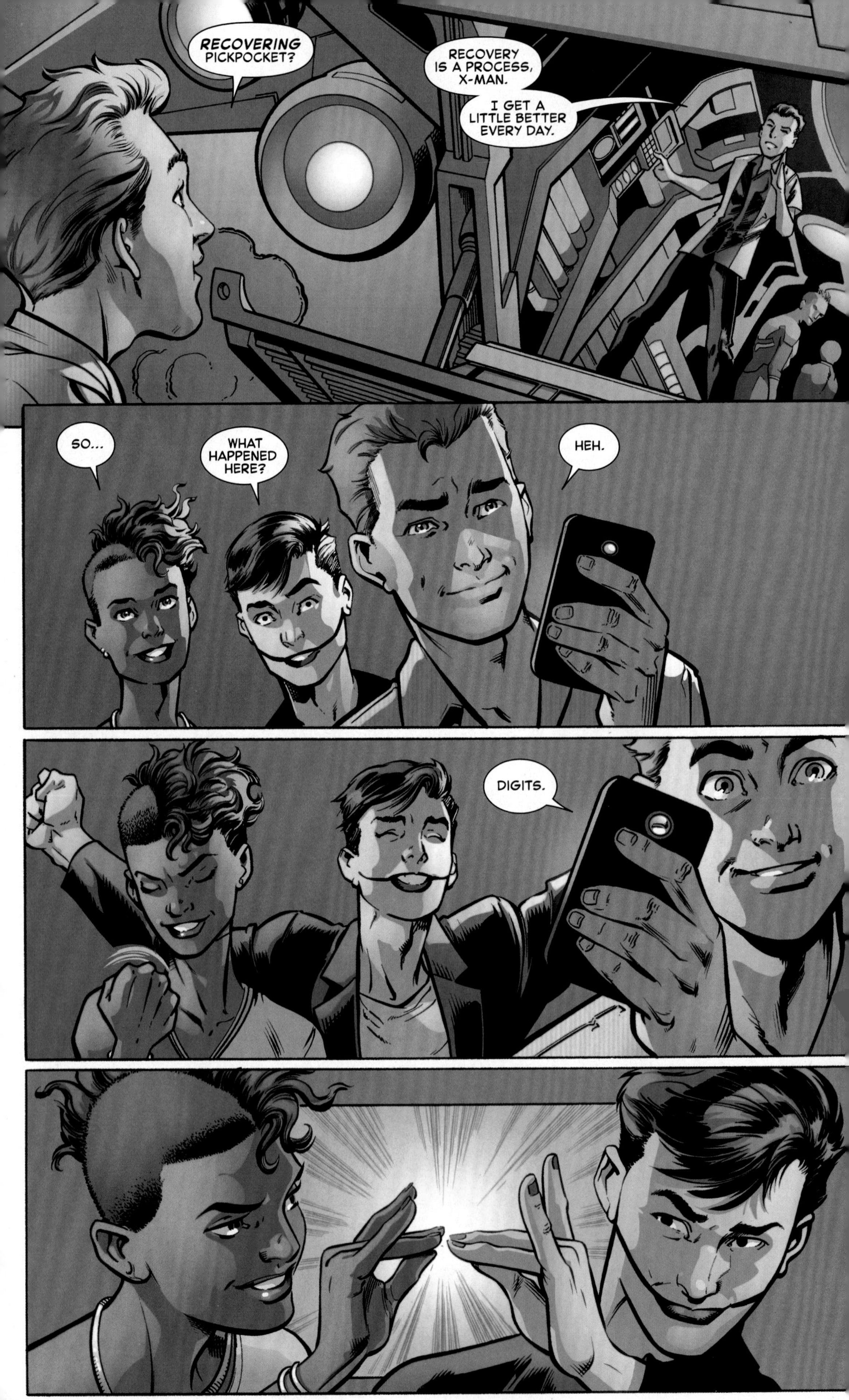

RECOVERING PICKPOCKET?
RECOVERY IS A PROCESS, X-MAN.
I GET A LITTLE BETTER EVERY DAY.
SO...
WHAT HAPPENED HERE?
HEH.
DIGITS.

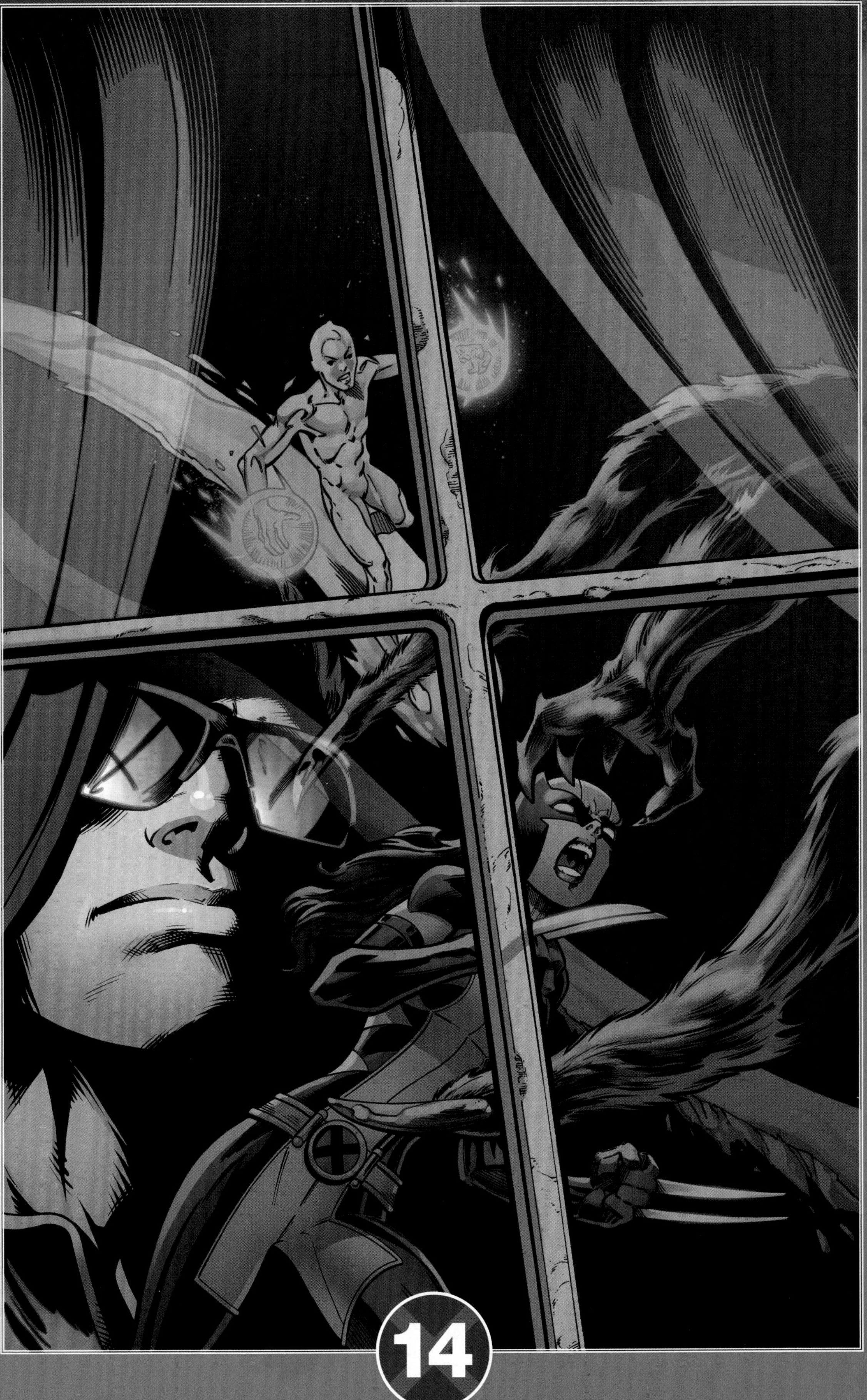
14

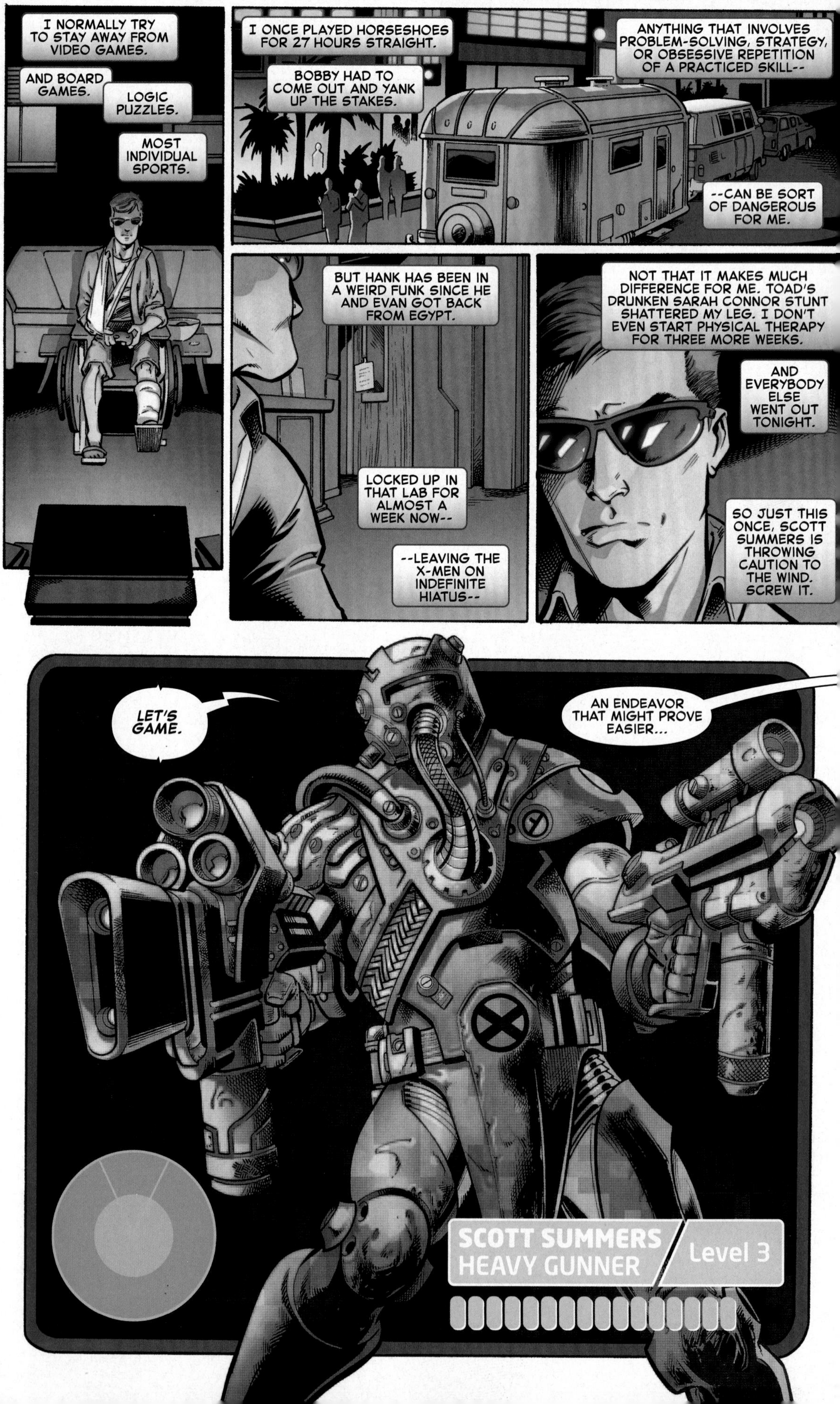
I NORMALLY TRY TO STAY AWAY FROM VIDEO GAMES.
AND BOARD GAMES.
LOGIC PUZZLES.
MOST INDIVIDUAL SPORTS.
I ONCE PLAYED HORSESHOES FOR 27 HOURS STRAIGHT.
BOBBY HAD TO COME OUT AND YANK UP THE STAKES.
ANYTHING THAT INVOLVES PROBLEM-SOLVING, STRATEGY, OR OBSESSIVE REPETITION OF A PRACTICED SKILL--
--CAN BE SORT OF DANGEROUS FOR ME.
BUT HANK HAS BEEN IN A WEIRD FUNK SINCE HE AND EVAN GOT BACK FROM EGYPT.
LOCKED UP IN THAT LAB FOR ALMOST A WEEK NOW--
--LEAVING THE X-MEN ON INDEFINITE HIATUS--
NOT THAT IT MAKES MUCH DIFFERENCE FOR ME. TOAD'S DRUNKEN SARAH CONNOR STUNT SHATTERED MY LEG. I DON'T EVEN START PHYSICAL THERAPY FOR THREE MORE WEEKS.
AND EVERYBODY ELSE WENT OUT TONIGHT.
SO JUST THIS ONCE, SCOTT SUMMERS IS THROWING CAUTION TO THE WIND. SCREW IT.
LET'S GAME.
AN ENDEAVOR THAT MIGHT PROVE EASIER...
SCOTT SUMMERS
HEAVY GUNNER
Level 3

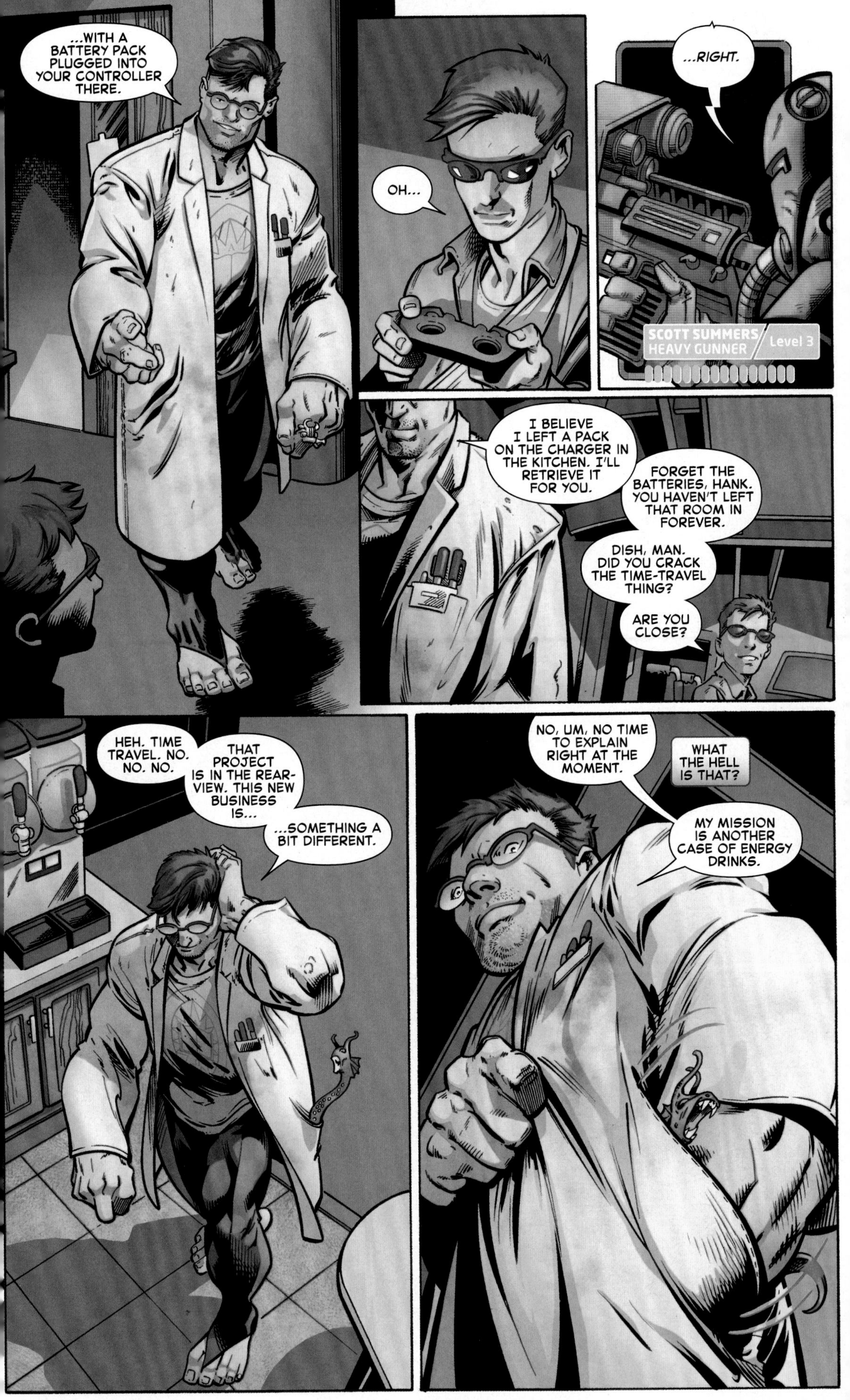
...WITH A BATTERY PACK PLUGGED INTO YOUR CONTROLLER THERE.
OH...
...RIGHT.
SCOTT SUMMERS
HEAVY GUNNER
Level 3
I BELIEVE I LEFT A PACK ON THE CHARGER IN THE KITCHEN. I'LL RETRIEVE IT FOR YOU.
FORGET THE BATTERIES, HANK. YOU HAVEN'T LEFT THAT ROOM IN FOREVER.
DISH, MAN. DID YOU CRACK THE TIME-TRAVEL THING?
ARE YOU CLOSE?
HEH. TIME TRAVEL. NO. NO. NO.
THAT PROJECT IS IN THE REAR-VIEW. THIS NEW BUSINESS IS...
...SOMETHING A BIT DIFFERENT.
NO, UM, NO TIME TO EXPLAIN RIGHT AT THE MOMENT.
WHAT THE HELL IS THAT?
MY MISSION IS ANOTHER CASE OF ENERGY DRINKS.

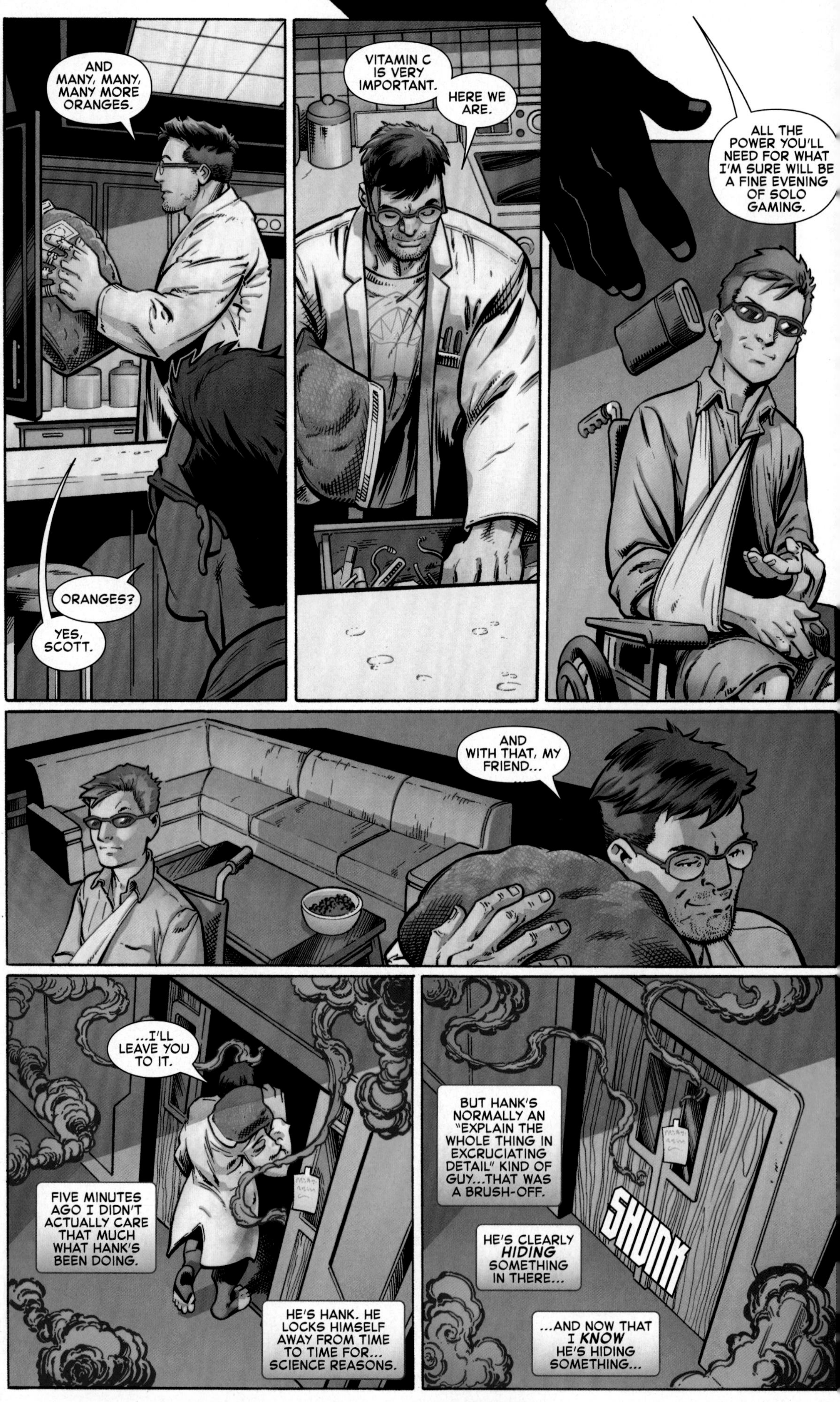
AND MANY, MANY, MANY MORE ORANGES.
ORANGES?
YES, SCOTT.
VITAMIN C IS VERY IMPORTANT.
HERE WE ARE.
ALL THE POWER YOU'LL NEED FOR WHAT I'M SURE WILL BE A FINE EVENING OF SOLO GAMING.
AND WITH THAT, MY FRIEND...
...I'LL LEAVE YOU TO IT.
FIVE MINUTES AGO I DIDN'T ACTUALLY CARE THAT MUCH WHAT HANK'S BEEN DOING.
HE'S HANK. HE LOCKS HIMSELF AWAY FROM TIME TO TIME FOR... SCIENCE REASONS.
BUT HANK'S NORMALLY AN "EXPLAIN THE WHOLE THING IN EXCRUCIATING DETAIL" KIND OF GUY...THAT WAS A BRUSH-OFF.
HE'S CLEARLY HIDING SOMETHING IN THERE...
...AND NOW THAT I KNOW HE'S HIDING SOMETHING...
SHUNK

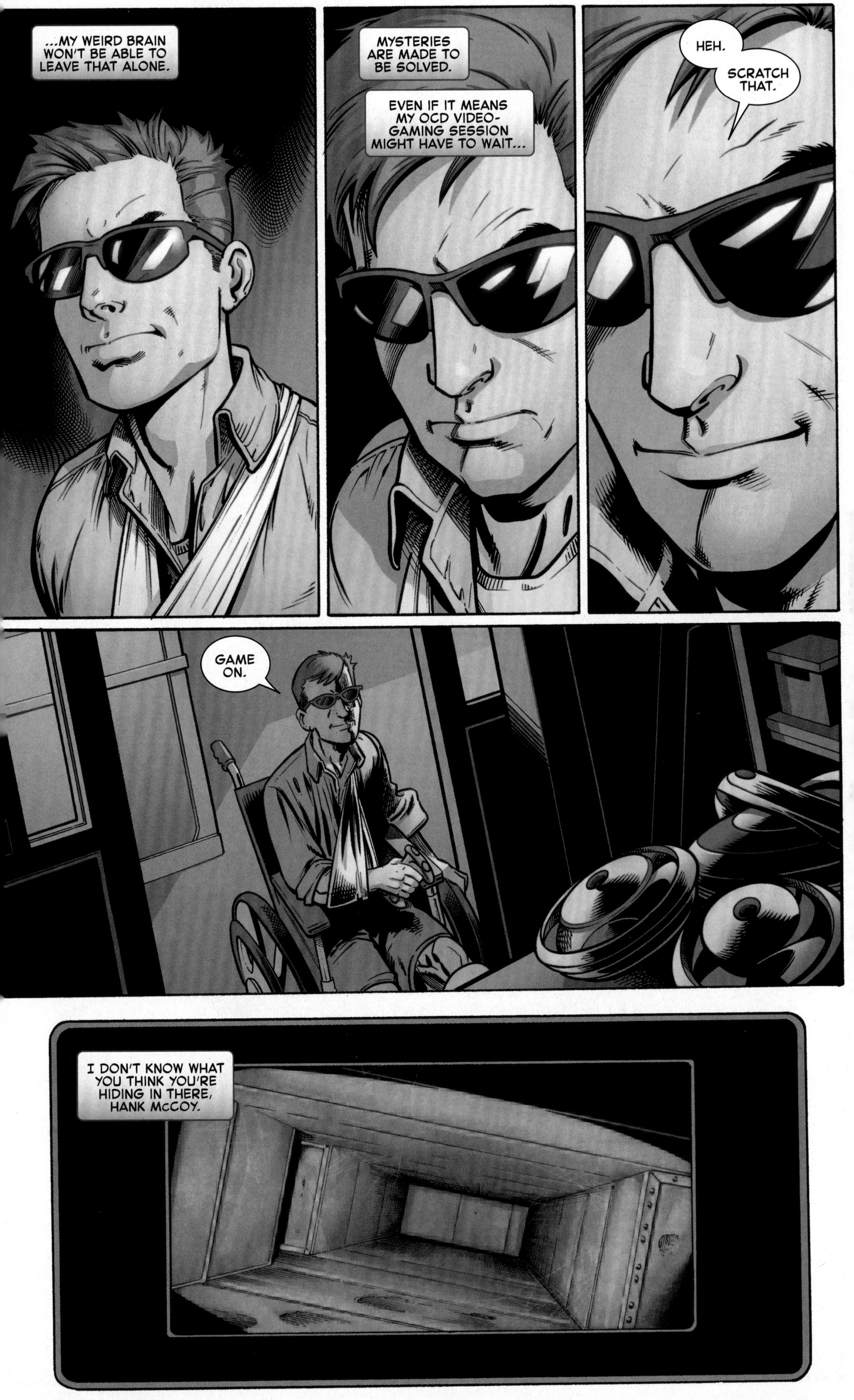
...MY WEIRD BRAIN WON'T BE ABLE TO LEAVE THAT ALONE.
MYSTERIES ARE MADE TO BE SOLVED.
EVEN IF IT MEANS MY OCD VIDEO-GAMING SESSION MIGHT HAVE TO WAIT...
HEH.
SCRATCH THAT.
GAME ON.
I DON'T KNOW WHAT YOU THINK YOU'RE HIDING IN THERE, HANK McCOY.

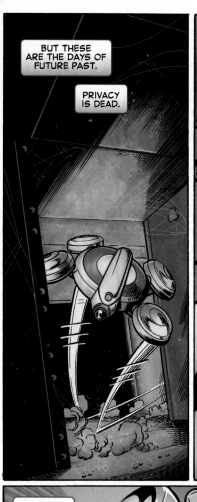

BUT THESE ARE THE DAYS OF FUTURE PAST.

PRIVACY IS DEAD.

AND THIS HORRIFYING PEEPING-TOM BOT...

...IS ABOUT TO GET...

...ALL UP IN...

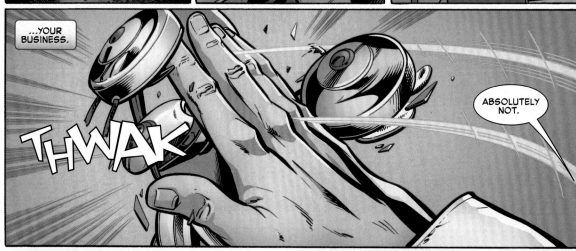

...YOUR BUSINESS.

THWAK

ABSOLUTELY NOT.

HMM...

GAME OVER
CONTINUE IN

9

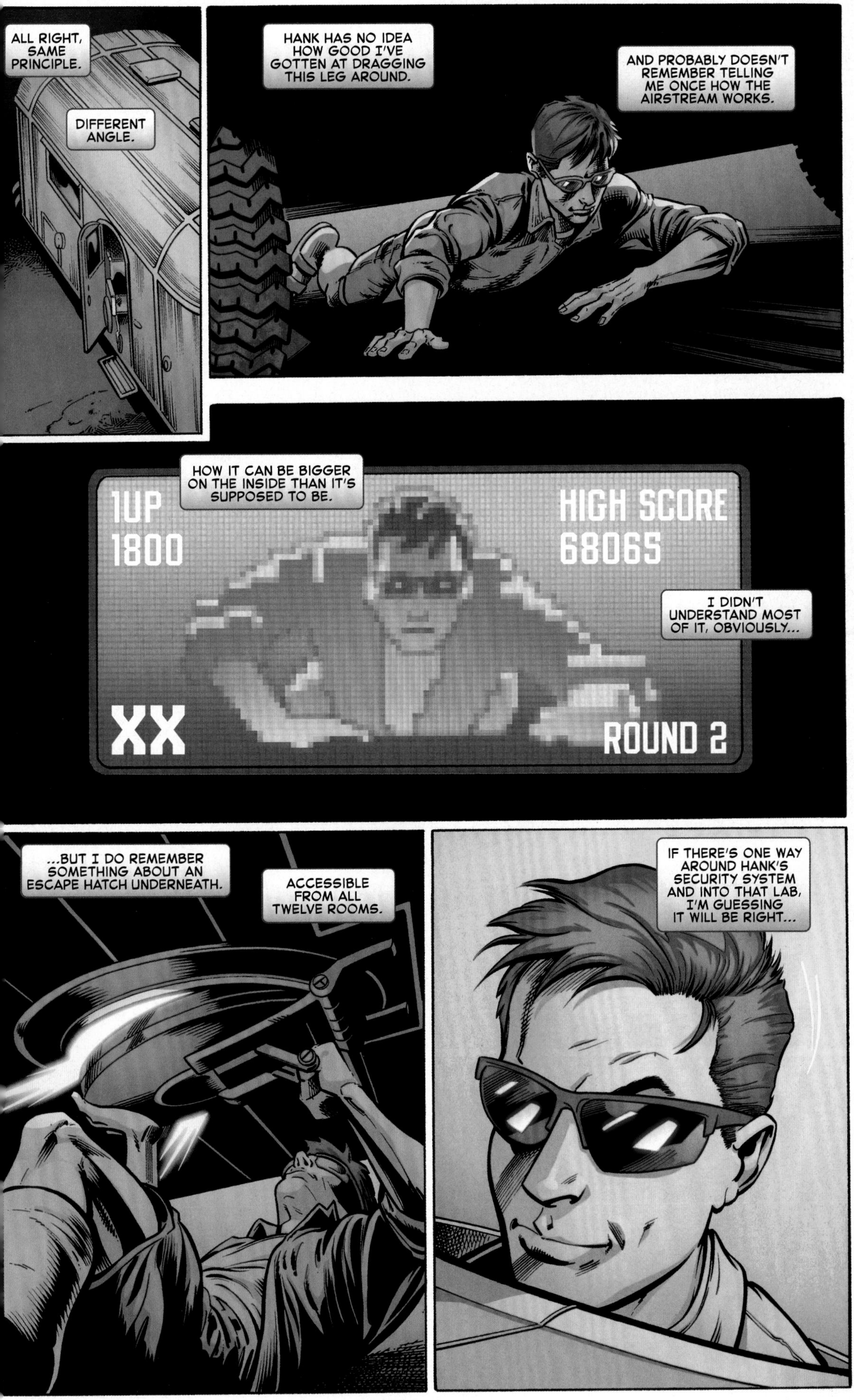

ALL RIGHT, SAME PRINCIPLE.
DIFFERENT ANGLE.
HANK HAS NO IDEA HOW GOOD I'VE GOTTEN AT DRAGGING THIS LEG AROUND.
AND PROBABLY DOESN'T REMEMBER TELLING ME ONCE HOW THE AIRSTREAM WORKS.
HOW IT CAN BE BIGGER ON THE INSIDE THAN IT'S SUPPOSED TO BE.
1UP
1800
HIGH SCORE
68065
I DIDN'T UNDERSTAND MOST OF IT, OBVIOUSLY...
XX
ROUND 2
...BUT I DO REMEMBER SOMETHING ABOUT AN ESCAPE HATCH UNDERNEATH.
ACCESSIBLE FROM ALL TWELVE ROOMS.
IF THERE'S ONE WAY AROUND HANK'S SECURITY SYSTEM AND INTO THAT LAB, I'M GUESSING IT WILL BE RIGHT...

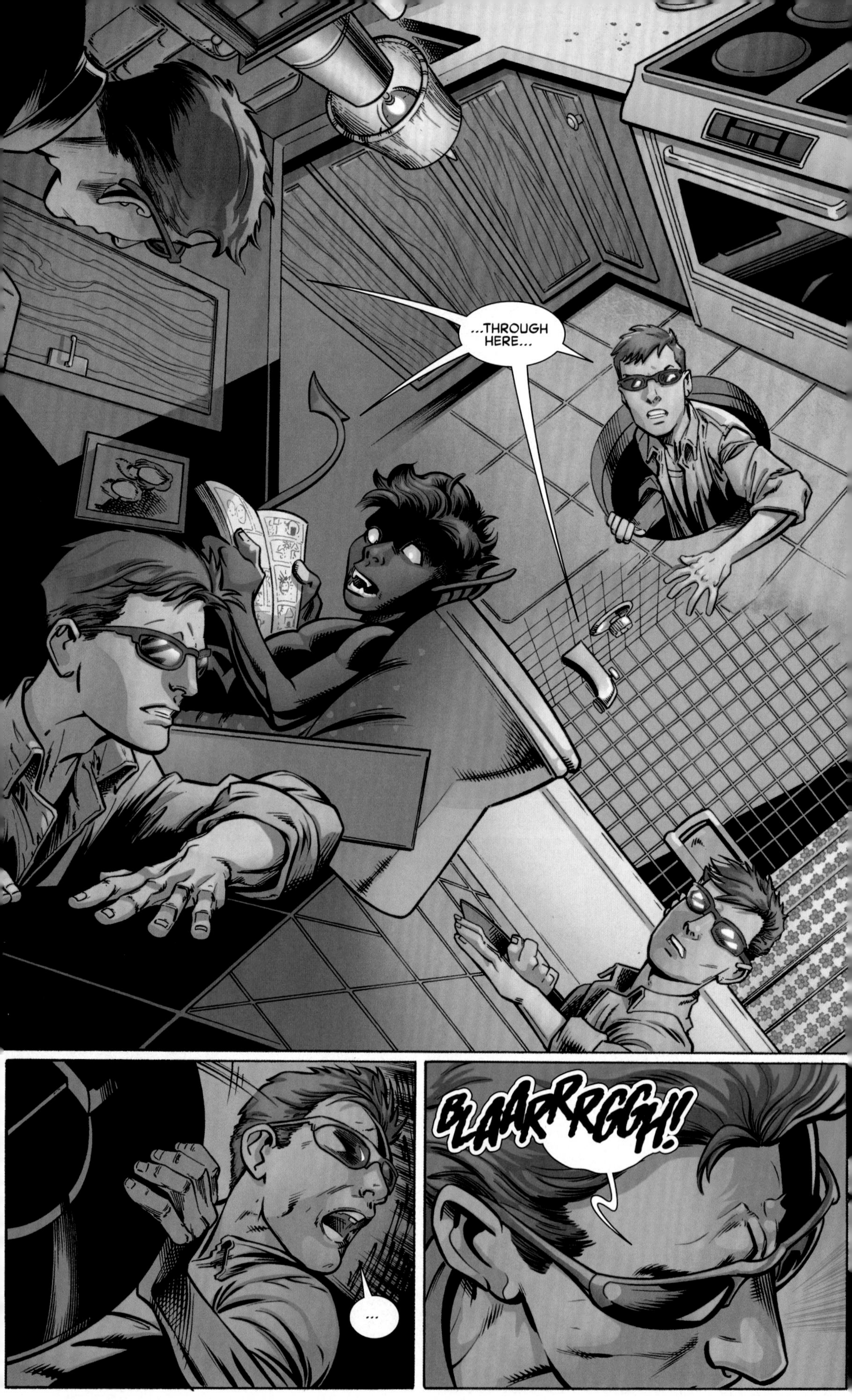
...THROUGH HERE...
...
BLAARRRGGH!

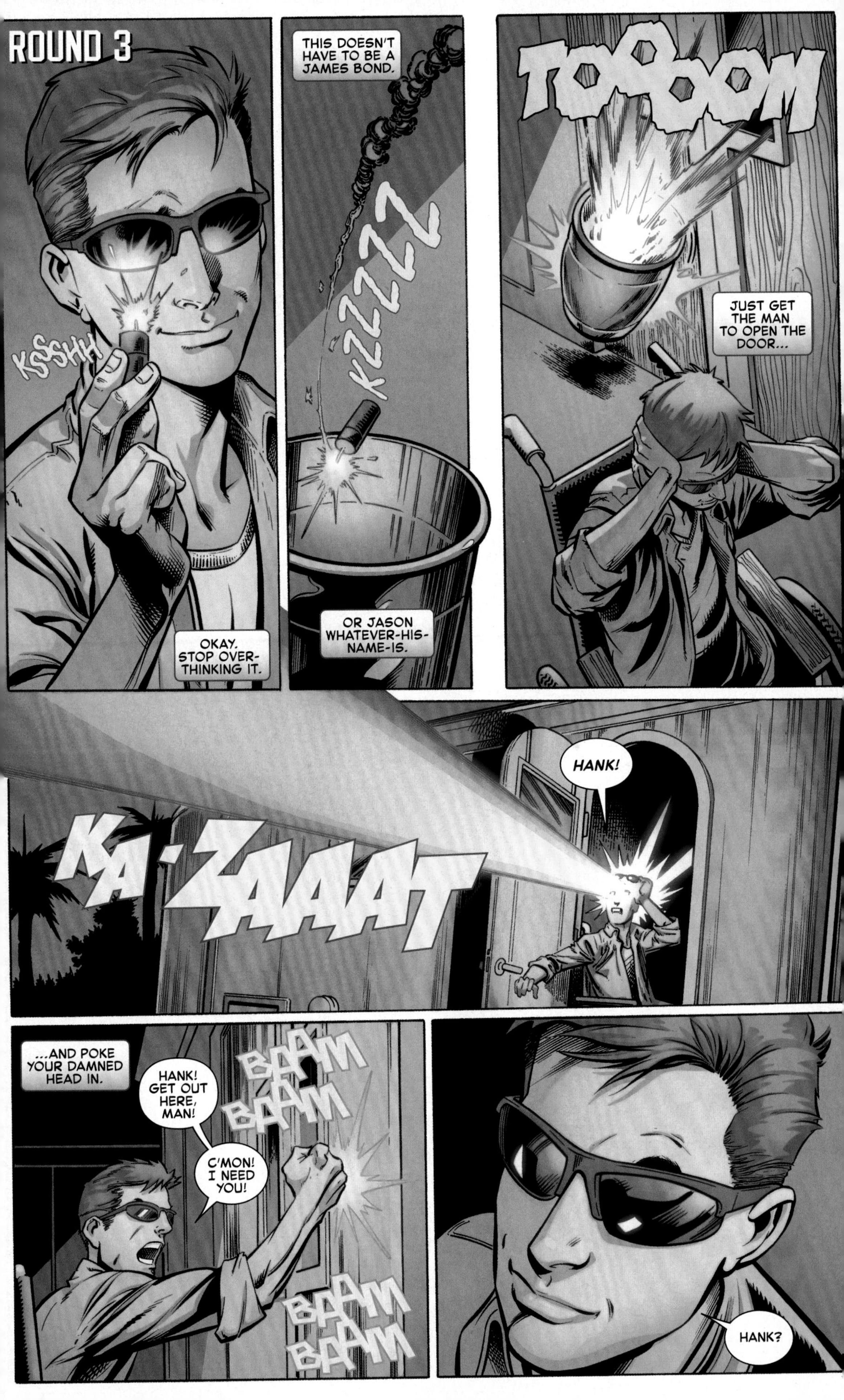
ROUND 3
KSSSHH
OKAY. STOP OVER-THINKING IT.
THIS DOESN'T HAVE TO BE A JAMES BOND.
KZZZZZZ
OR JASON WHATEVER-HIS-NAME-IS.
TOOOOM
JUST GET THE MAN TO OPEN THE DOOR...
HANK!
KA-ZAAAAT
...AND POKE YOUR DAMNED HEAD IN.
HANK! GET OUT HERE, MAN!
BAAM BAAM
C'MON! I NEED YOU!
BAAM BAAM
HANK?

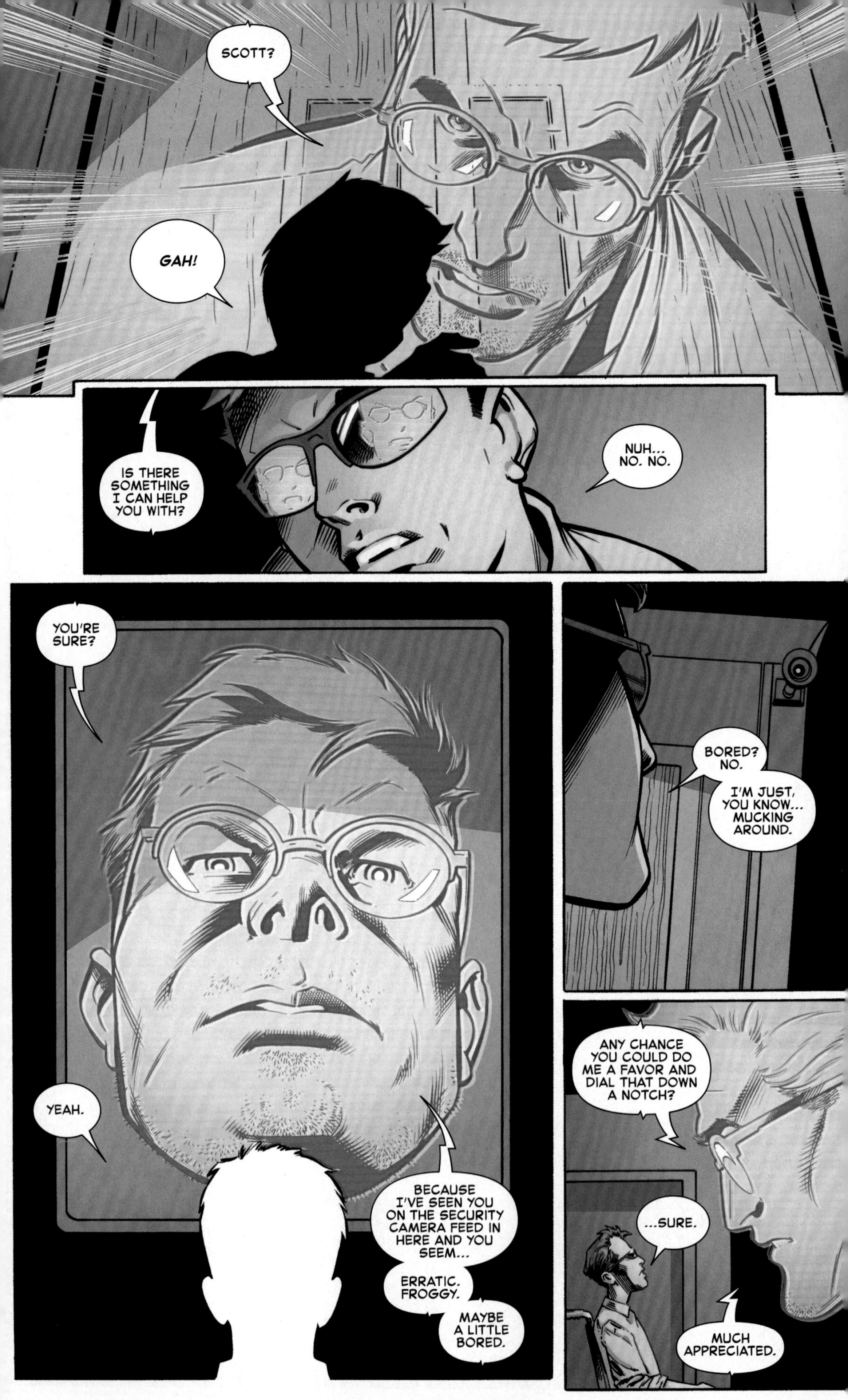
SCOTT?
GAH!
IS THERE SOMETHING I CAN HELP YOU WITH?
NUH... NO. NO.
YOU'RE SURE?
YEAH.
BECAUSE I'VE SEEN YOU ON THE SECURITY CAMERA FEED IN HERE AND YOU SEEM...
ERRATIC. FROGGY.
MAYBE A LITTLE BORED.
BORED? NO.
I'M JUST, YOU KNOW... MUCKING AROUND.
ANY CHANCE YOU COULD DO ME A FAVOR AND DIAL THAT DOWN A NOTCH?
...SURE.
MUCH APPRECIATED.

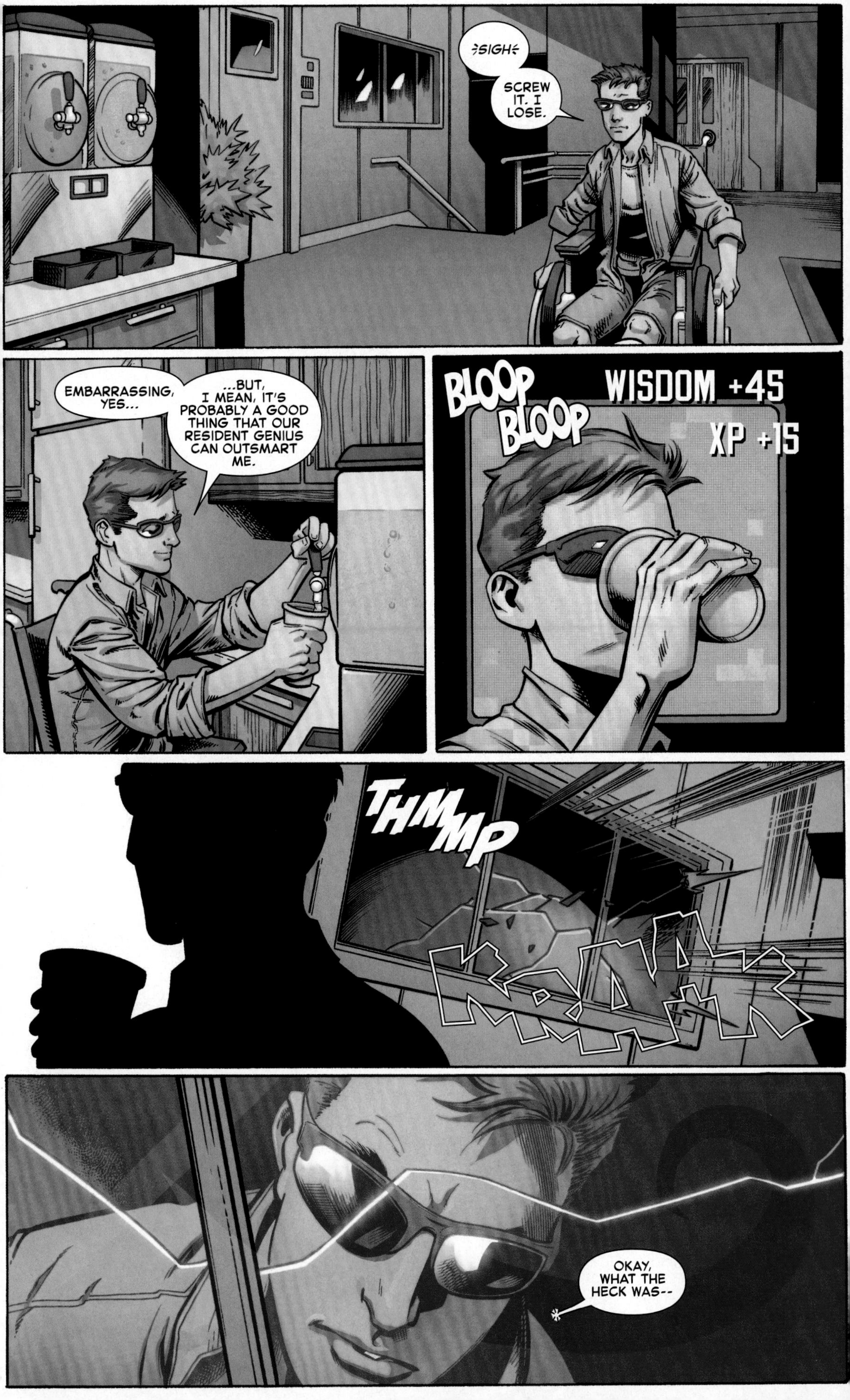

SIGH
SCREW IT. I LOSE.
EMBARRASSING, YES...
...BUT, I MEAN, IT'S PROBABLY A GOOD THING THAT OUR RESIDENT GENIUS CAN OUTSMART ME.
BLOOP BLOOP
WISDOM +45
XP +15
THMMMP
KRAAK
OKAY, WHAT THE HECK WAS--

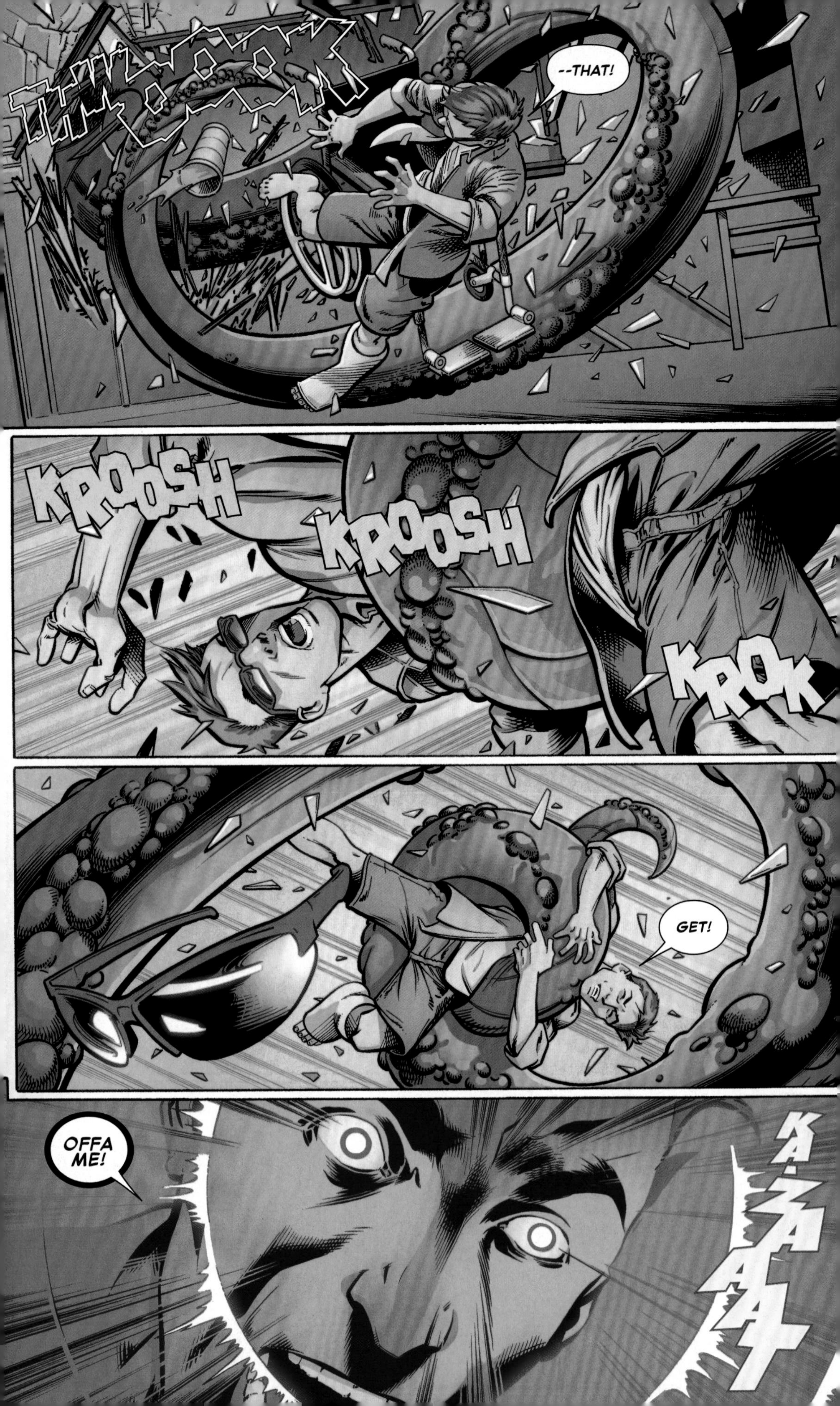
THWOOOM
--THAT!
KROOSH
KROOSH
KROK
GET!
OFFA ME!
KA-ZAAAT

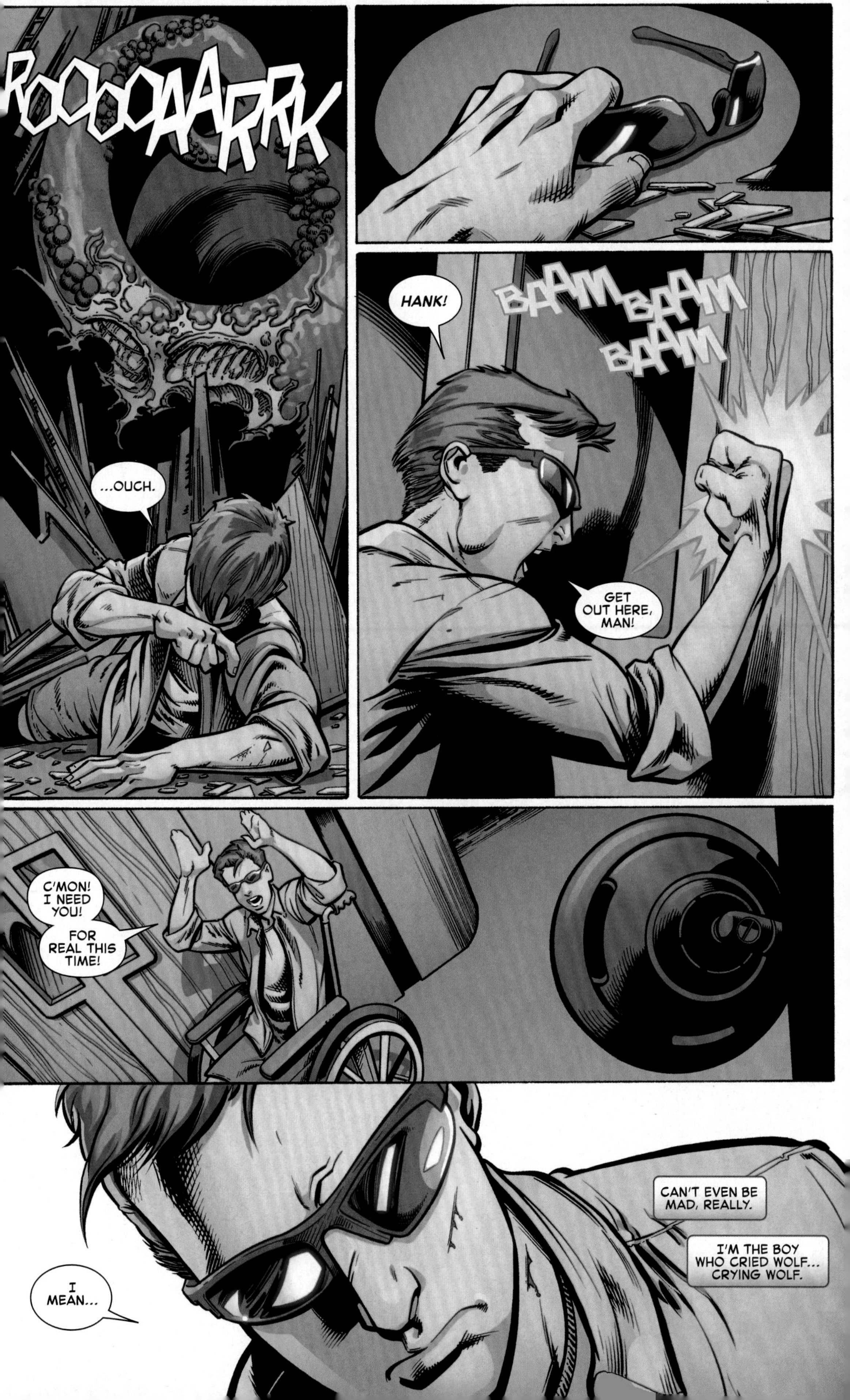
ROOOOAARRRK
...OUCH.
HANK!
BAAM BAAM BAAM
GET OUT HERE, MAN!
C'MON! I NEED YOU!
FOR REAL THIS TIME!
CAN'T EVEN BE MAD, REALLY.
I'M THE BOY WHO CRIED WOLF... CRYING WOLF.
I MEAN...

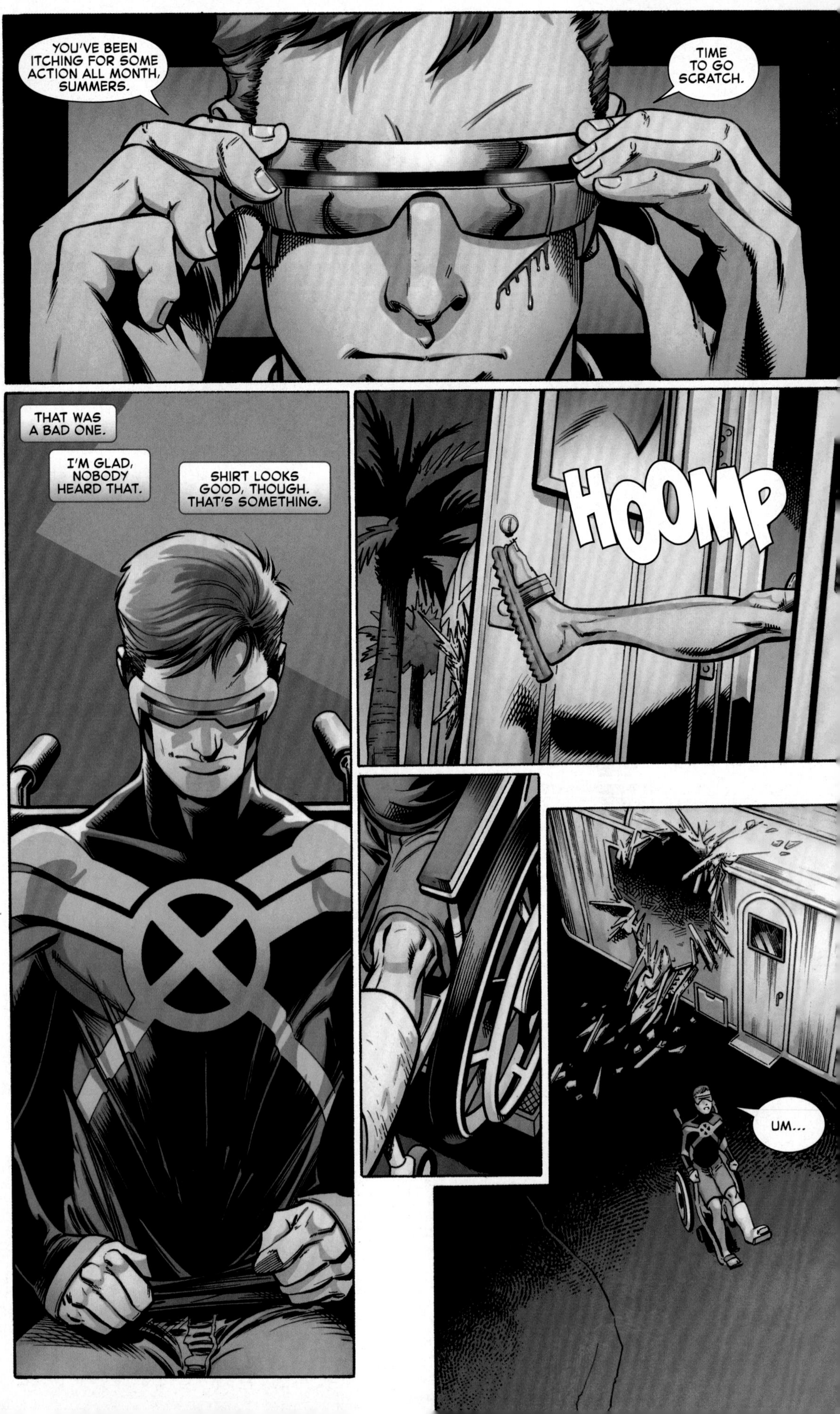
YOU'VE BEEN ITCHING FOR SOME ACTION ALL MONTH, SUMMERS.
TIME TO GO SCRATCH.
THAT WAS A BAD ONE.
I'M GLAD, NOBODY HEARD THAT.
SHIRT LOOKS GOOD, THOUGH. THAT'S SOMETHING.
HOOMP
UM...

THREE-STORY BRAIN-BLEED HORROR SHOW.

DOESN'T MATTER. JUST BREAK IT DOWN.

THE TENTACLES ARE A NONSTARTER. CAN'T TAKE THEM ALL OUT AND IF I GET TOO CLOSE I'M TOAST.

THAT LEAVES THE GROSS, TOOTHY MEAT TRUNK--

--THE GIANT GOOGLY EYEBALL.

THERE'S ONLY SO MUCH STRATEGY TO BE HAD WHEN FIGHTING SOMETHING LIKE THIS.

BUT IF I'VE LEARNED ANYTHING FROM EVERY BOSS STAGE EVER...

IT'S THAT YOU *ALWAYS*.

SHOOT.

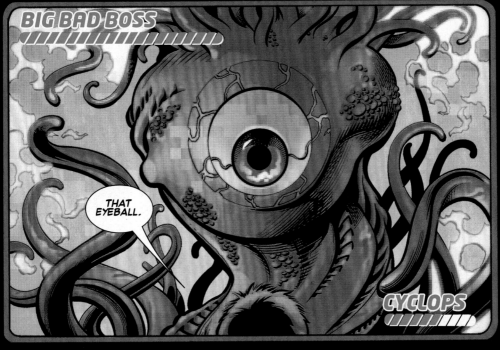

BIG BAD BOSS

THAT EYEBALL.

CYCLOPS

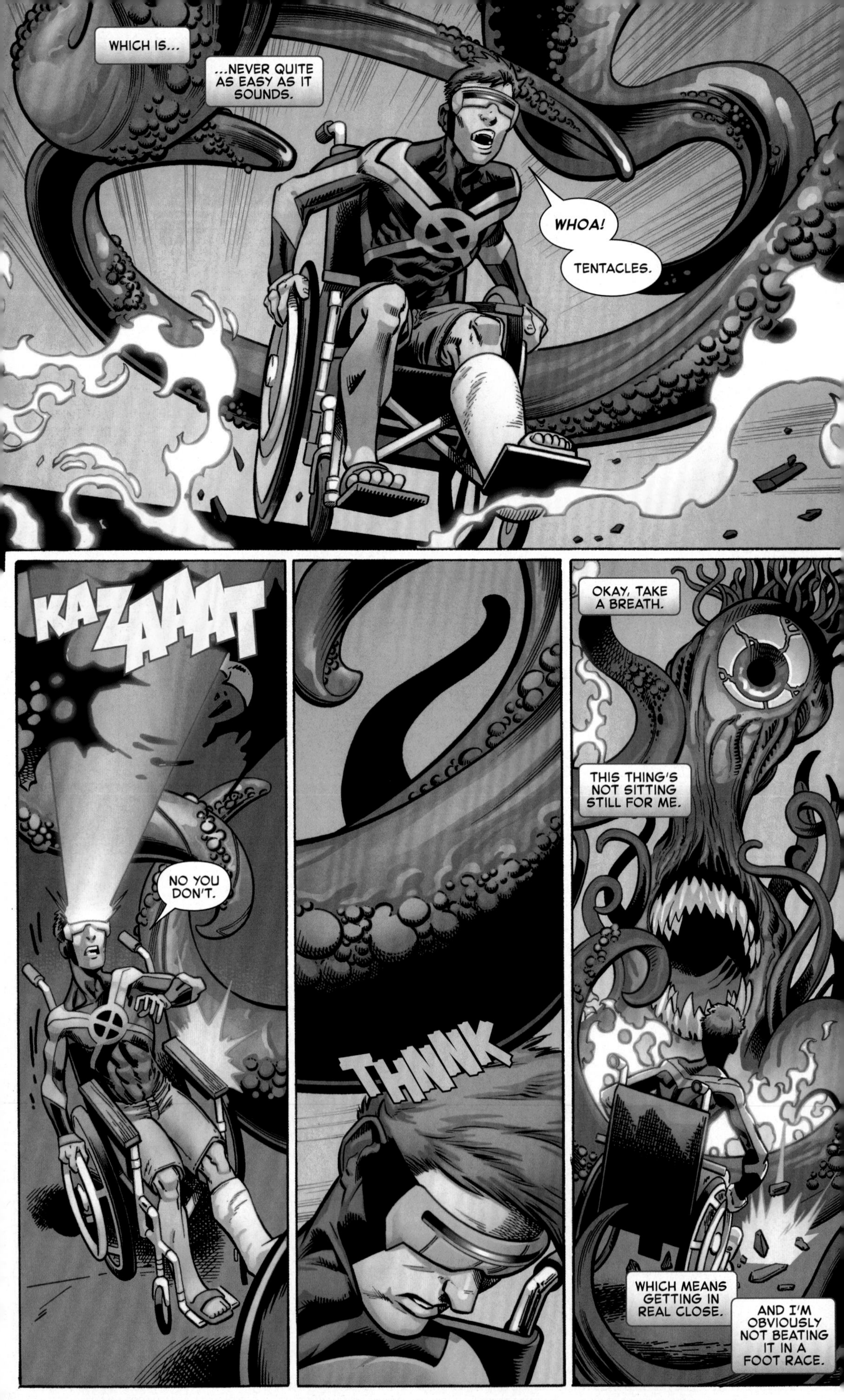
WHICH IS...
...NEVER QUITE AS EASY AS IT SOUNDS.
WHOA!
TENTACLES.
KAZAAAT
NO YOU DON'T.
THNNK
OKAY, TAKE A BREATH.
THIS THING'S NOT SITTING STILL FOR ME.
WHICH MEANS GETTING IN REAL CLOSE.
AND I'M OBVIOUSLY NOT BEATING IT IN A FOOT RACE.

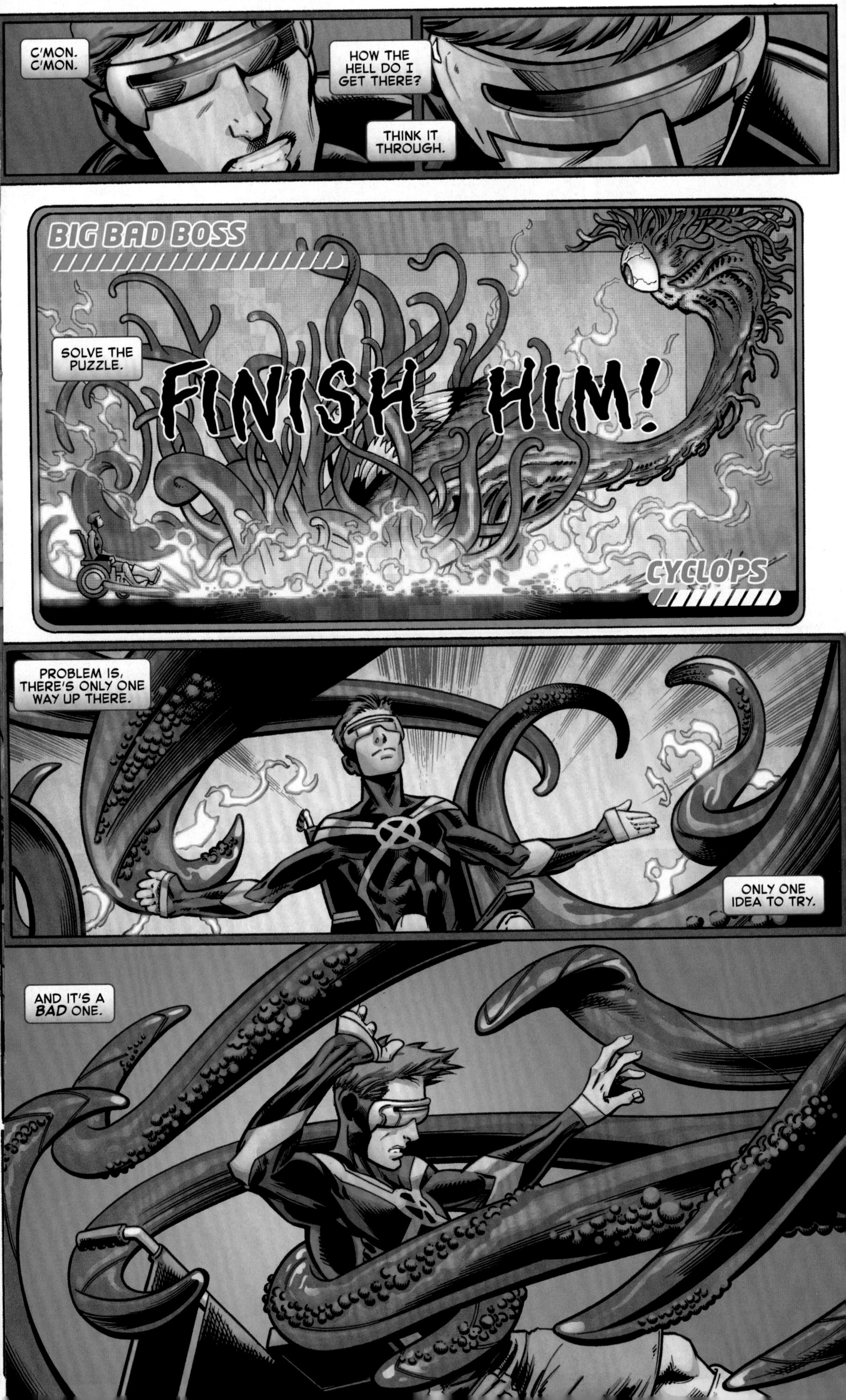
C'MON. C'MON.
HOW THE HELL DO I GET THERE?
THINK IT THROUGH.
BIG BAD BOSS
SOLVE THE PUZZLE.
FINISH HIM!
CYCLOPS
PROBLEM IS, THERE'S ONLY ONE WAY UP THERE.
ONLY ONE IDEA TO TRY.
AND IT'S A *BAD* ONE.

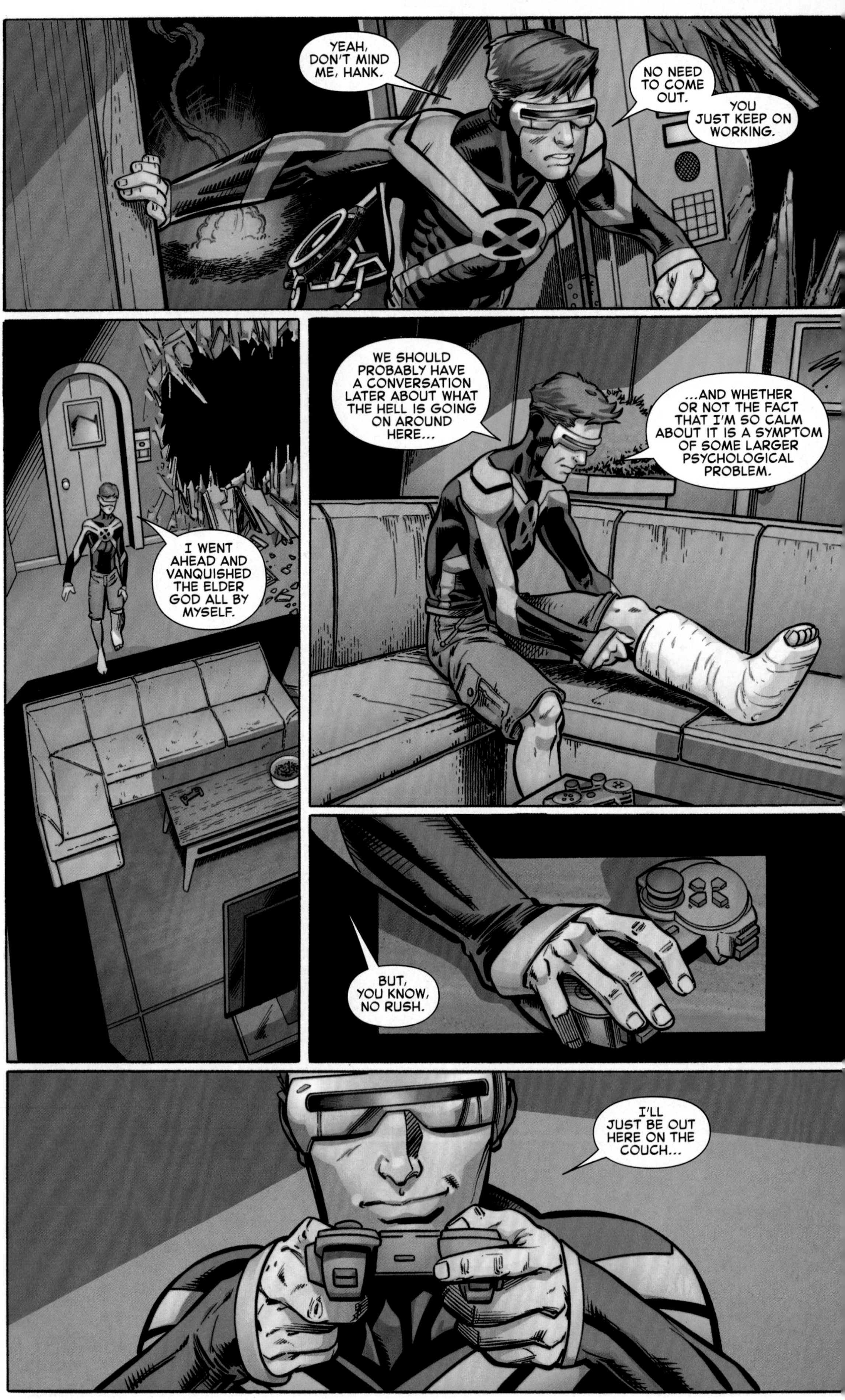
YEAH, DON'T MIND ME, HANK.
NO NEED TO COME OUT.
YOU JUST KEEP ON WORKING.
I WENT AHEAD AND VANQUISHED THE ELDER GOD ALL BY MYSELF.
WE SHOULD PROBABLY HAVE A CONVERSATION LATER ABOUT WHAT THE HELL IS GOING ON AROUND HERE...
...AND WHETHER OR NOT THE FACT THAT I'M SO CALM ABOUT IT IS A SYMPTOM OF SOME LARGER PSYCHOLOGICAL PROBLEM.
BUT, YOU KNOW, NO RUSH.
I'LL JUST BE OUT HERE ON THE COUCH...

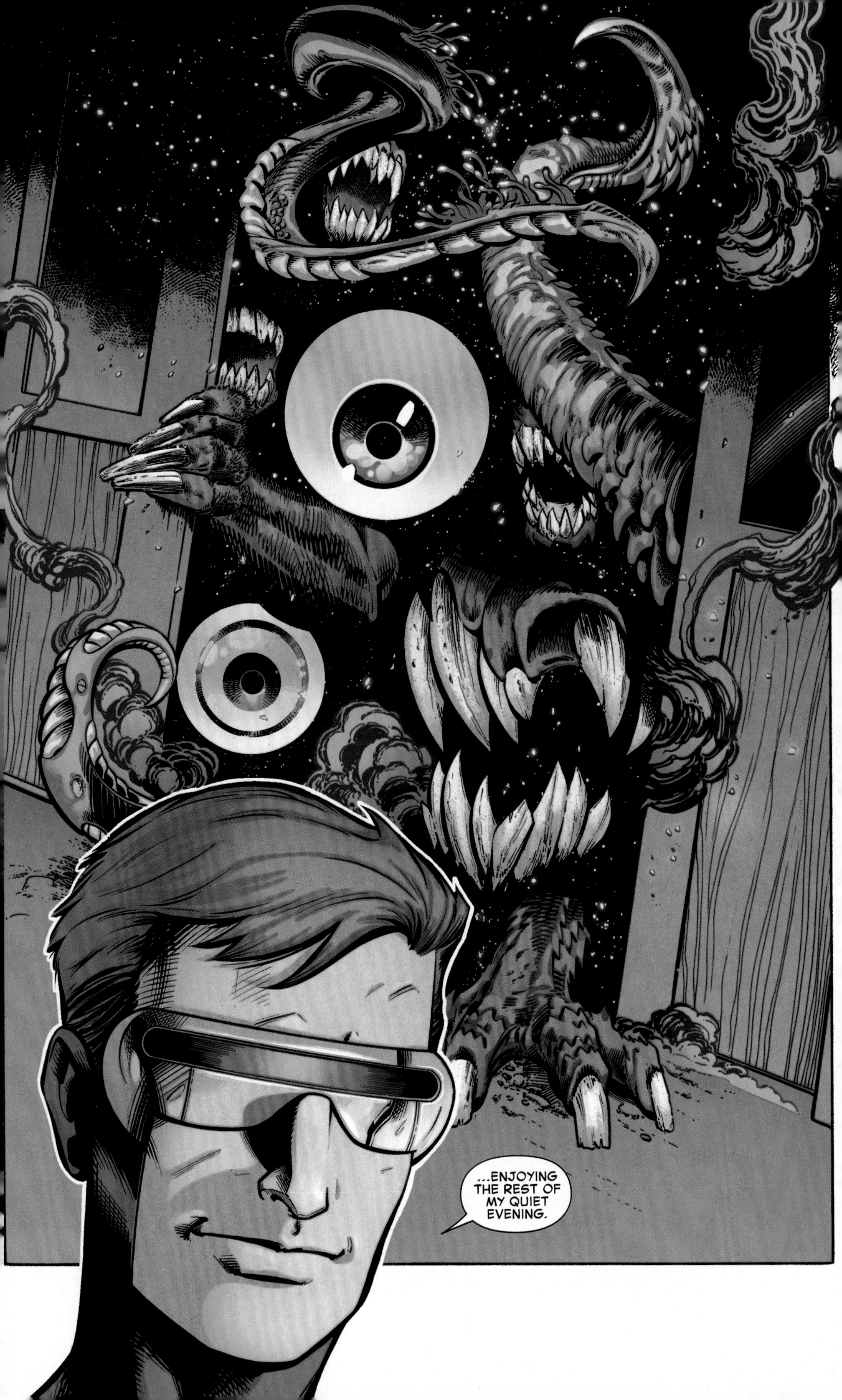
...ENJOYING THE REST OF MY QUIET EVENING.

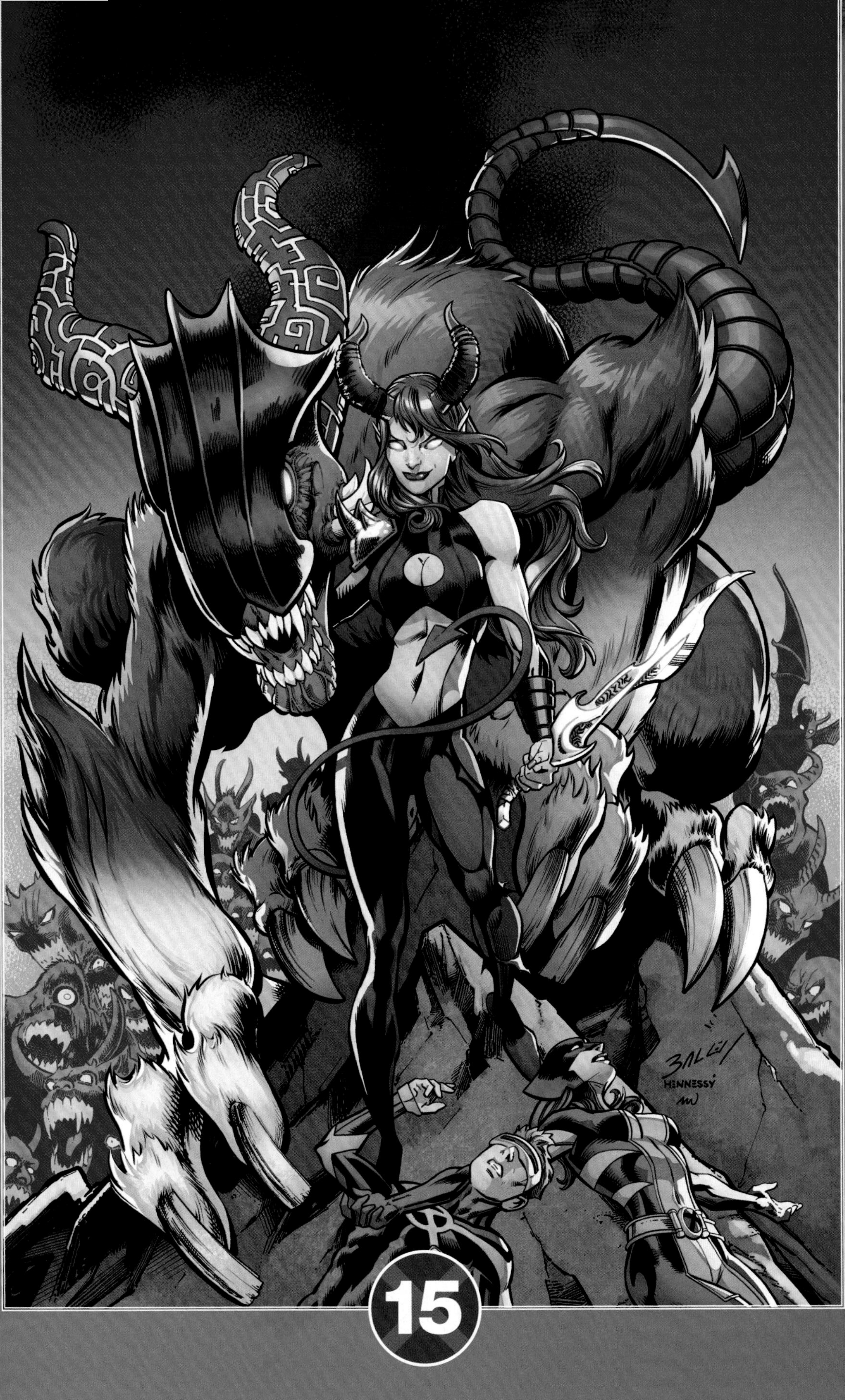
HENNESSY
15

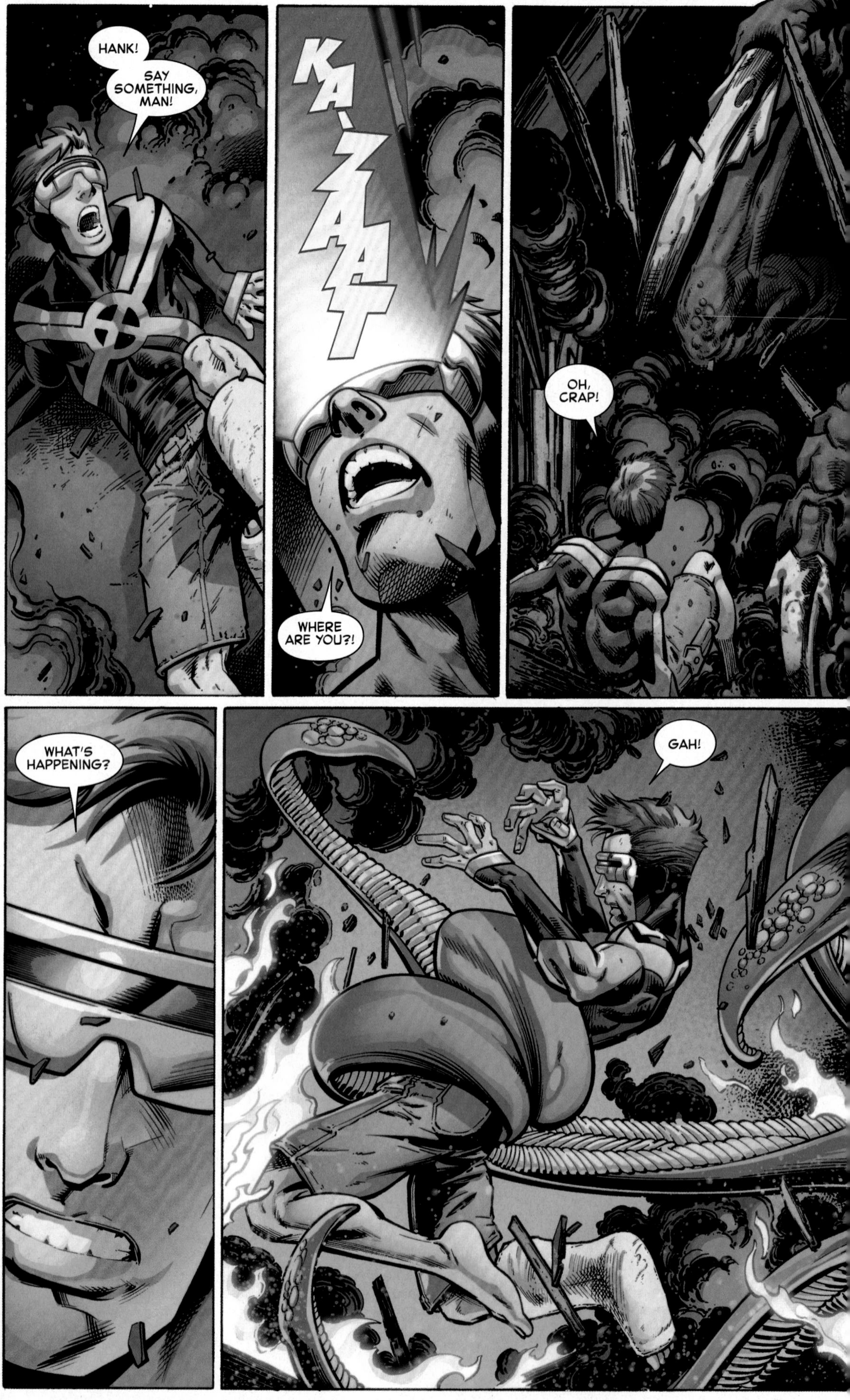
HANK!
SAY SOMETHING, MAN!
KA-ZAAT
WHERE ARE YOU?!
OH, CRAP!
WHAT'S HAPPENING?
GAH!

HANK...

SOMETHING'S GOT ME!

KA-ZAAT!

WHAT'S GOT ME?!

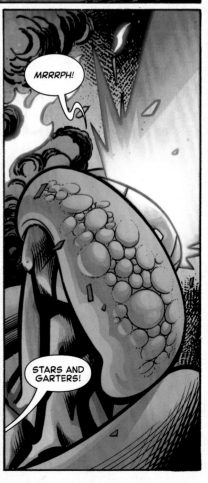

MRRRPH!

STARS AND GARTERS!

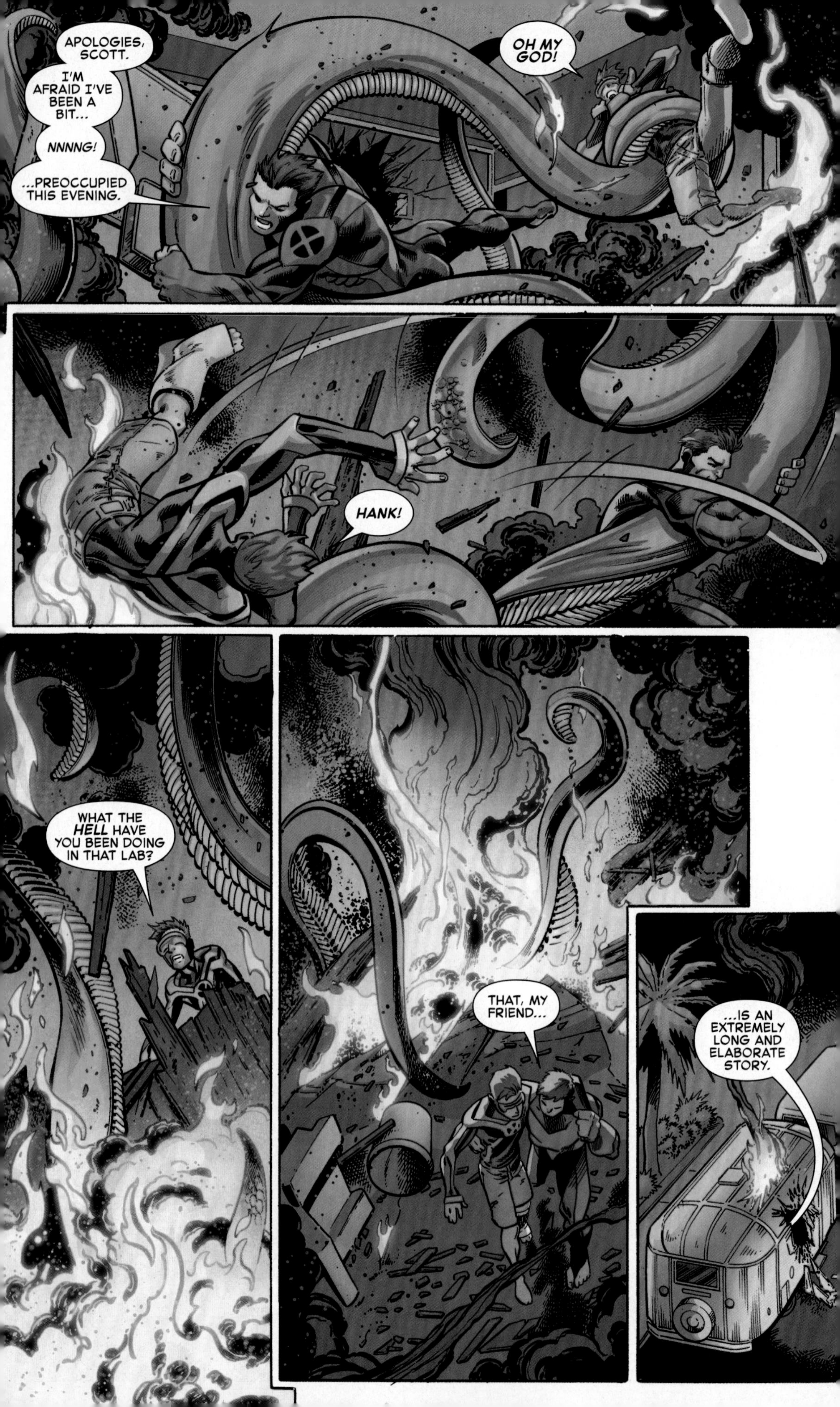

APOLOGIES, SCOTT.
I'M AFRAID I'VE BEEN A BIT...
NNNNG!
...PREOCCUPIED THIS EVENING.
OH MY GOD!
HANK!
WHAT THE HELL HAVE YOU BEEN DOING IN THAT LAB?
THAT, MY FRIEND...
...IS AN EXTREMELY LONG AND ELABORATE STORY.

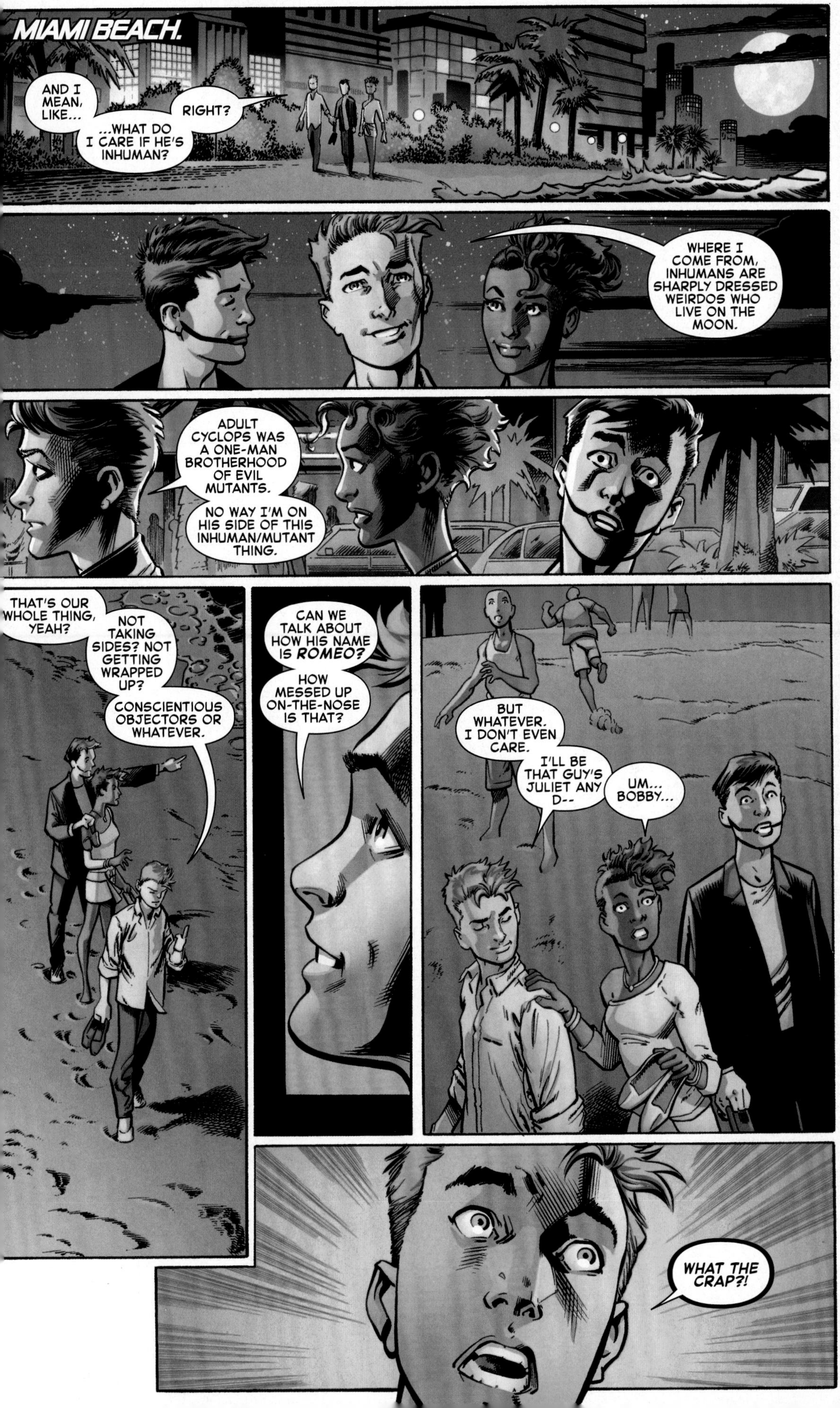
MIAMI BEACH.
AND I MEAN, LIKE...
...WHAT DO I CARE IF HE'S INHUMAN?
RIGHT?
WHERE I COME FROM, INHUMANS ARE SHARPLY DRESSED WEIRDOS WHO LIVE ON THE MOON.
ADULT CYCLOPS WAS A ONE-MAN BROTHERHOOD OF EVIL MUTANTS.
NO WAY I'M ON HIS SIDE OF THIS INHUMAN/MUTANT THING.
THAT'S OUR WHOLE THING, YEAH?
NOT TAKING SIDES? NOT GETTING WRAPPED UP?
CONSCIENTIOUS OBJECTORS OR WHATEVER.
CAN WE TALK ABOUT HOW HIS NAME IS ROMEO?
HOW MESSED UP ON-THE-NOSE IS THAT?
BUT WHATEVER. I DON'T EVEN CARE.
I'LL BE THAT GUY'S JULIET ANY D--
UM... BOBBY...
WHAT THE CRAP?!

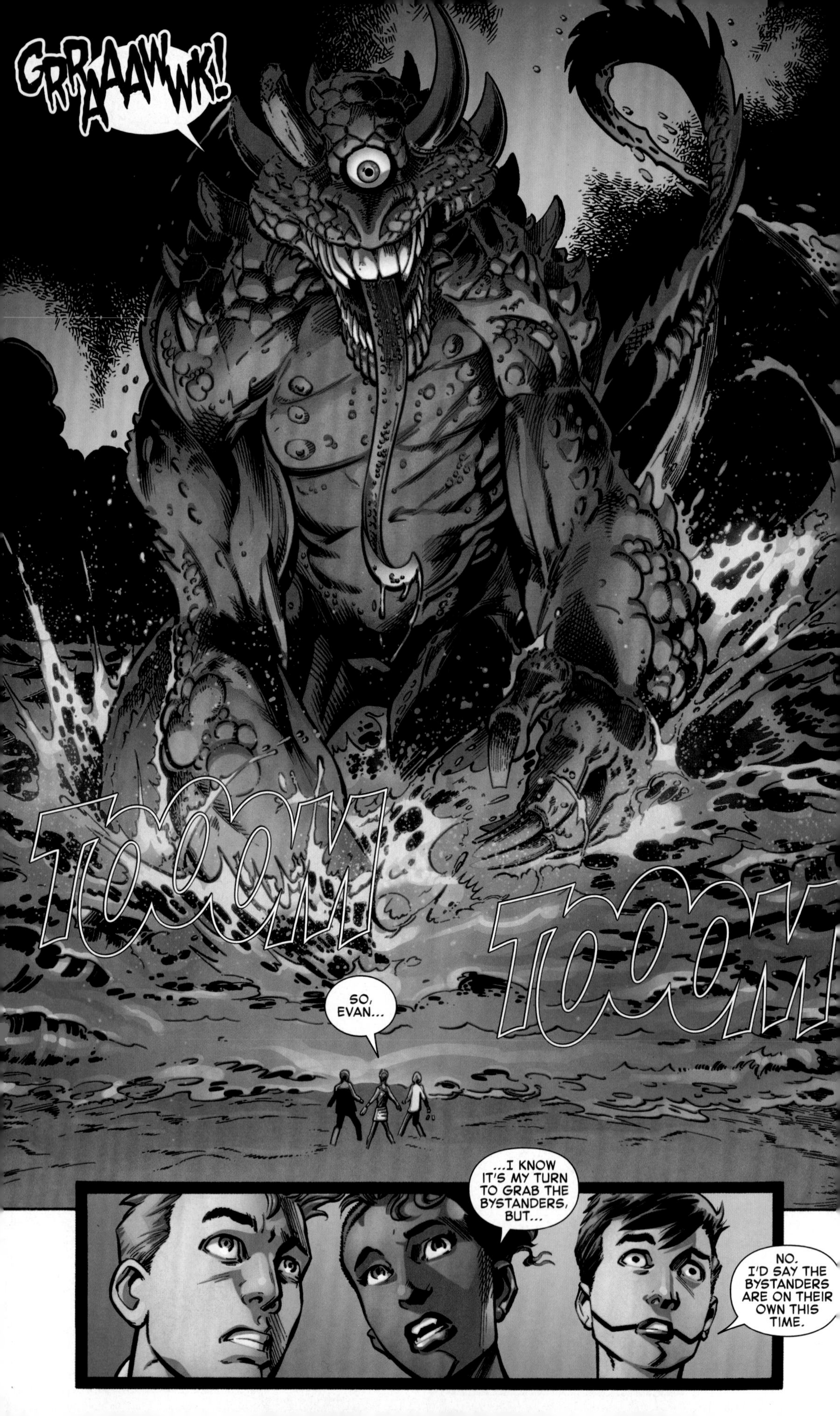
GRRAAAWWK!
TOOOM
TOOOM
SO, EVAN...
...I KNOW IT'S MY TURN TO GRAB THE BYSTANDERS, BUT...
NO. I'D SAY THE BYSTANDERS ARE ON THEIR OWN THIS TIME.

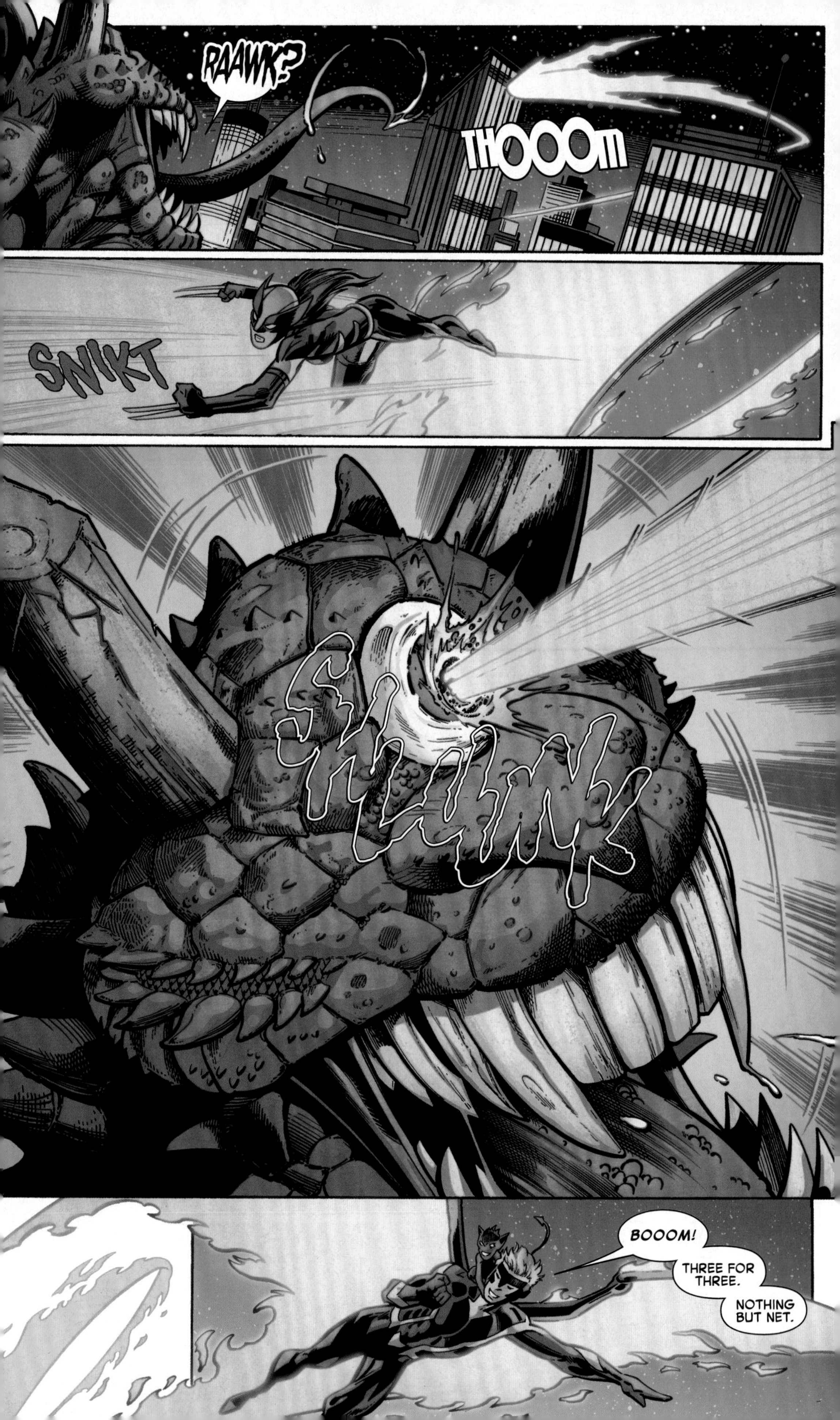
RAAWK?
THOOOM
SNIKT
SHHUNK
BOOOM!
THREE FOR THREE.
NOTHING BUT NET.

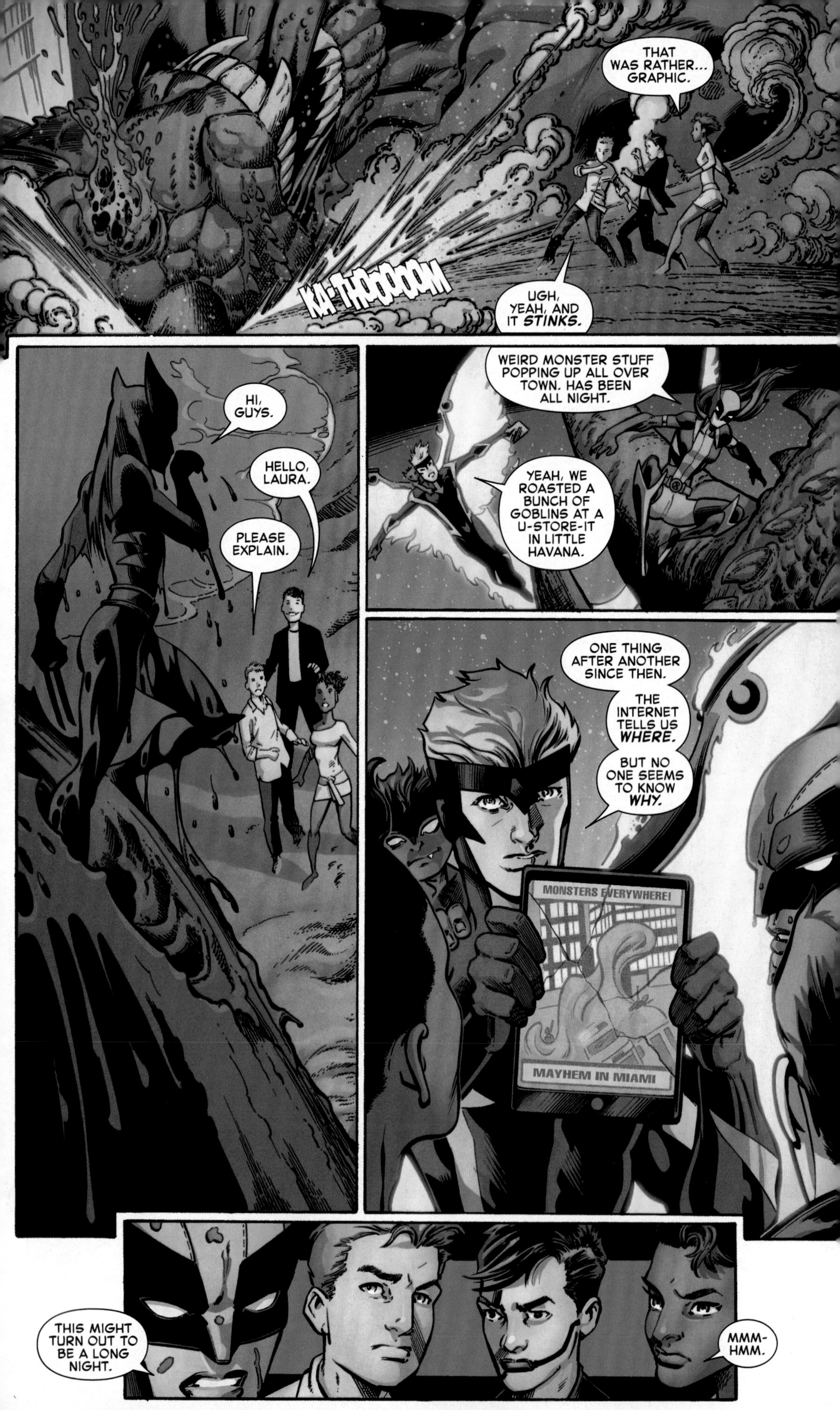
THAT WAS RATHER... GRAPHIC.
KA-THOOOOOM
UGH, YEAH, AND IT STINKS.
HI, GUYS.
HELLO, LAURA.
PLEASE EXPLAIN.
WEIRD MONSTER STUFF POPPING UP ALL OVER TOWN. HAS BEEN ALL NIGHT.
YEAH, WE ROASTED A BUNCH OF GOBLINS AT A U-STORE-IT IN LITTLE HAVANA.
ONE THING AFTER ANOTHER SINCE THEN.
THE INTERNET TELLS US WHERE.
BUT NO ONE SEEMS TO KNOW WHY.
MONSTERS EVERYWHERE!
MAYHEM IN MIAMI
THIS MIGHT TURN OUT TO BE A LONG NIGHT.
MMM-HMM.

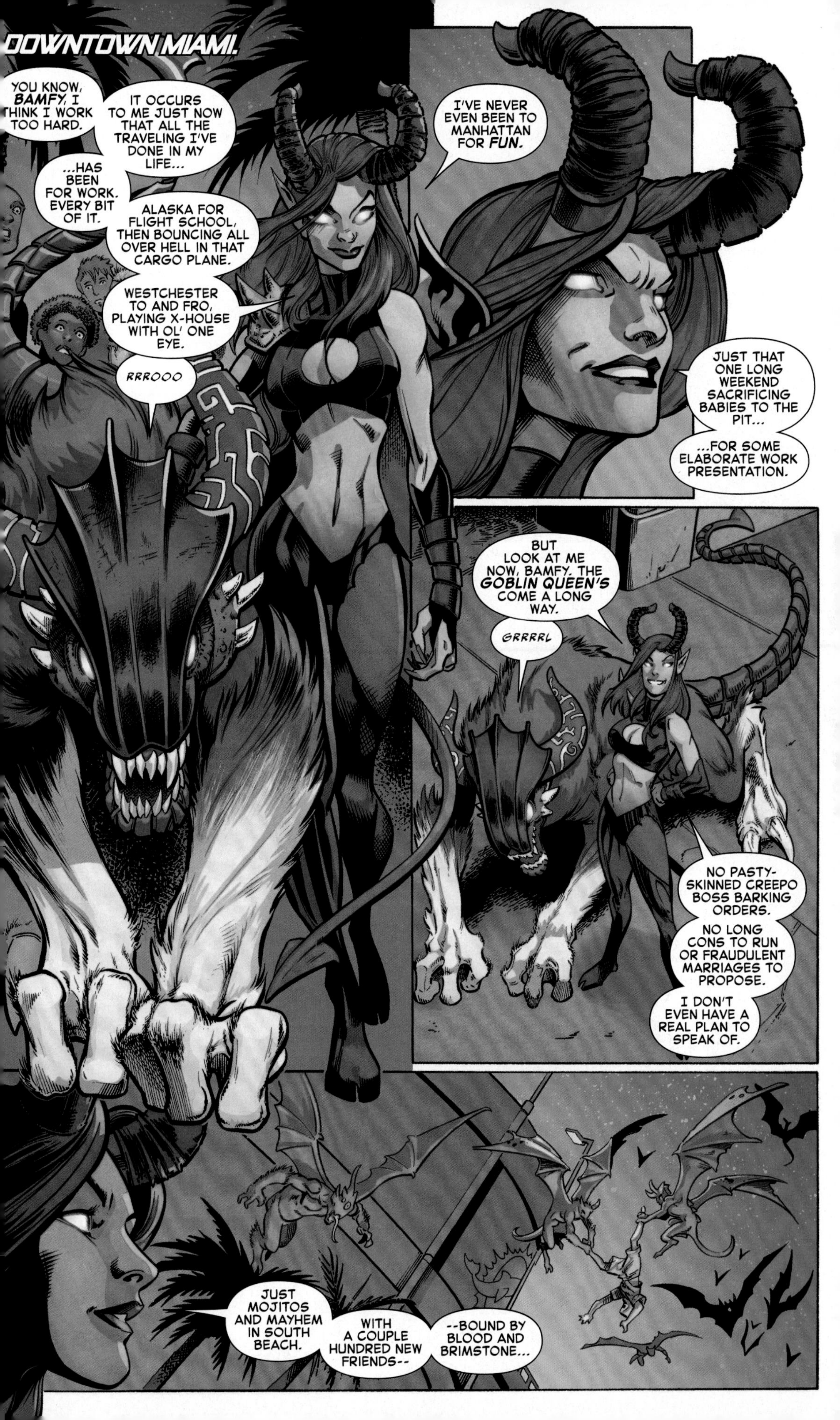
DOWNTOWN MIAMI.
YOU KNOW, BAMFY, I THINK I WORK TOO HARD.
IT OCCURS TO ME JUST NOW THAT ALL THE TRAVELING I'VE DONE IN MY LIFE...
...HAS BEEN FOR WORK. EVERY BIT OF IT.
ALASKA FOR FLIGHT SCHOOL, THEN BOUNCING ALL OVER HELL IN THAT CARGO PLANE.
WESTCHESTER TO AND FRO, PLAYING X-HOUSE WITH OL' ONE EYE.
RRROOO
I'VE NEVER EVEN BEEN TO MANHATTAN FOR FUN.
JUST THAT ONE LONG WEEKEND SACRIFICING BABIES TO THE PIT...
...FOR SOME ELABORATE WORK PRESENTATION.
BUT LOOK AT ME NOW, BAMFY. THE GOBLIN QUEEN'S COME A LONG WAY.
GRRRRL
NO PASTY-SKINNED CREEPO BOSS BARKING ORDERS.
NO LONG CONS TO RUN OR FRAUDULENT MARRIAGES TO PROPOSE.
I DON'T EVEN HAVE A REAL PLAN TO SPEAK OF.
JUST MOJITOS AND MAYHEM IN SOUTH BEACH.
WITH A COUPLE HUNDRED NEW FRIENDS--
--BOUND BY BLOOD AND BRIMSTONE...

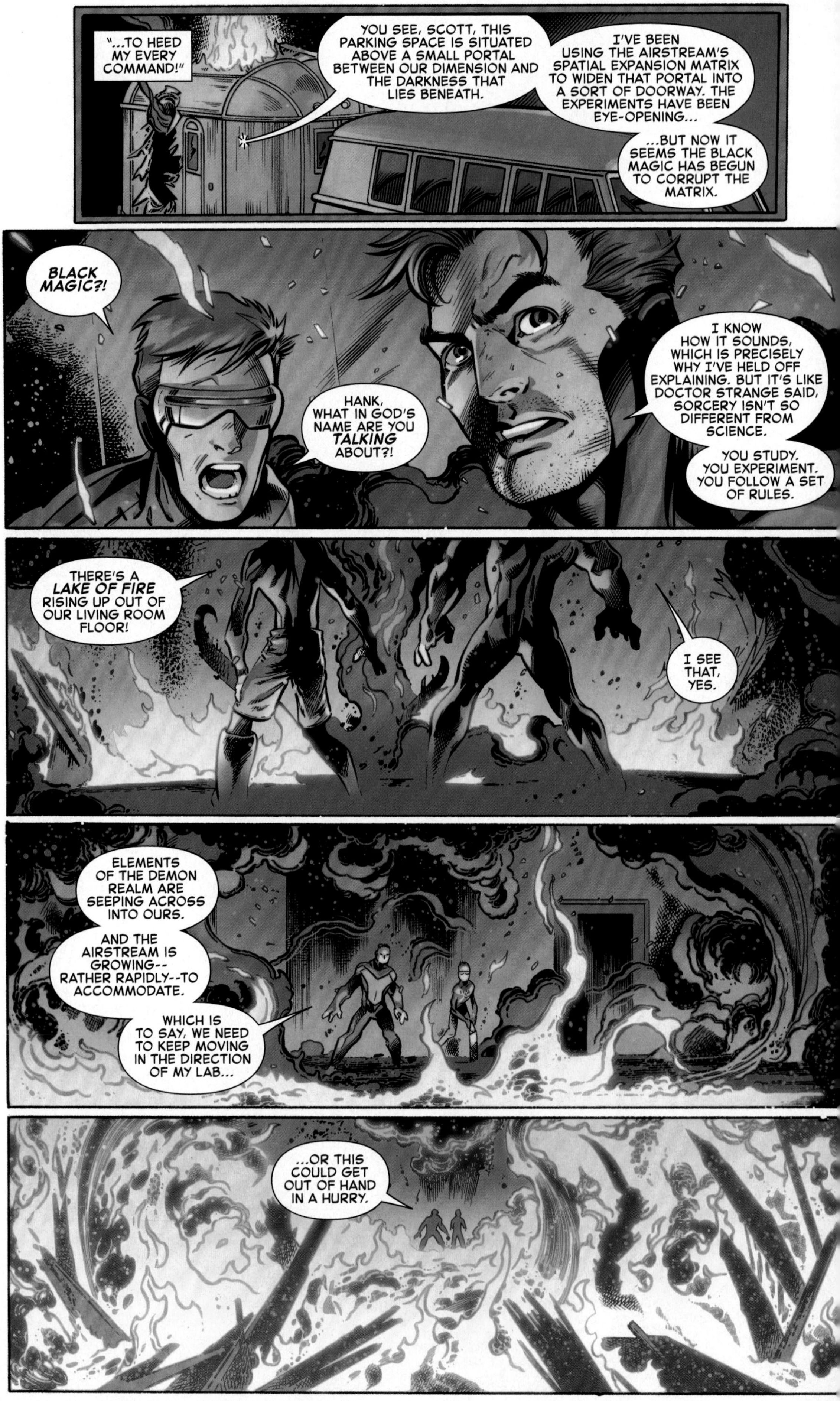
"...TO HEED MY EVERY COMMAND!"
YOU SEE, SCOTT, THIS PARKING SPACE IS SITUATED ABOVE A SMALL PORTAL BETWEEN OUR DIMENSION AND THE DARKNESS THAT LIES BENEATH.
I'VE BEEN USING THE AIRSTREAM'S SPATIAL EXPANSION MATRIX TO WIDEN THAT PORTAL INTO A SORT OF DOORWAY. THE EXPERIMENTS HAVE BEEN EYE-OPENING...
...BUT NOW IT SEEMS THE BLACK MAGIC HAS BEGUN TO CORRUPT THE MATRIX.
BLACK MAGIC?!
HANK, WHAT IN GOD'S NAME ARE YOU *TALKING* ABOUT?!
I KNOW HOW IT SOUNDS, WHICH IS PRECISELY WHY I'VE HELD OFF EXPLAINING. BUT IT'S LIKE DOCTOR STRANGE SAID, SORCERY ISN'T SO DIFFERENT FROM SCIENCE.
YOU STUDY. YOU EXPERIMENT. YOU FOLLOW A SET OF RULES.
THERE'S A *LAKE OF FIRE* RISING UP OUT OF OUR LIVING ROOM FLOOR!
I SEE THAT, YES.
ELEMENTS OF THE DEMON REALM ARE SEEPING ACROSS INTO OURS.
AND THE AIRSTREAM IS GROWING-- RATHER RAPIDLY--TO ACCOMMODATE.
WHICH IS TO SAY, WE NEED TO KEEP MOVING IN THE DIRECTION OF MY LAB...
...OR THIS COULD GET OUT OF HAND IN A HURRY.

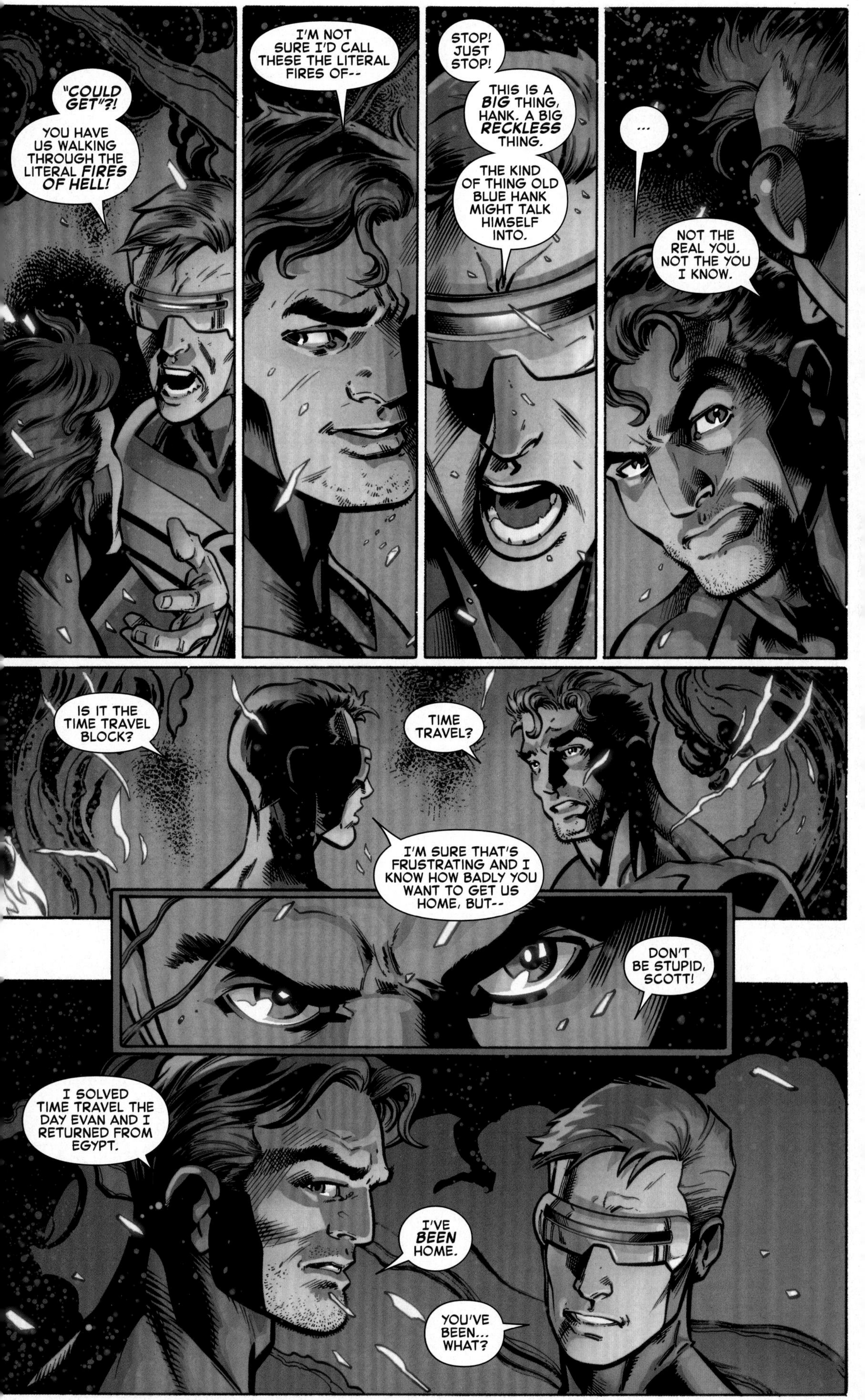
"COULD GET"?!
YOU HAVE US WALKING THROUGH THE LITERAL FIRES OF HELL!
I'M NOT SURE I'D CALL THESE THE LITERAL FIRES OF--
STOP! JUST STOP!
THIS IS A BIG THING, HANK. A BIG RECKLESS THING.
THE KIND OF THING OLD BLUE HANK MIGHT TALK HIMSELF INTO.
...
NOT THE REAL YOU. NOT THE YOU I KNOW.
IS IT THE TIME TRAVEL BLOCK?
TIME TRAVEL?
I'M SURE THAT'S FRUSTRATING AND I KNOW HOW BADLY YOU WANT TO GET US HOME, BUT--
DON'T BE STUPID, SCOTT!
I SOLVED TIME TRAVEL THE DAY EVAN AND I RETURNED FROM EGYPT.
I'VE BEEN HOME.
YOU'VE BEEN... WHAT?

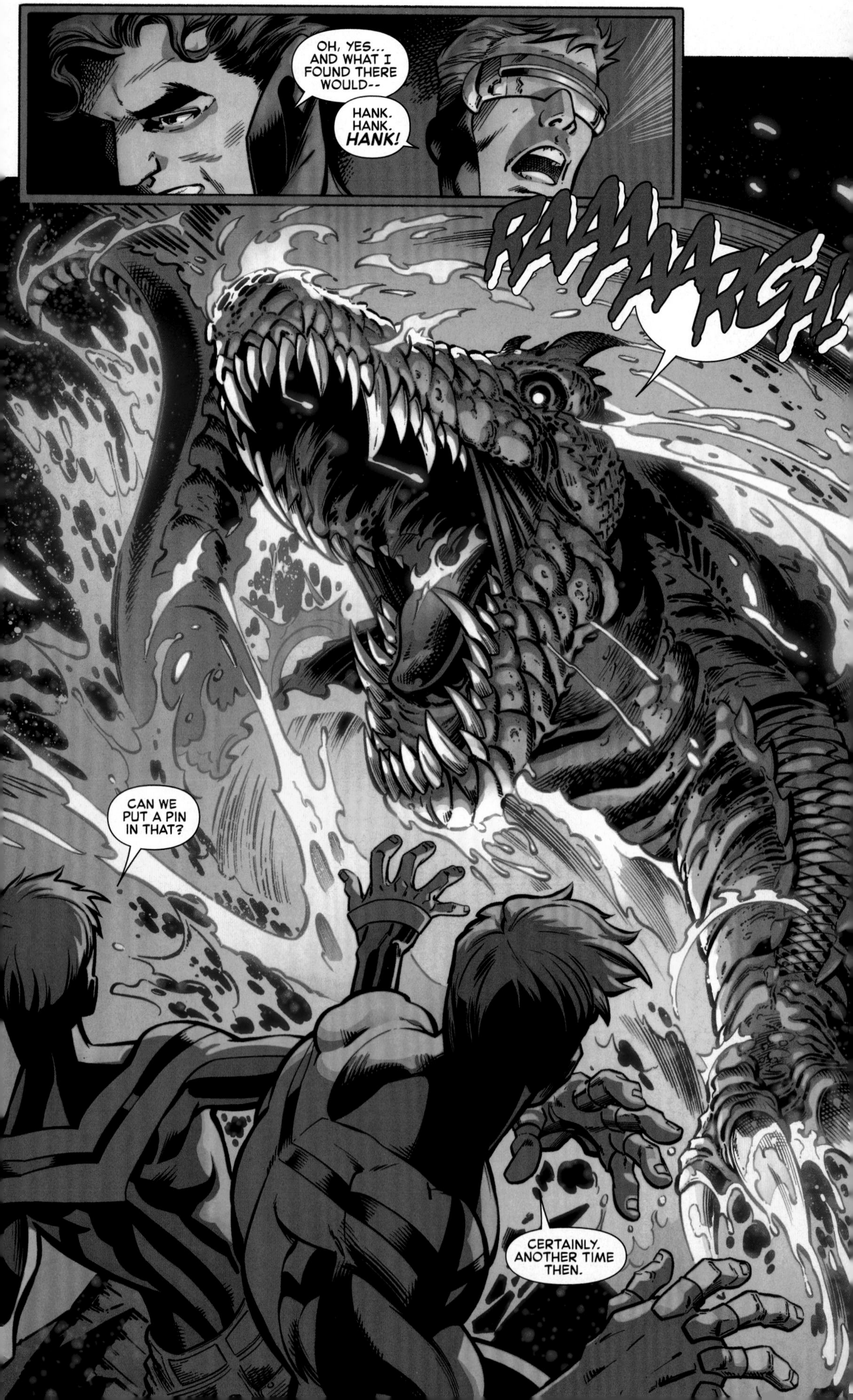
OH, YES... AND WHAT I FOUND THERE WOULD--
HANK. HANK. HANK!
RAAAAARGH!!
CAN WE PUT A PIN IN THAT?
CERTAINLY. ANOTHER TIME THEN.

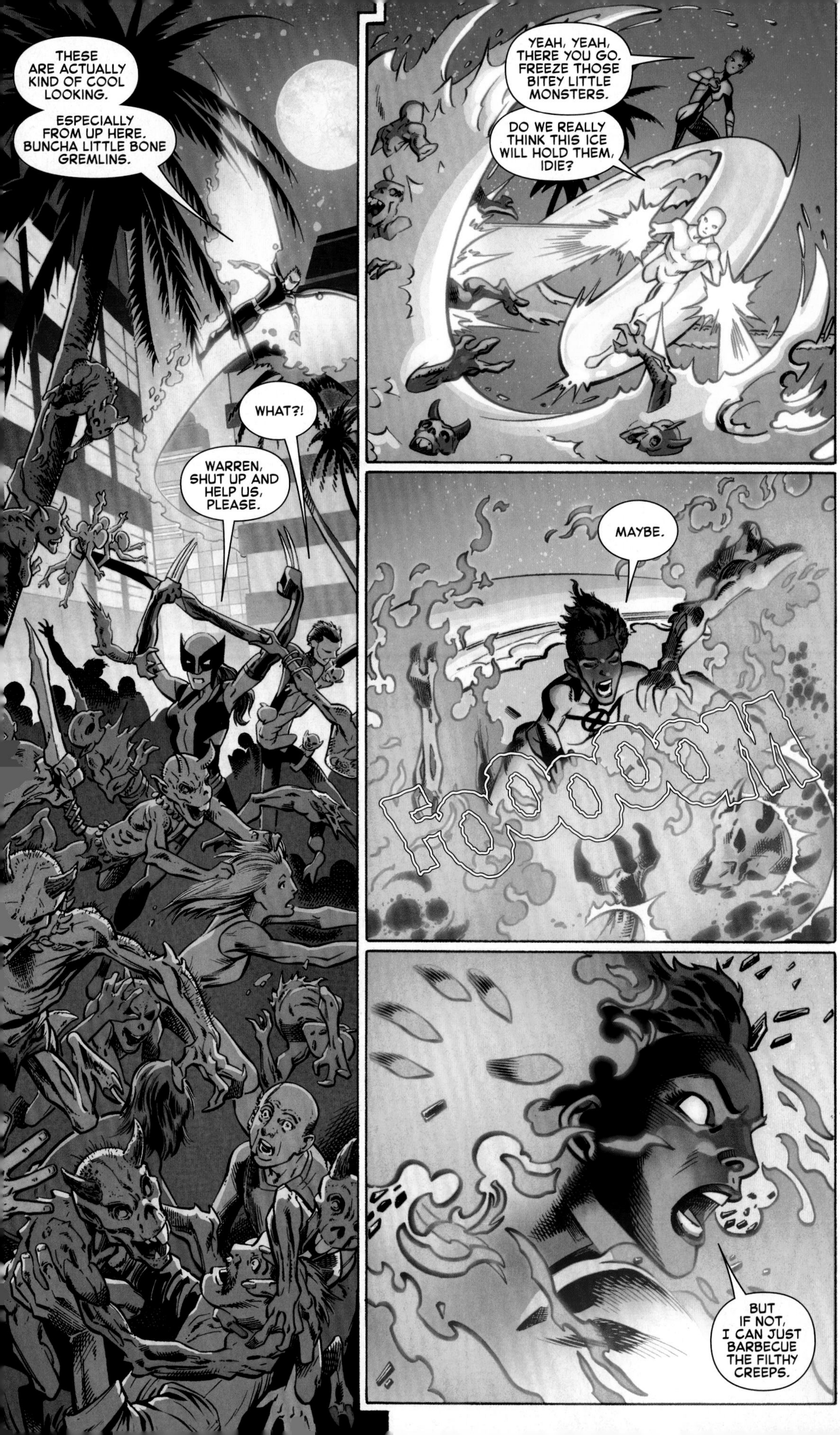
THESE ARE ACTUALLY KIND OF COOL LOOKING.
ESPECIALLY FROM UP HERE. BUNCHA LITTLE BONE GREMLINS.
WHAT?!
WARREN, SHUT UP AND HELP US, PLEASE.
YEAH, YEAH, THERE YOU GO. FREEZE THOSE BITEY LITTLE MONSTERS.
DO WE REALLY THINK THIS ICE WILL HOLD THEM, IDIE?
MAYBE.
FOOOOOM
BUT IF NOT, I CAN JUST BARBECUE THE FILTHY CREEPS.

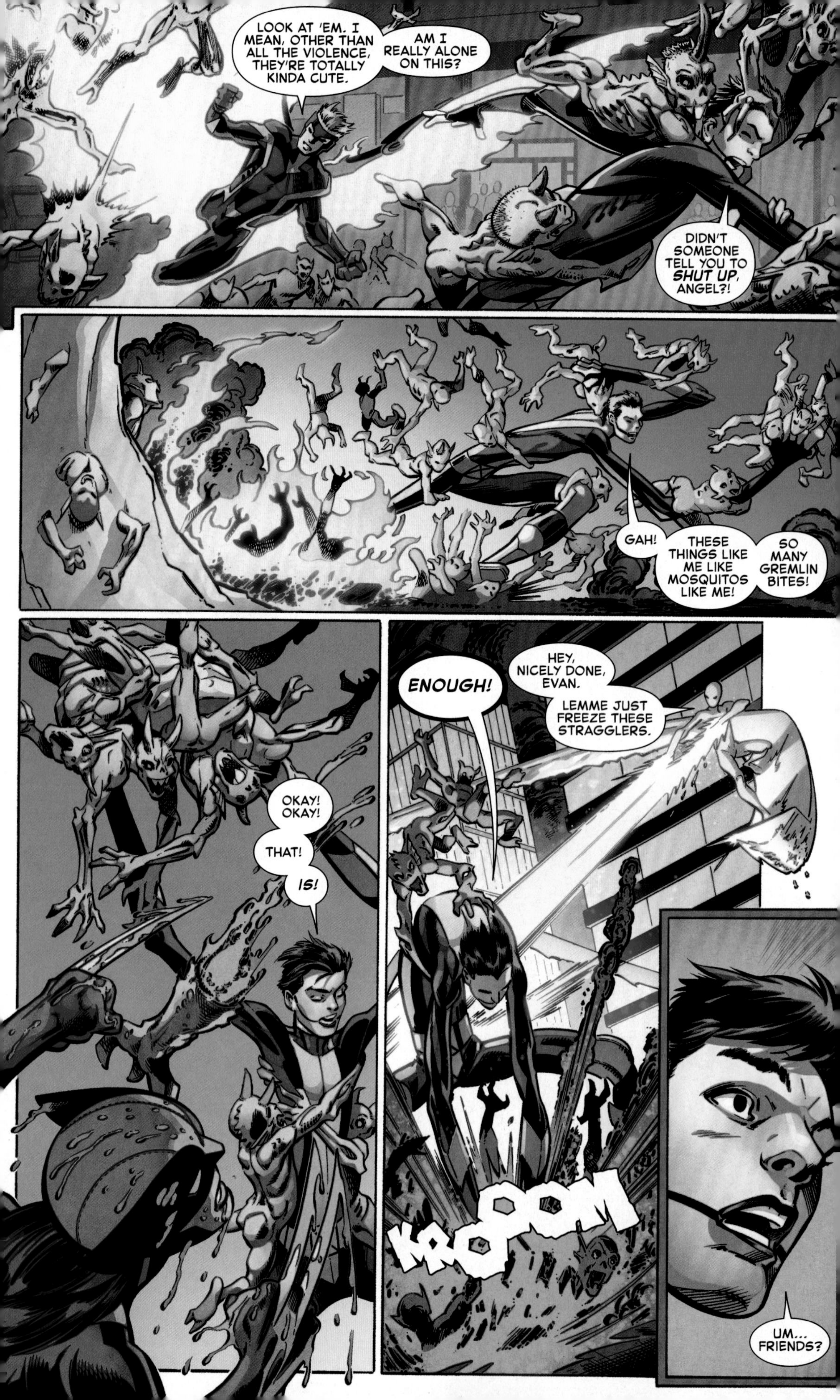
LOOK AT 'EM. I MEAN, OTHER THAN ALL THE VIOLENCE, THEY'RE TOTALLY KINDA CUTE.
AM I REALLY ALONE ON THIS?
DIDN'T SOMEONE TELL YOU TO SHUT UP, ANGEL?!
GAH!
THESE THINGS LIKE ME LIKE MOSQUITOS LIKE ME!
SO MANY GREMLIN BITES!
OKAY! OKAY!
THAT!
IS!
ENOUGH!
HEY, NICELY DONE, EVAN.
LEMME JUST FREEZE THESE STRAGGLERS.
KROOOM
UM... FRIENDS?

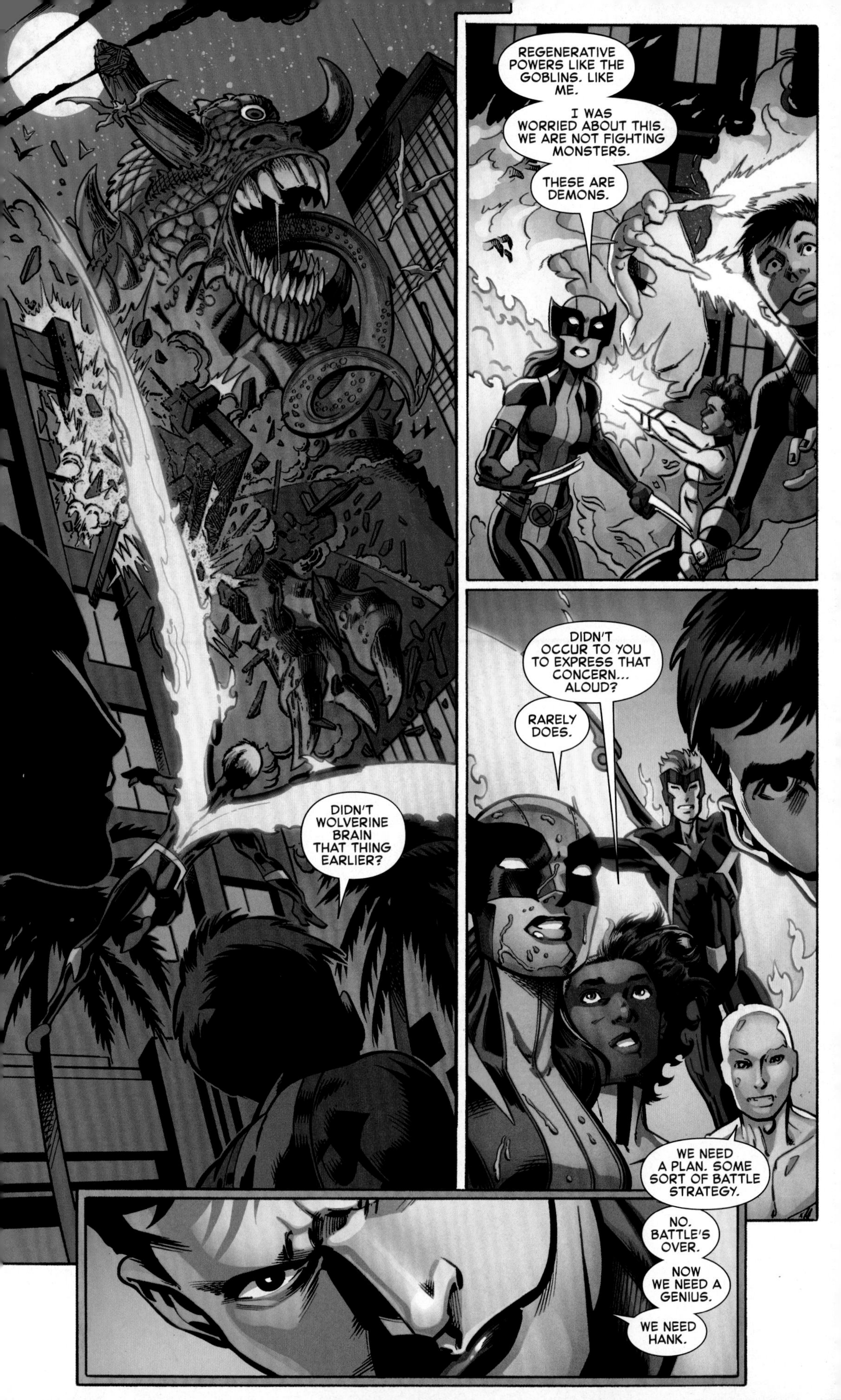

DIDN'T WOLVERINE BRAIN THAT THING EARLIER?
REGENERATIVE POWERS LIKE THE GOBLINS. LIKE ME.
I WAS WORRIED ABOUT THIS. WE ARE NOT FIGHTING MONSTERS.
THESE ARE DEMONS.
DIDN'T OCCUR TO YOU TO EXPRESS THAT CONCERN... ALOUD?
RARELY DOES.
WE NEED A PLAN. SOME SORT OF BATTLE STRATEGY.
NO. BATTLE'S OVER.
NOW WE NEED A GENIUS.
WE NEED HANK.

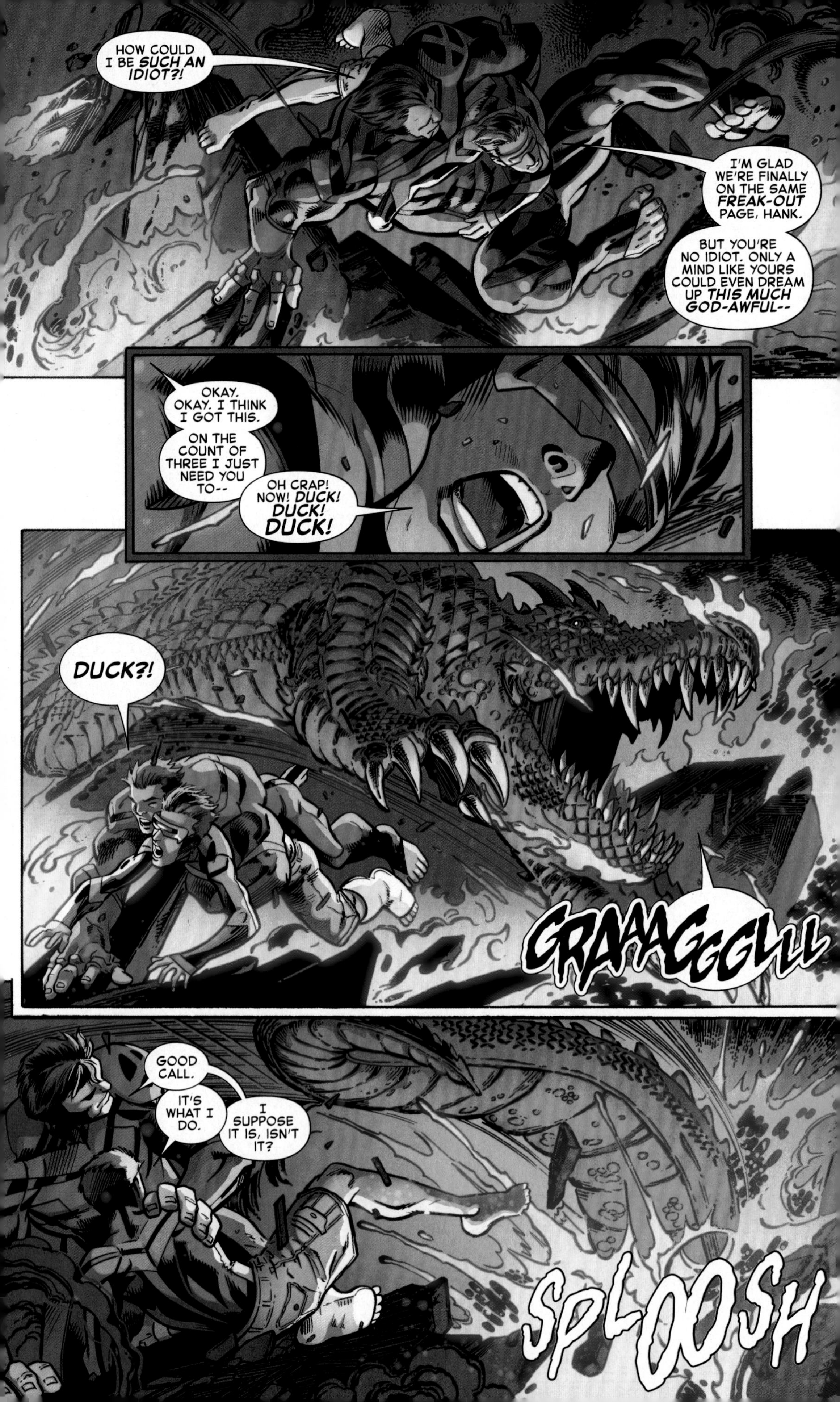

HOW COULD I BE SUCH AN IDIOT?!
I'M GLAD WE'RE FINALLY ON THE SAME FREAK-OUT PAGE, HANK.
BUT YOU'RE NO IDIOT. ONLY A MIND LIKE YOURS COULD EVEN DREAM UP THIS MUCH GOD-AWFUL--
OKAY. OKAY. I THINK I GOT THIS.
ON THE COUNT OF THREE I JUST NEED YOU TO--
OH CRAP! NOW! DUCK! DUCK! DUCK!
DUCK?!
GRAAAGGGLLL
GOOD CALL.
IT'S WHAT I DO.
I SUPPOSE IT IS, ISN'T IT?
SPLOOSH

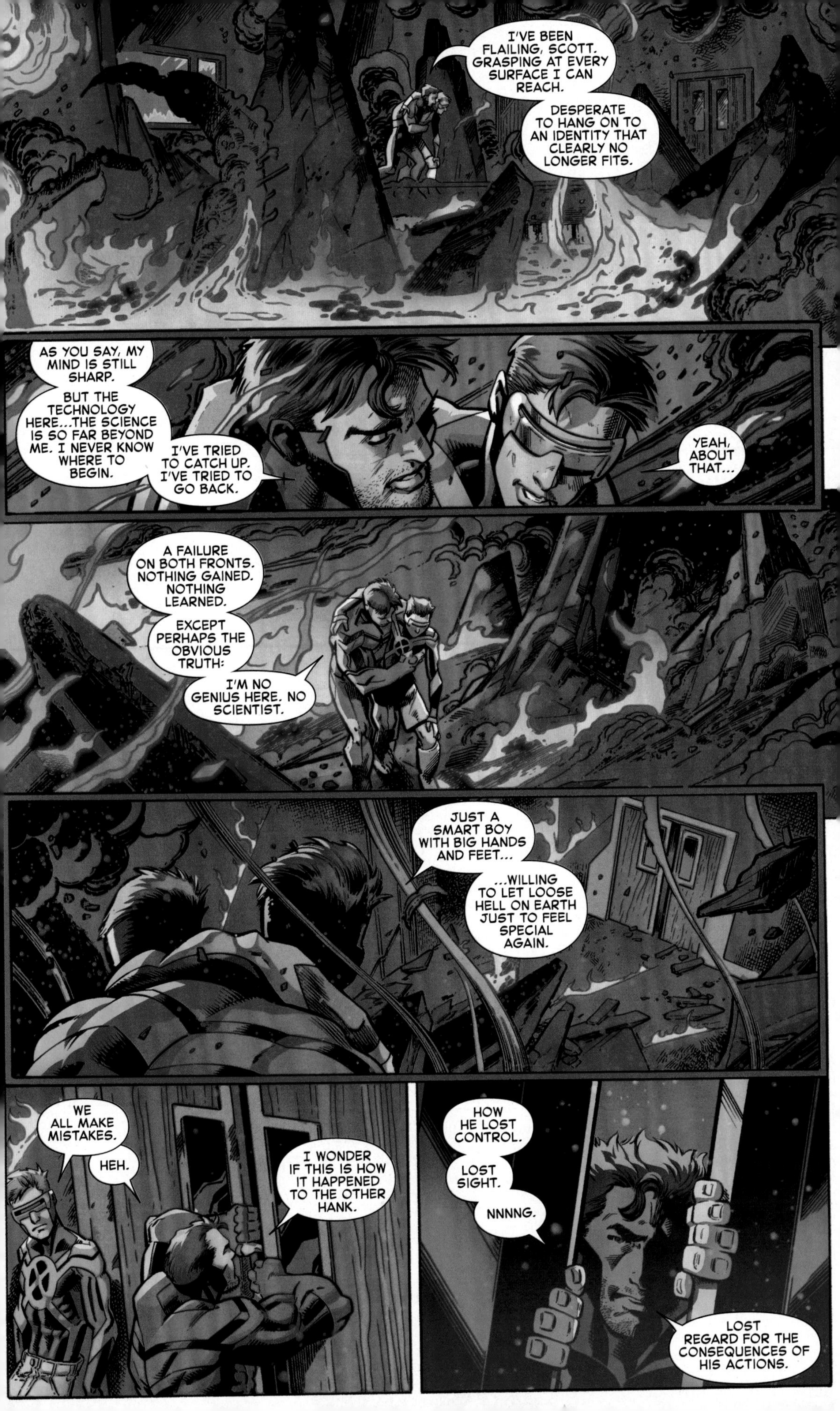
I'VE BEEN FLAILING, SCOTT. GRASPING AT EVERY SURFACE I CAN REACH.
DESPERATE TO HANG ON TO AN IDENTITY THAT CLEARLY NO LONGER FITS.
AS YOU SAY, MY MIND IS STILL SHARP.
BUT THE TECHNOLOGY HERE...THE SCIENCE IS SO FAR BEYOND ME. I NEVER KNOW WHERE TO BEGIN.
I'VE TRIED TO CATCH UP. I'VE TRIED TO GO BACK.
YEAH, ABOUT THAT...
A FAILURE ON BOTH FRONTS. NOTHING GAINED. NOTHING LEARNED.
EXCEPT PERHAPS THE OBVIOUS TRUTH:
I'M NO GENIUS HERE. NO SCIENTIST.
JUST A SMART BOY WITH BIG HANDS AND FEET...
...WILLING TO LET LOOSE HELL ON EARTH JUST TO FEEL SPECIAL AGAIN.
WE ALL MAKE MISTAKES.
HEH.
I WONDER IF THIS IS HOW IT HAPPENED TO THE OTHER HANK.
HOW HE LOST CONTROL.
LOST SIGHT.
NNNNG.
LOST REGARD FOR THE CONSEQUENCES OF HIS ACTIONS.

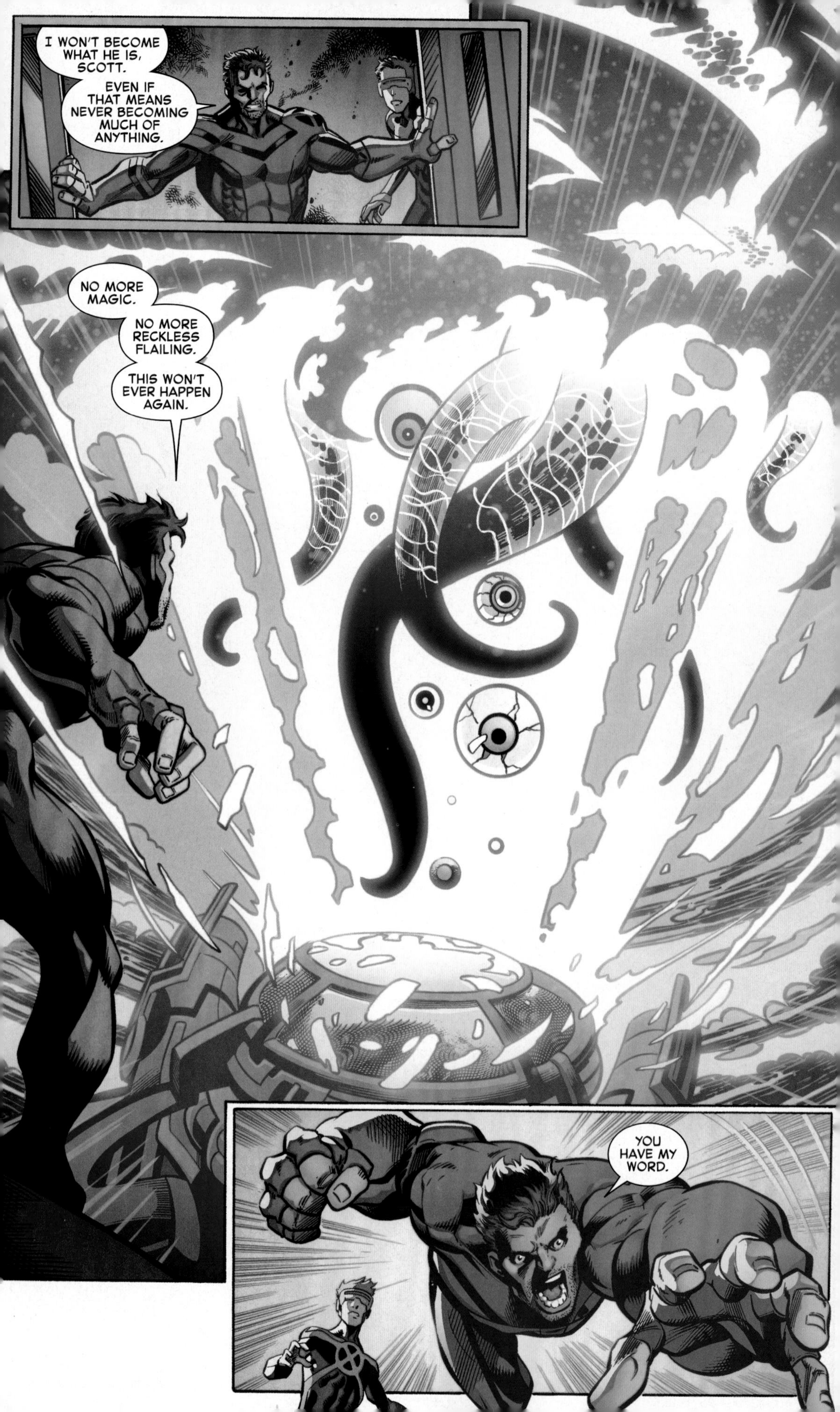
I WON'T BECOME WHAT HE IS, SCOTT.
EVEN IF THAT MEANS NEVER BECOMING MUCH OF ANYTHING.
NO MORE MAGIC.
NO MORE RECKLESS FLAILING.
THIS WON'T EVER HAPPEN AGAIN.
YOU HAVE MY WORD.

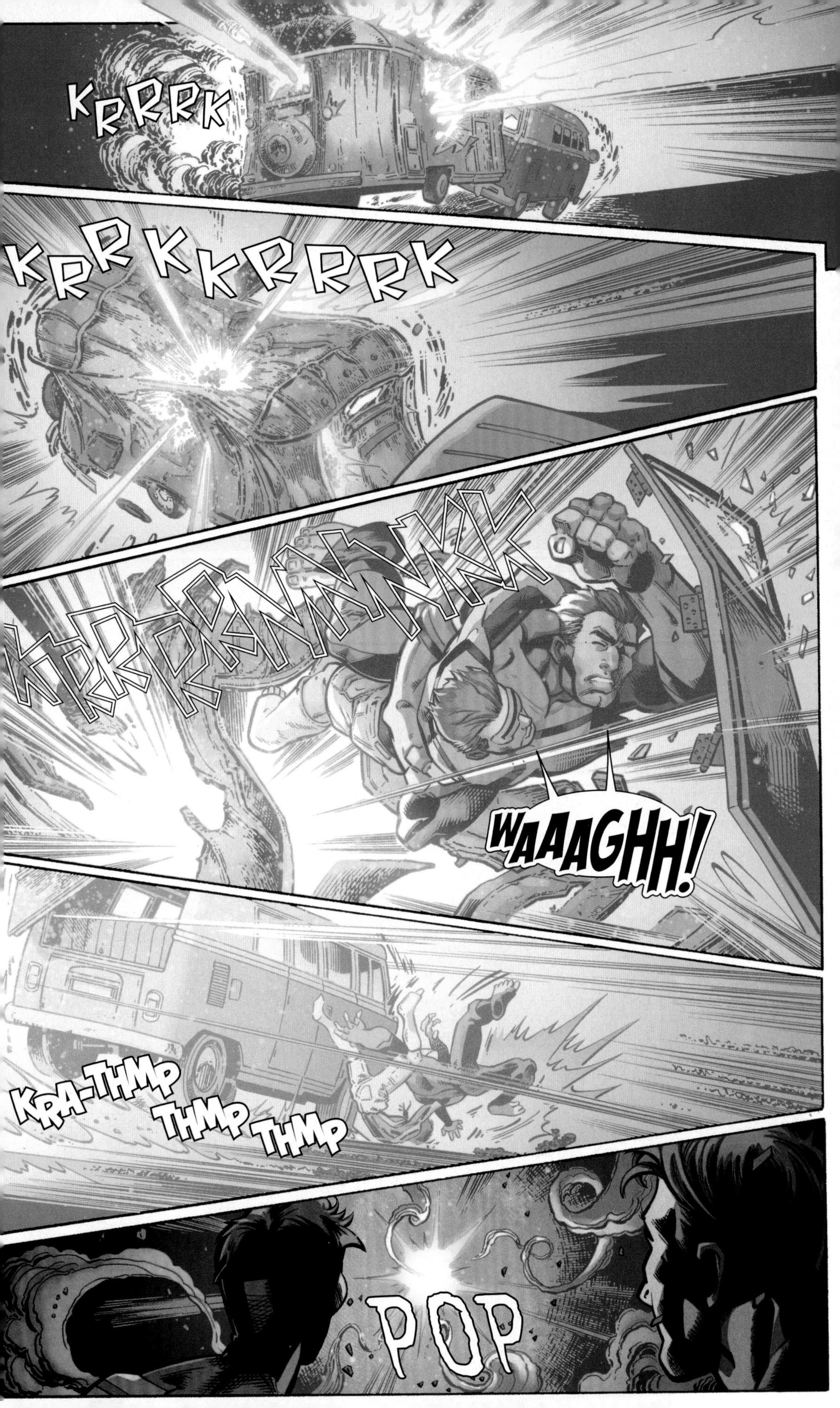
KRRRK
KRRKKRRRRK
KRRRRRAAANNNKK
WAAAGHH!
KRA-THMP
THMP THMP
POP

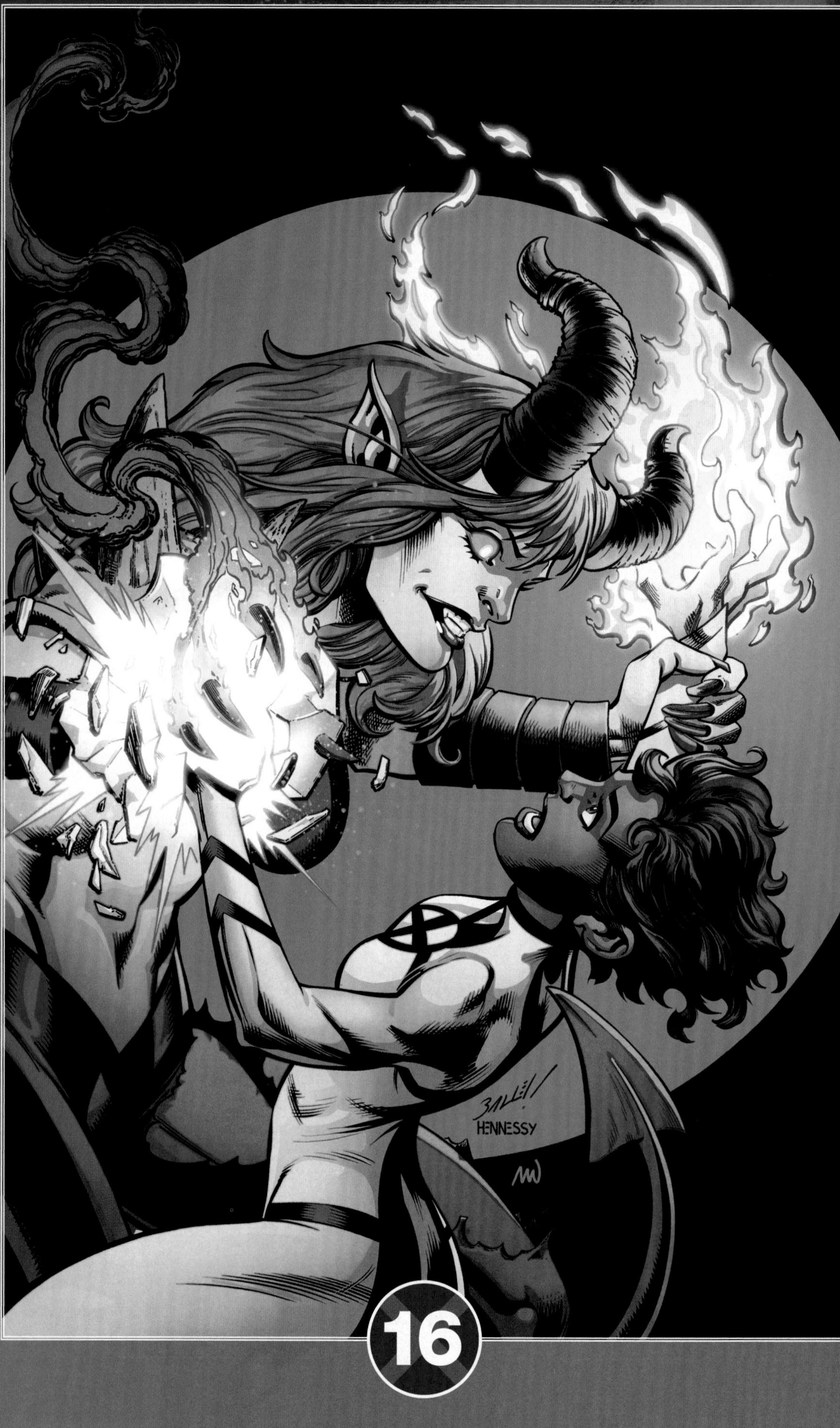
BAGLEY
HENNESSY
16

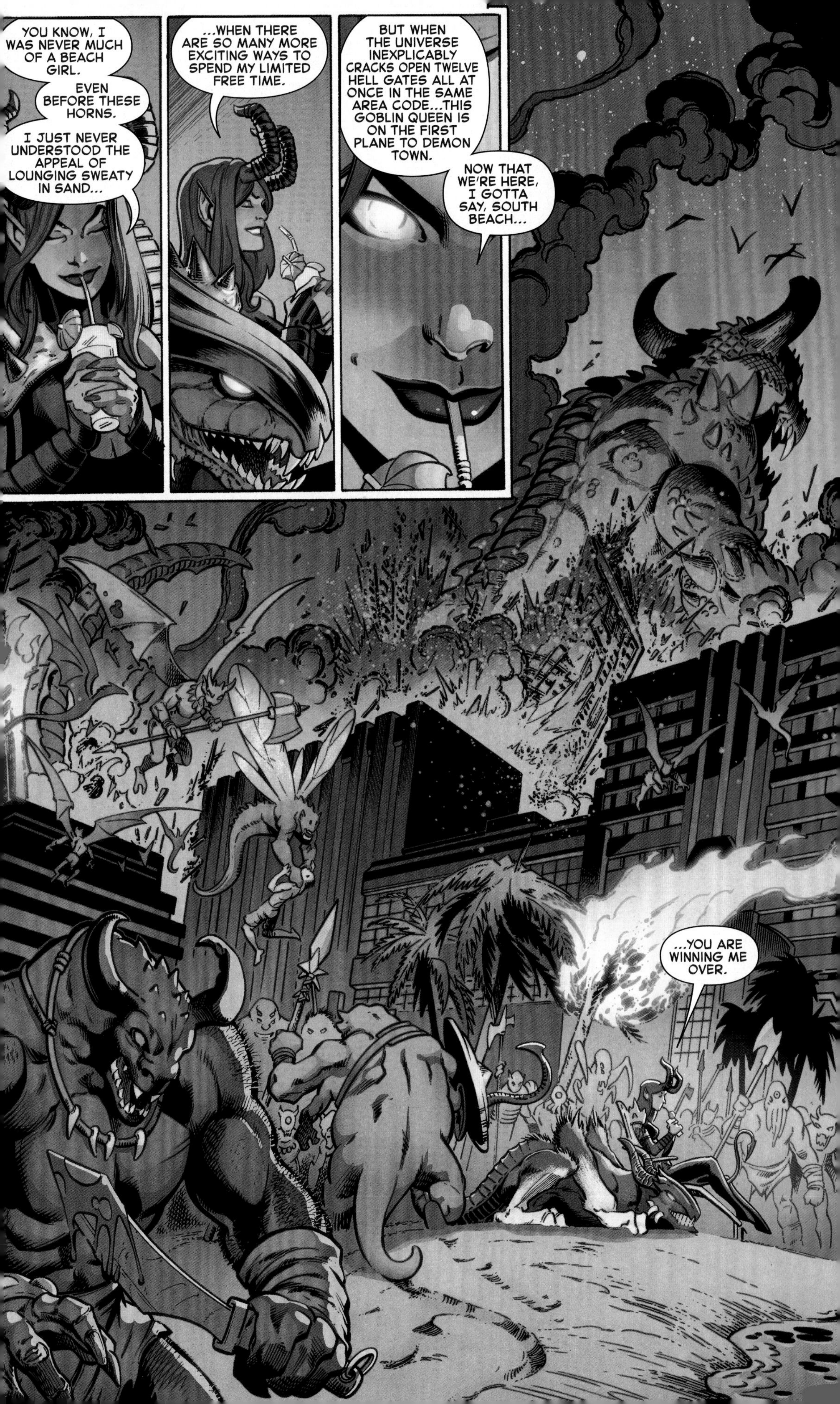
YOU KNOW, I WAS NEVER MUCH OF A BEACH GIRL.
EVEN BEFORE THESE HORNS.
I JUST NEVER UNDERSTOOD THE APPEAL OF LOUNGING SWEATY IN SAND...
...WHEN THERE ARE SO MANY MORE EXCITING WAYS TO SPEND MY LIMITED FREE TIME.
BUT WHEN THE UNIVERSE INEXPLICABLY CRACKS OPEN TWELVE HELL GATES ALL AT ONCE IN THE SAME AREA CODE...THIS GOBLIN QUEEN IS ON THE FIRST PLANE TO DEMON TOWN.
NOW THAT WE'RE HERE, I GOTTA SAY, SOUTH BEACH...
...YOU ARE WINNING ME OVER.

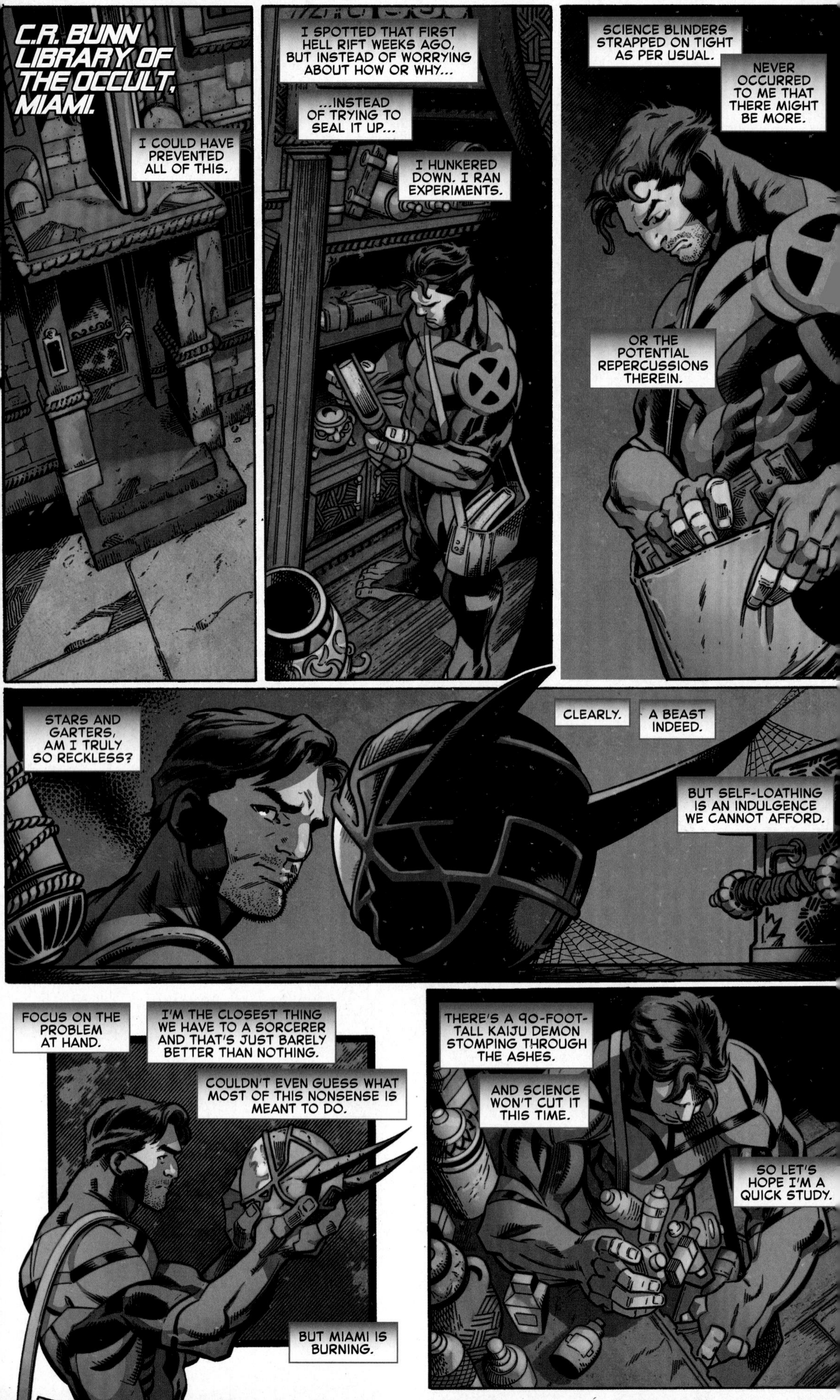
C.R. BUNN LIBRARY OF THE OCCULT, MIAMI.
I COULD HAVE PREVENTED ALL OF THIS.
I SPOTTED THAT FIRST HELL RIFT WEEKS AGO, BUT INSTEAD OF WORRYING ABOUT HOW OR WHY...
...INSTEAD OF TRYING TO SEAL IT UP...
I HUNKERED DOWN. I RAN EXPERIMENTS.
SCIENCE BLINDERS STRAPPED ON TIGHT AS PER USUAL.
NEVER OCCURRED TO ME THAT THERE MIGHT BE MORE.
OR THE POTENTIAL REPERCUSSIONS THEREIN.
STARS AND GARTERS, AM I TRULY SO RECKLESS?
CLEARLY.
A BEAST INDEED.
BUT SELF-LOATHING IS AN INDULGENCE WE CANNOT AFFORD.
FOCUS ON THE PROBLEM AT HAND.
I'M THE CLOSEST THING WE HAVE TO A SORCERER AND THAT'S JUST BARELY BETTER THAN NOTHING.
COULDN'T EVEN GUESS WHAT MOST OF THIS NONSENSE IS MEANT TO DO.
BUT MIAMI IS BURNING.
THERE'S A 90-FOOT-TALL KAIJU DEMON STOMPING THROUGH THE ASHES.
AND SCIENCE WON'T CUT IT THIS TIME.
SO LET'S HOPE I'M A QUICK STUDY.

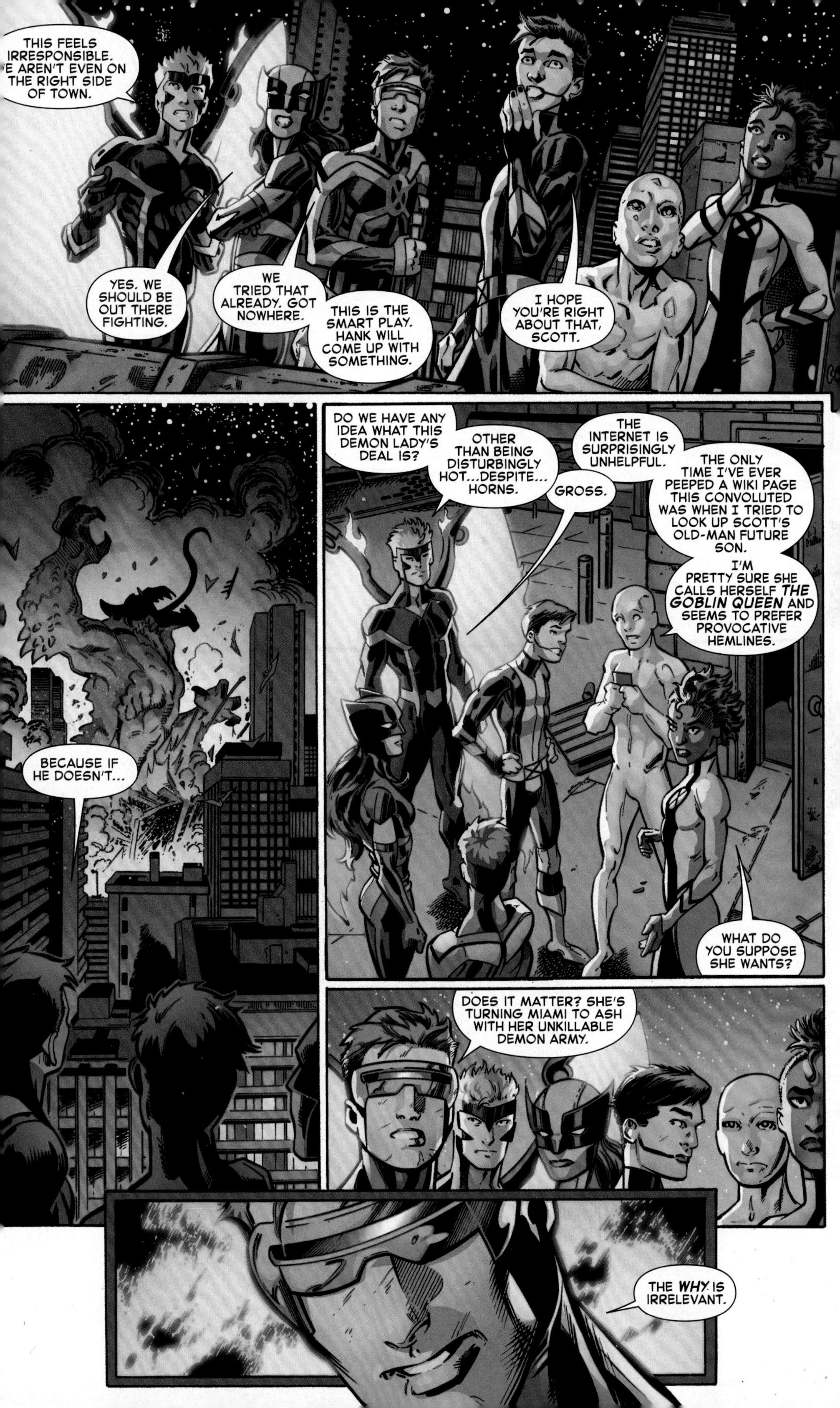

THIS FEELS IRRESPONSIBLE. E AREN'T EVEN ON THE RIGHT SIDE OF TOWN.
YES. WE SHOULD BE OUT THERE FIGHTING.
WE TRIED THAT ALREADY. GOT NOWHERE.
THIS IS THE SMART PLAY. HANK WILL COME UP WITH SOMETHING.
I HOPE YOU'RE RIGHT ABOUT THAT, SCOTT.
BECAUSE IF HE DOESN'T...
DO WE HAVE ANY IDEA WHAT THIS DEMON LADY'S DEAL IS?
OTHER THAN BEING DISTURBINGLY HOT...DESPITE... HORNS.
GROSS.
THE INTERNET IS SURPRISINGLY UNHELPFUL.
THE ONLY TIME I'VE EVER PEEPED A WIKI PAGE THIS CONVOLUTED WAS WHEN I TRIED TO LOOK UP SCOTT'S OLD-MAN FUTURE SON.
I'M PRETTY SURE SHE CALLS HERSELF ***THE GOBLIN QUEEN*** AND SEEMS TO PREFER PROVOCATIVE HEMLINES.
WHAT DO YOU SUPPOSE SHE WANTS?
DOES IT MATTER? SHE'S TURNING MIAMI TO ASH WITH HER UNKILLABLE DEMON ARMY.
THE ***WHY*** IS IRRELEVANT.

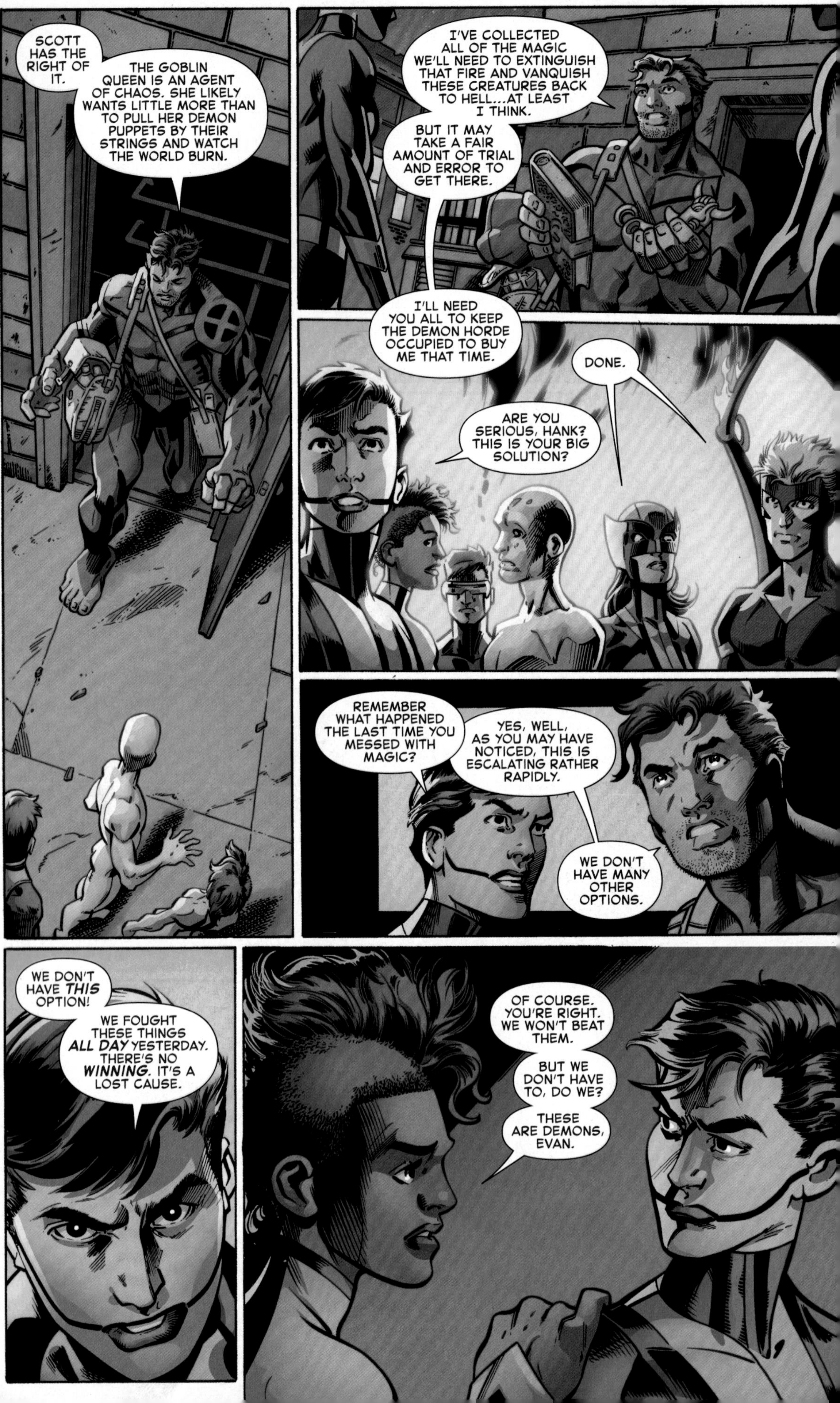

SCOTT HAS THE RIGHT OF IT.
THE GOBLIN QUEEN IS AN AGENT OF CHAOS. SHE LIKELY WANTS LITTLE MORE THAN TO PULL HER DEMON PUPPETS BY THEIR STRINGS AND WATCH THE WORLD BURN.
I'VE COLLECTED ALL OF THE MAGIC WE'LL NEED TO EXTINGUISH THAT FIRE AND VANQUISH THESE CREATURES BACK TO HELL...AT LEAST I THINK.
BUT IT MAY TAKE A FAIR AMOUNT OF TRIAL AND ERROR TO GET THERE.
I'LL NEED YOU ALL TO KEEP THE DEMON HORDE OCCUPIED TO BUY ME THAT TIME.
DONE.
ARE YOU SERIOUS, HANK? THIS IS YOUR BIG SOLUTION?
REMEMBER WHAT HAPPENED THE LAST TIME YOU MESSED WITH MAGIC?
YES, WELL, AS YOU MAY HAVE NOTICED, THIS IS ESCALATING RATHER RAPIDLY.
WE DON'T HAVE MANY OTHER OPTIONS.
WE DON'T HAVE *THIS* OPTION!
WE FOUGHT THESE THINGS *ALL DAY* YESTERDAY. THERE'S NO *WINNING*. IT'S A LOST CAUSE.
OF COURSE. YOU'RE RIGHT. WE WON'T BEAT THEM.
BUT WE DON'T HAVE TO, DO WE?
THESE ARE DEMONS, EVAN.

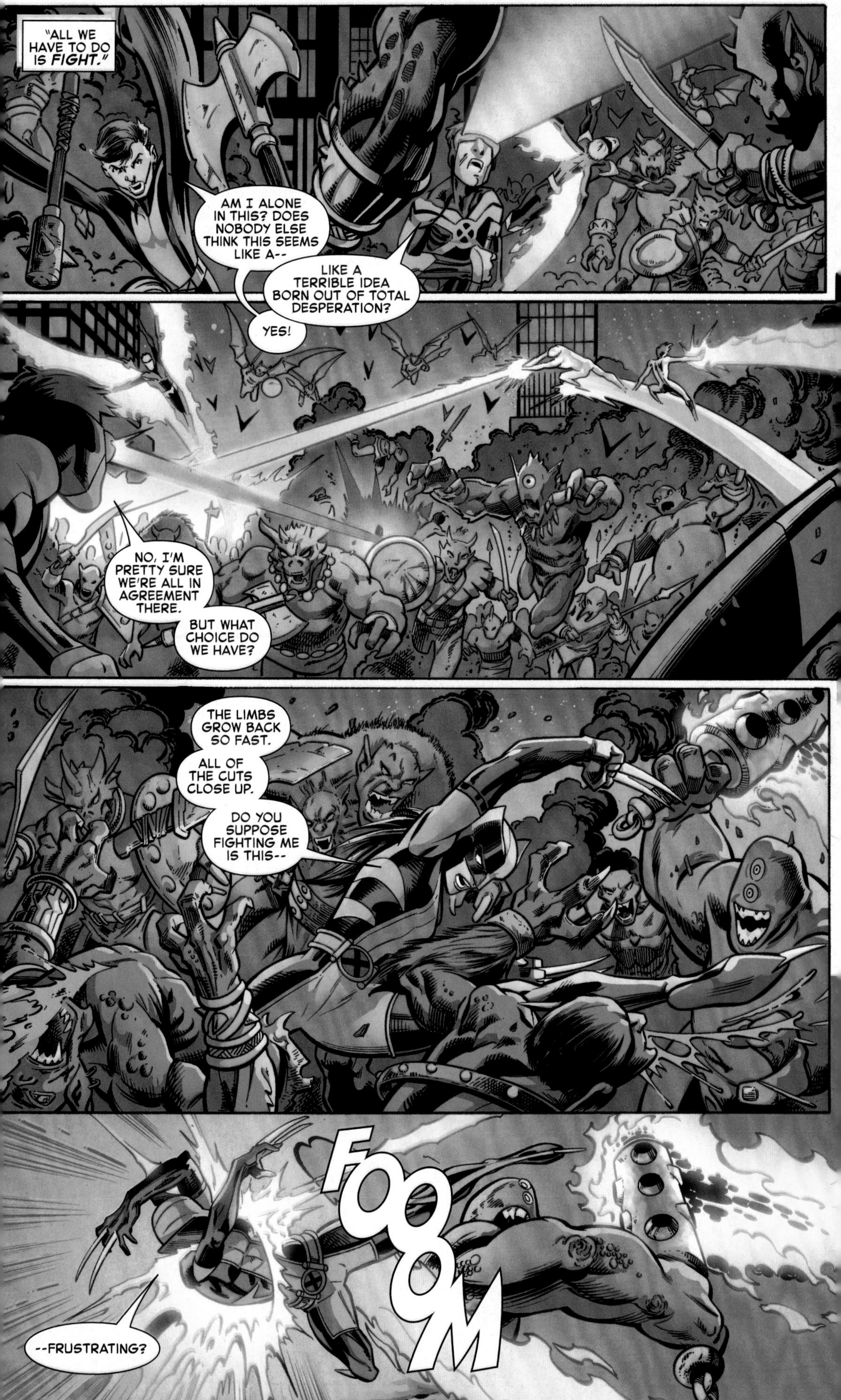
"ALL WE HAVE TO DO IS *FIGHT*."
AM I ALONE IN THIS? DOES NOBODY ELSE THINK THIS SEEMS LIKE A--
LIKE A TERRIBLE IDEA BORN OUT OF TOTAL DESPERATION?
YES!
NO, I'M PRETTY SURE WE'RE ALL IN AGREEMENT THERE.
BUT WHAT CHOICE DO WE HAVE?
THE LIMBS GROW BACK SO FAST.
ALL OF THE CUTS CLOSE UP.
DO YOU SUPPOSE FIGHTING ME IS THIS--
FOOOM
--FRUSTRATING?

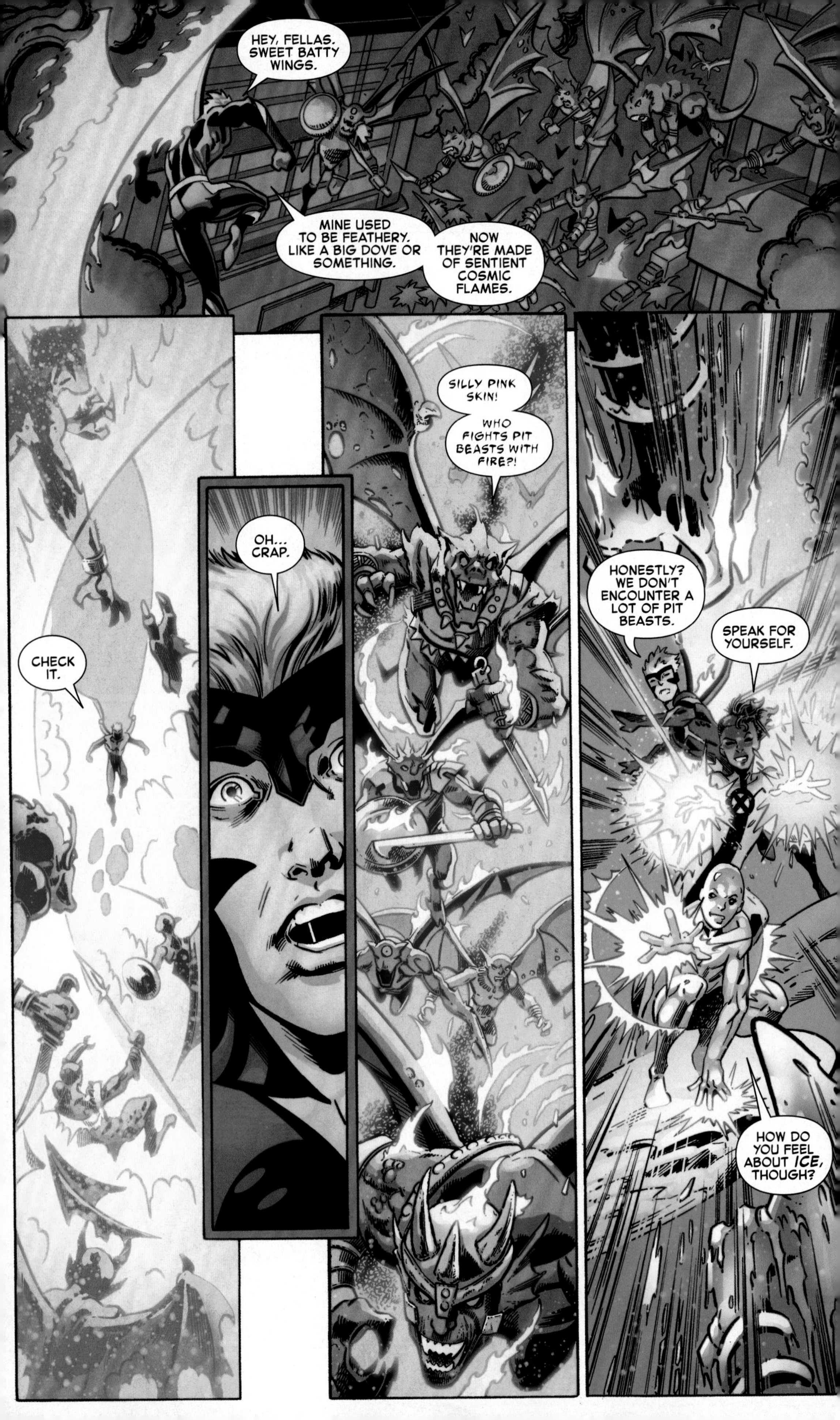
HEY, FELLAS. SWEET BATTY WINGS.
MINE USED TO BE FEATHERY. LIKE A BIG DOVE OR SOMETHING.
NOW THEY'RE MADE OF SENTIENT COSMIC FLAMES.
CHECK IT.
OH... CRAP.
SILLY PINK SKIN!
WHO FIGHTS PIT BEASTS WITH FIRE?!
HONESTLY? WE DON'T ENCOUNTER A LOT OF PIT BEASTS.
SPEAK FOR YOURSELF.
HOW DO YOU FEEL ABOUT ICE, THOUGH?

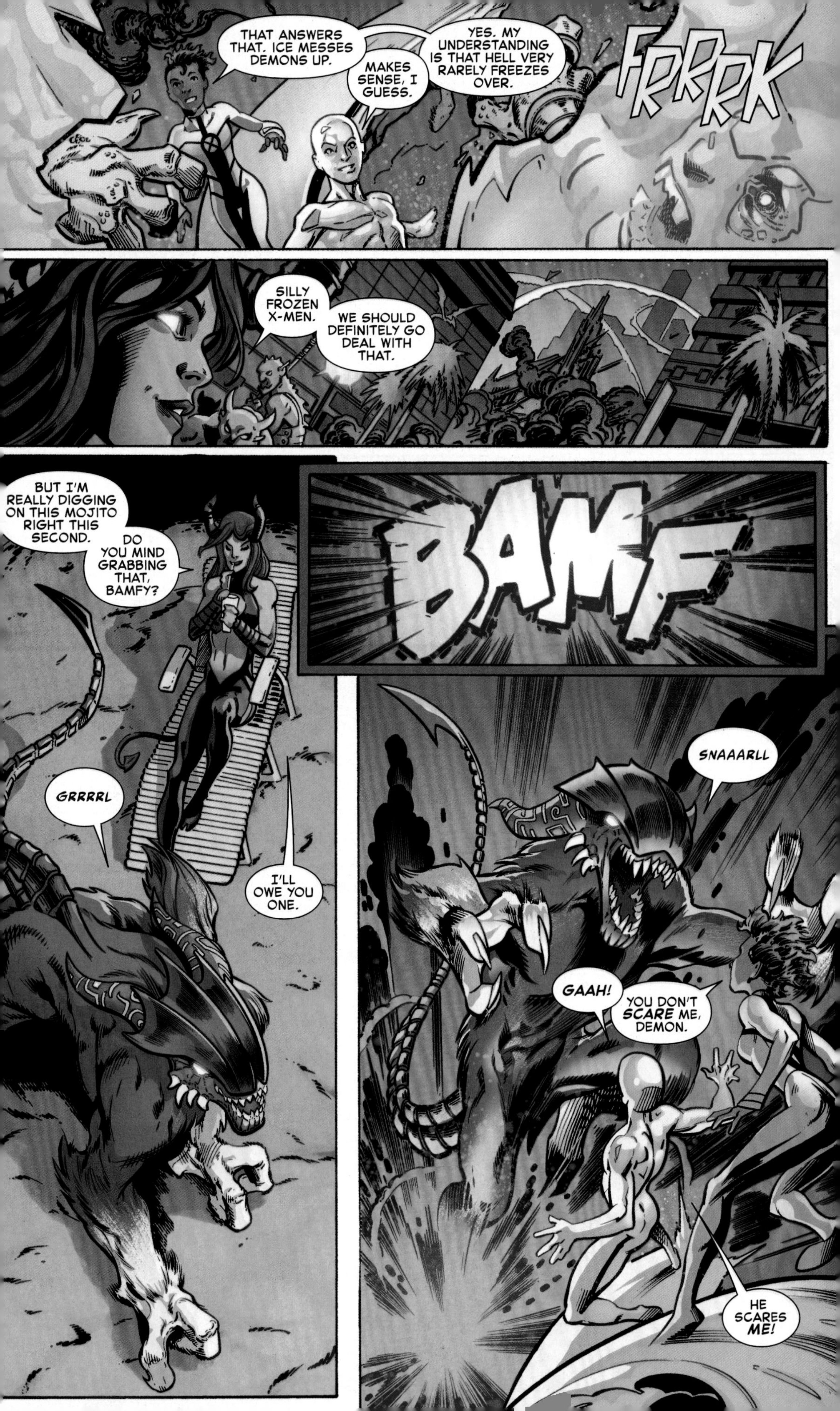
THAT ANSWERS THAT. ICE MESSES DEMONS UP.
MAKES SENSE, I GUESS.
YES. MY UNDERSTANDING IS THAT HELL VERY RARELY FREEZES OVER.
FRRRK
SILLY FROZEN X-MEN.
WE SHOULD DEFINITELY GO DEAL WITH THAT.
BUT I'M REALLY DIGGING ON THIS MOJITO RIGHT THIS SECOND.
DO YOU MIND GRABBING THAT, BAMFY?
GRRRRL
I'LL OWE YOU ONE.
BAMF
SNAAARLL
GAAH!
YOU DON'T SCARE ME, DEMON.
HE SCARES ME!

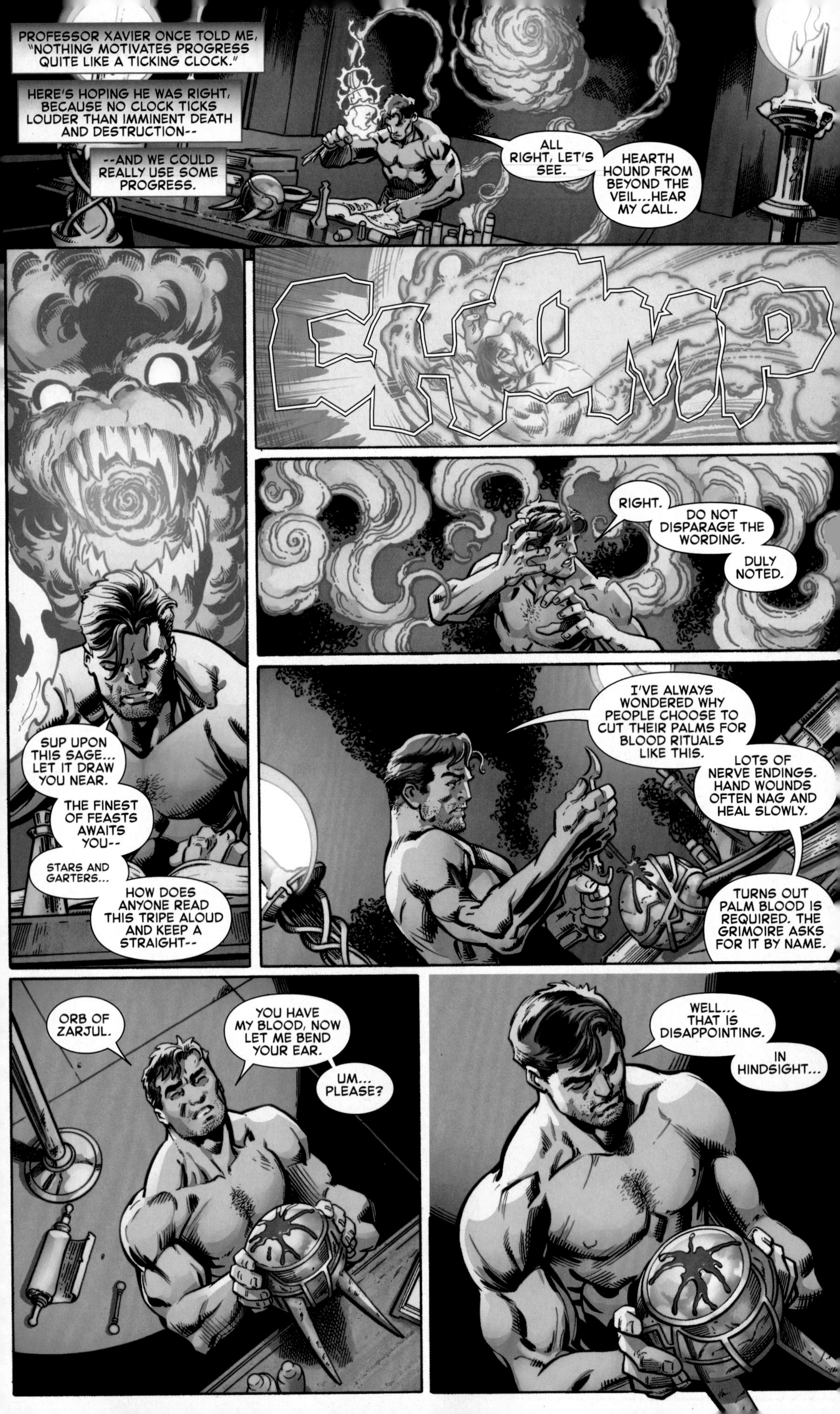
PROFESSOR XAVIER ONCE TOLD ME, "NOTHING MOTIVATES PROGRESS QUITE LIKE A TICKING CLOCK."
HERE'S HOPING HE WAS RIGHT, BECAUSE NO CLOCK TICKS LOUDER THAN IMMINENT DEATH AND DESTRUCTION--
--AND WE COULD REALLY USE SOME PROGRESS.
ALL RIGHT, LET'S SEE.
HEARTH HOUND FROM BEYOND THE VEIL...HEAR MY CALL.
SUP UPON THIS SAGE... LET IT DRAW YOU NEAR.
THE FINEST OF FEASTS AWAITS YOU--
STARS AND GARTERS...
HOW DOES ANYONE READ THIS TRIPE ALOUD AND KEEP A STRAIGHT--
CHOMP
RIGHT.
DO NOT DISPARAGE THE WORDING.
DULY NOTED.
I'VE ALWAYS WONDERED WHY PEOPLE CHOOSE TO CUT THEIR PALMS FOR BLOOD RITUALS LIKE THIS.
LOTS OF NERVE ENDINGS. HAND WOUNDS OFTEN NAG AND HEAL SLOWLY.
TURNS OUT PALM BLOOD IS REQUIRED. THE GRIMOIRE ASKS FOR IT BY NAME.
ORB OF ZARJUL.
YOU HAVE MY BLOOD, NOW LET ME BEND YOUR EAR.
UM... PLEASE?
WELL... THAT IS DISAPPOINTING.
IN HINDSIGHT...

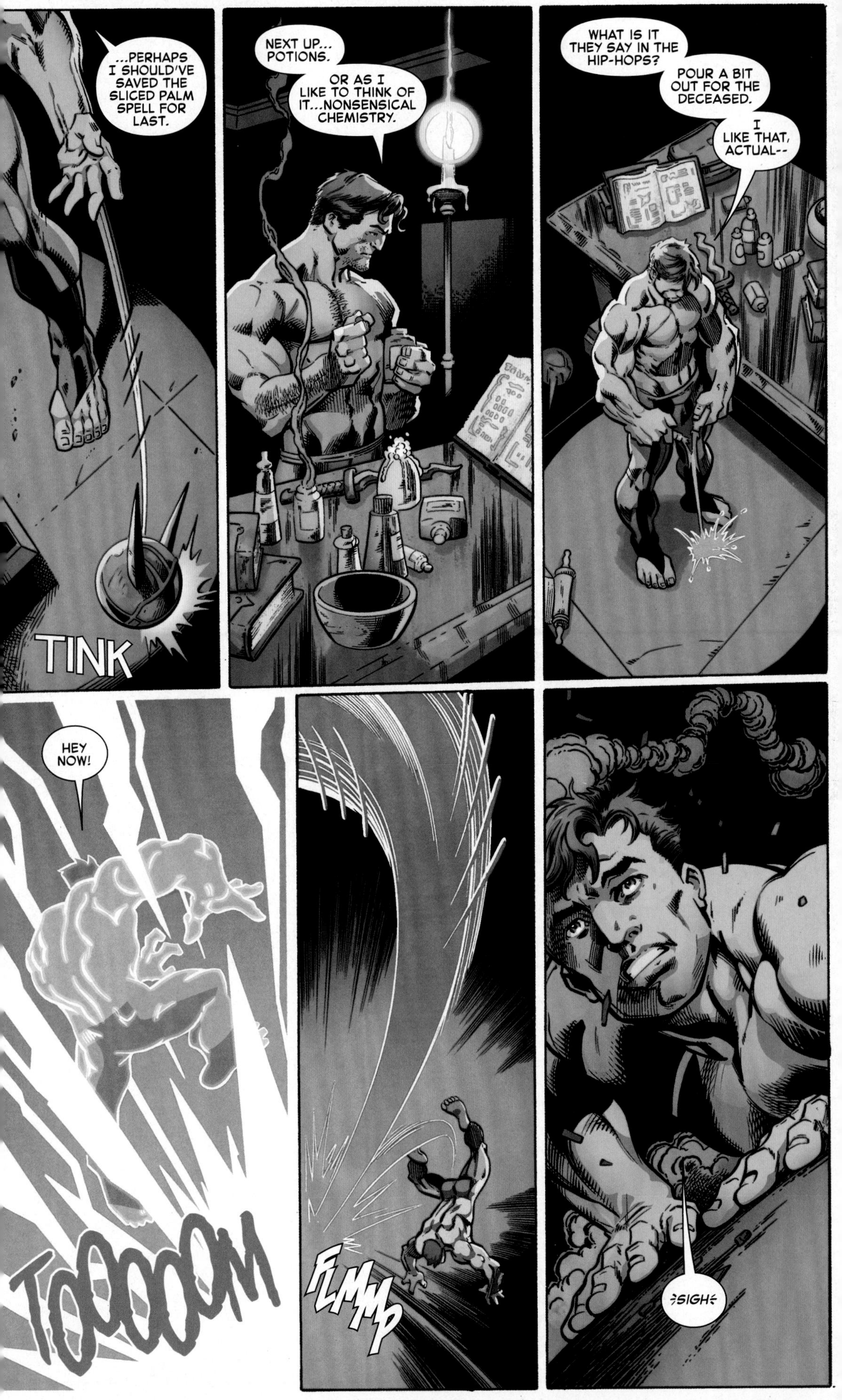
...PERHAPS I SHOULD'VE SAVED THE SLICED PALM SPELL FOR LAST.
TINK
NEXT UP... POTIONS.
OR AS I LIKE TO THINK OF IT...NONSENSICAL CHEMISTRY.
WHAT IS IT THEY SAY IN THE HIP-HOPS?
POUR A BIT OUT FOR THE DECEASED.
I LIKE THAT, ACTUAL--
HEY NOW!
TOOOOOM
FLMMP
SIGH

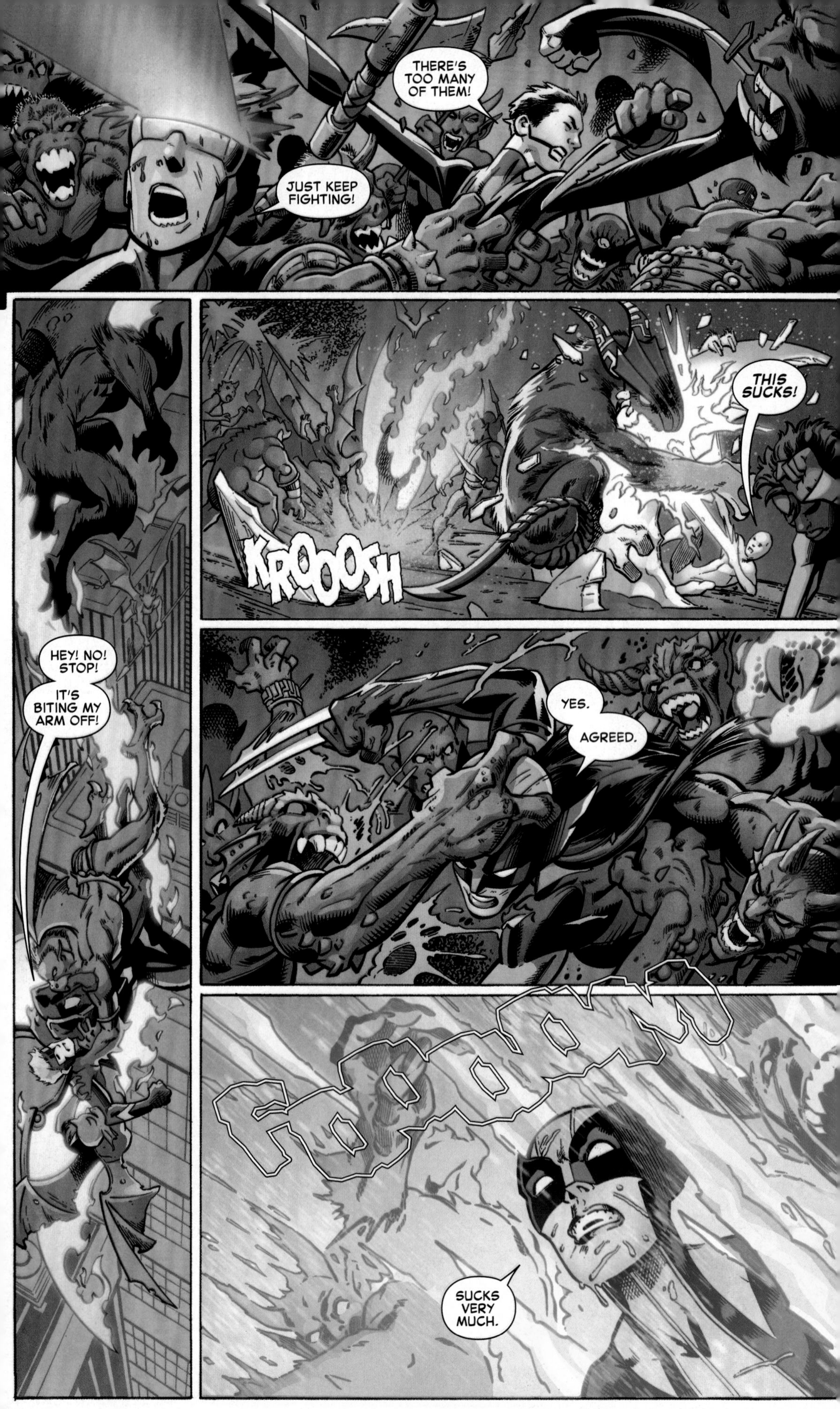
THERE'S TOO MANY OF THEM!
JUST KEEP FIGHTING!
HEY! NO! STOP!
IT'S BITING MY ARM OFF!
KROOOSH
THIS SUCKS!
YES.
AGREED.
SUCKS VERY MUCH.

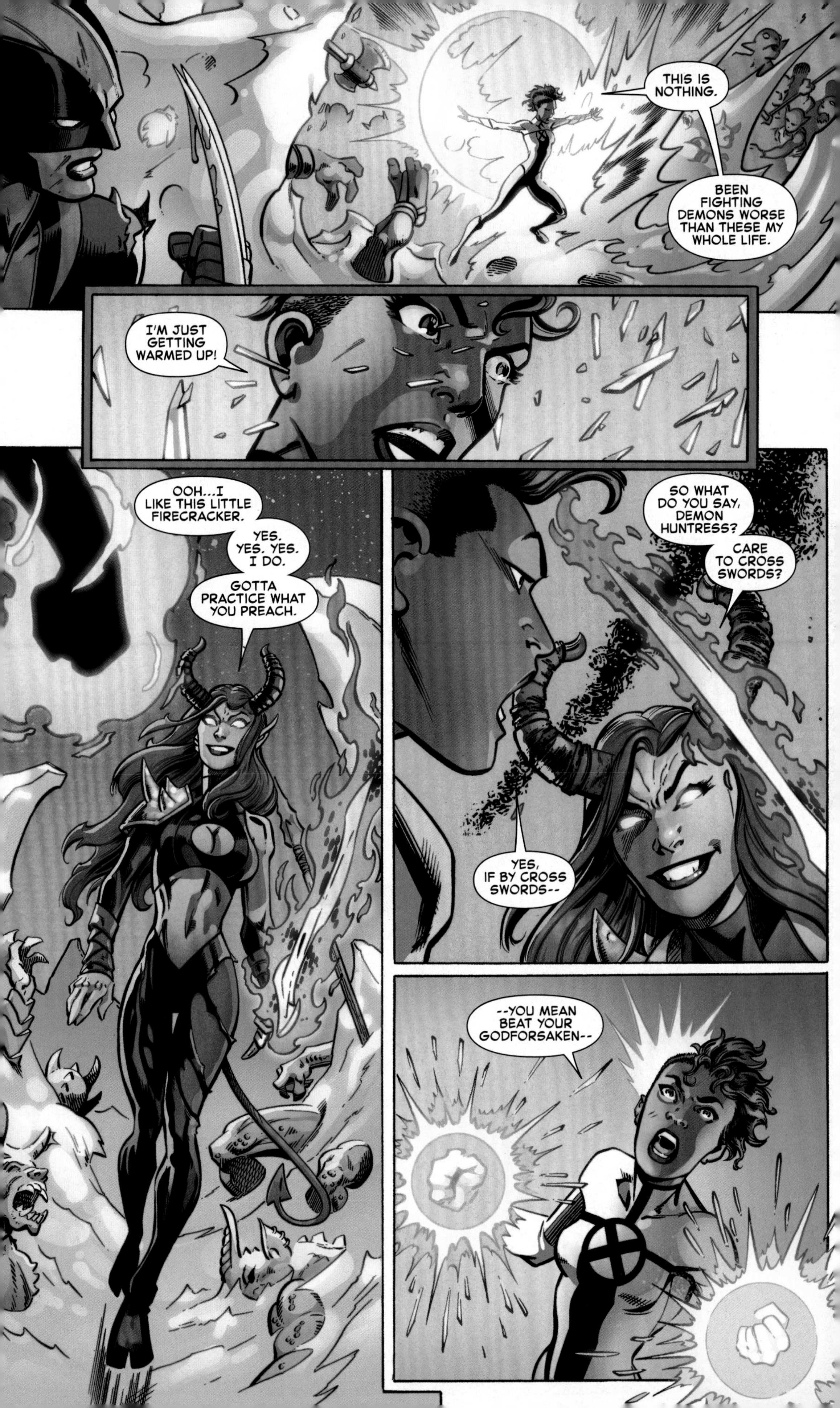

THIS IS NOTHING.
BEEN FIGHTING DEMONS WORSE THAN THESE MY WHOLE LIFE.
I'M JUST GETTING WARMED UP!
OOH...I LIKE THIS LITTLE FIRECRACKER.
YES. YES. YES. I DO.
GOTTA PRACTICE WHAT YOU PREACH.
SO WHAT DO YOU SAY, DEMON HUNTRESS?
CARE TO CROSS SWORDS?
YES, IF BY CROSS SWORDS--
--YOU MEAN BEAT YOUR GODFORSAKEN--

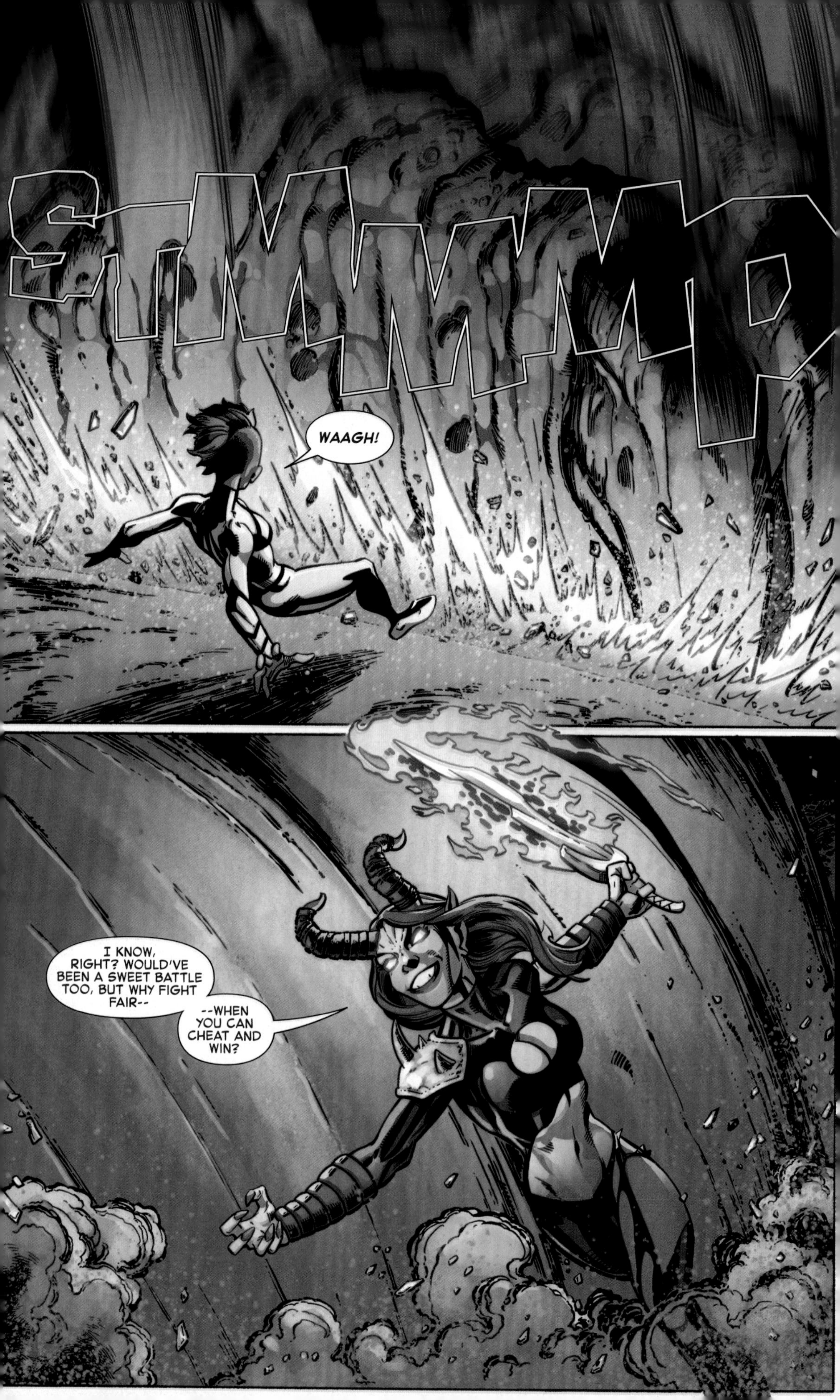
STMMMP
WAAGH!
I KNOW, RIGHT? WOULD'VE BEEN A SWEET BATTLE TOO, BUT WHY FIGHT FAIR--
--WHEN YOU CAN CHEAT AND WIN?

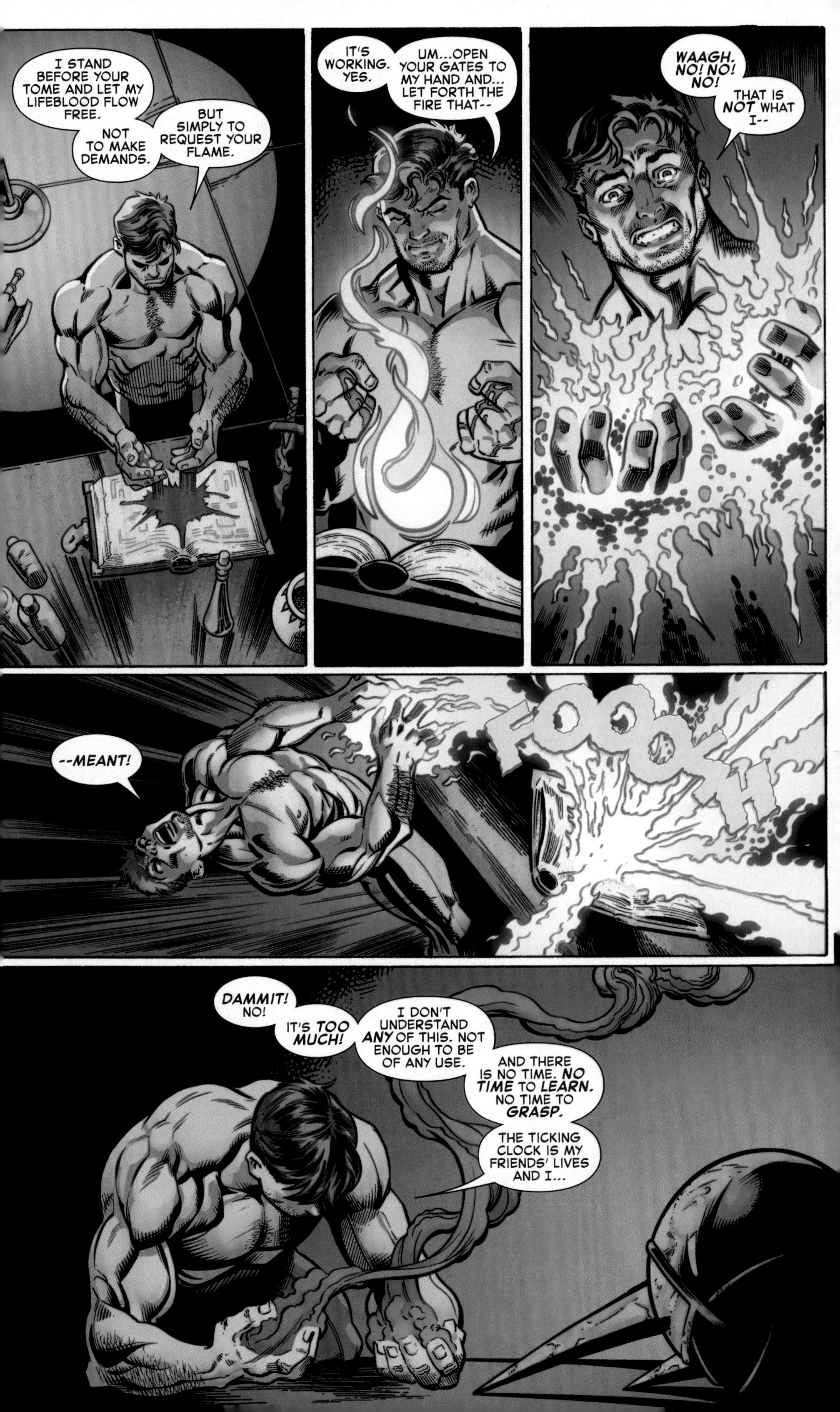
I STAND BEFORE YOUR TOME AND LET MY LIFEBLOOD FLOW FREE.
NOT TO MAKE DEMANDS.
BUT SIMPLY TO REQUEST YOUR FLAME.
IT'S WORKING. YES.
UM...OPEN YOUR GATES TO MY HAND AND... LET FORTH THE FIRE THAT--
WAAGH. NO! NO! NO!
THAT IS NOT WHAT I--
--MEANT!
FOOOSH
DAMMIT! NO!
IT'S TOO MUCH!
I DON'T UNDERSTAND ANY OF THIS. NOT ENOUGH TO BE OF ANY USE.
AND THERE IS NO TIME. NO TIME TO LEARN. NO TIME TO GRASP.
THE TICKING CLOCK IS MY FRIENDS' LIVES AND I...

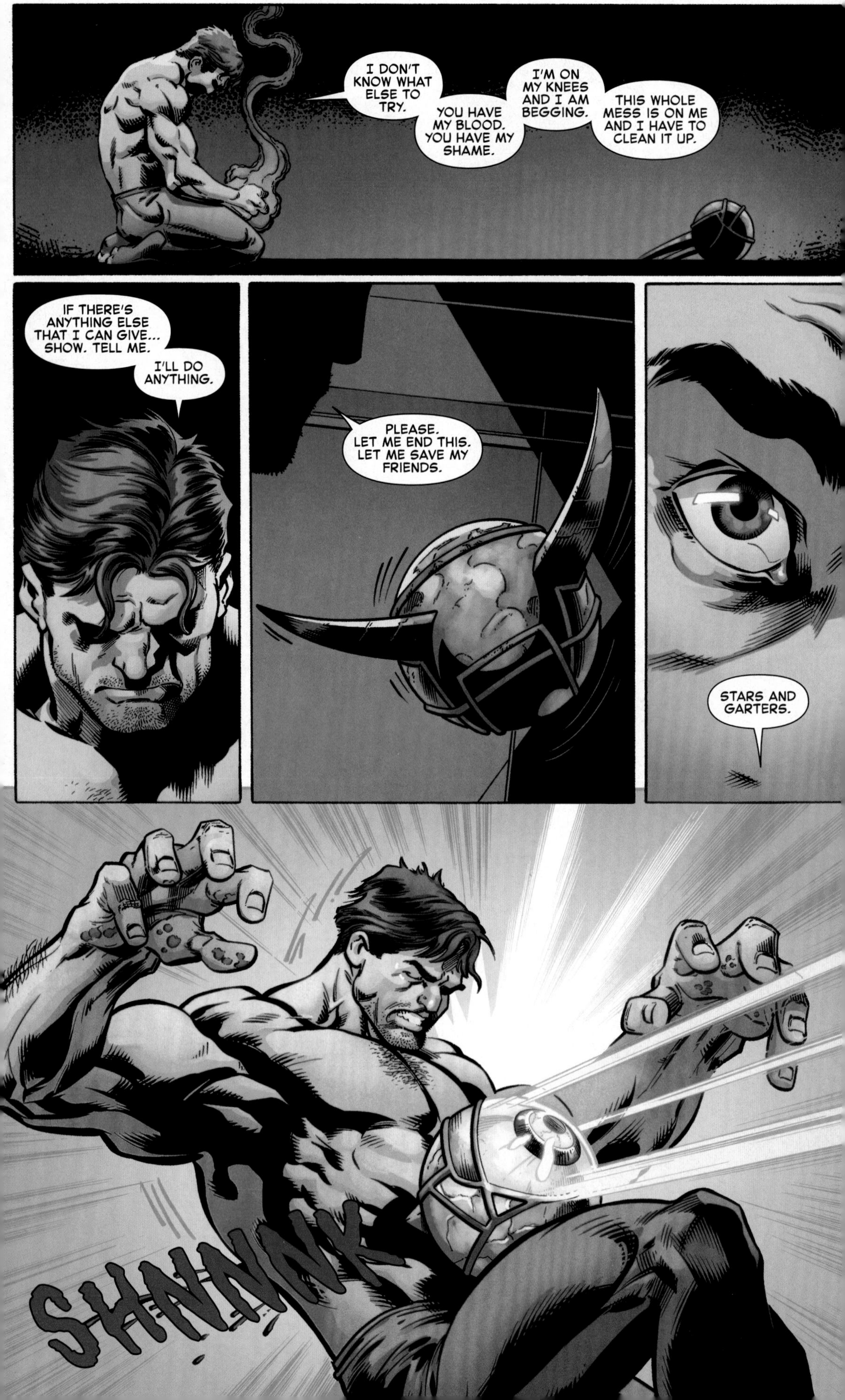
I DON'T KNOW WHAT ELSE TO TRY.
YOU HAVE MY BLOOD. YOU HAVE MY SHAME.
I'M ON MY KNEES AND I AM BEGGING.
THIS WHOLE MESS IS ON ME AND I HAVE TO CLEAN IT UP.
IF THERE'S ANYTHING ELSE THAT I CAN GIVE... SHOW. TELL ME.
I'LL DO ANYTHING.
PLEASE. LET ME END THIS. LET ME SAVE MY FRIENDS.
STARS AND GARTERS.
SHNNNK

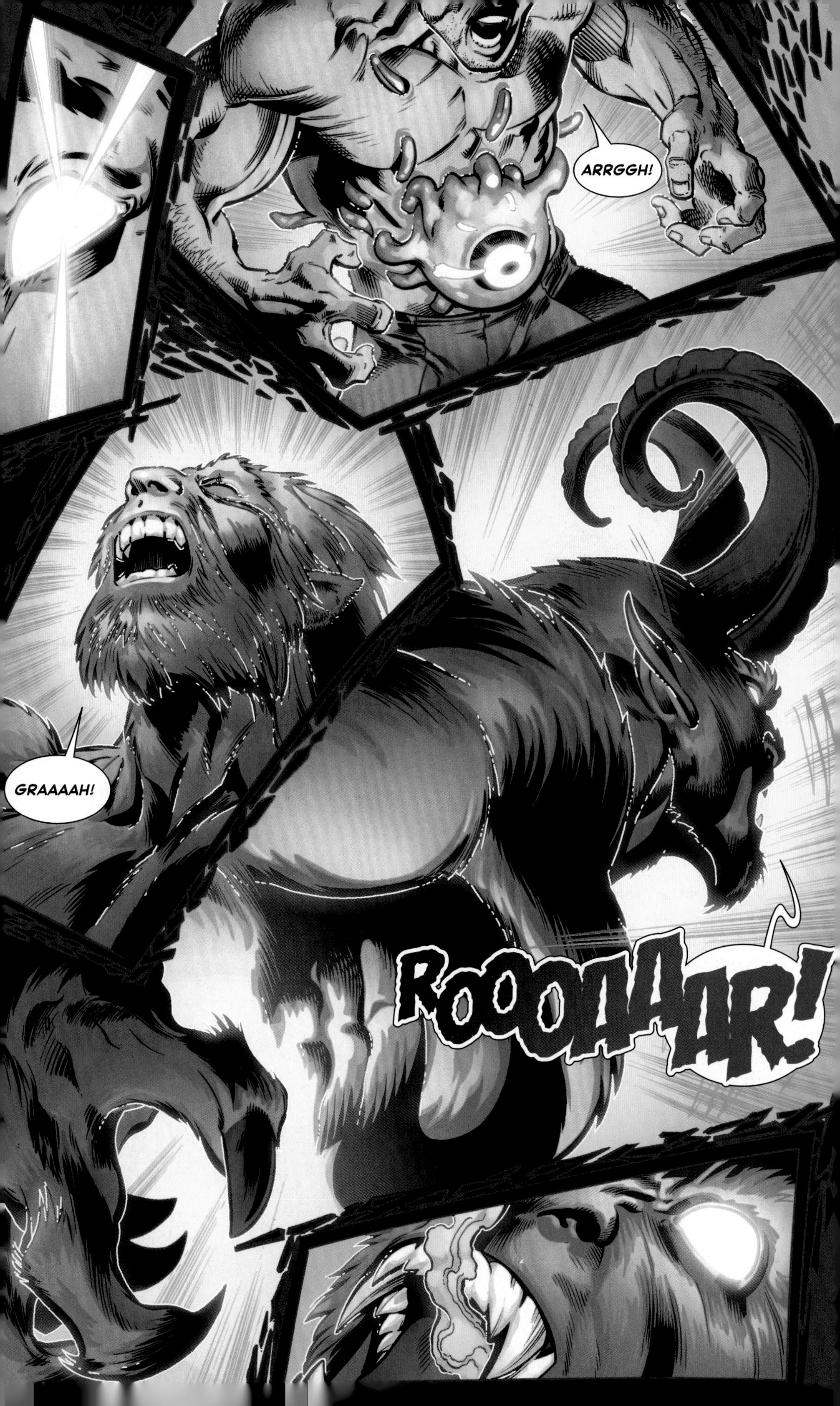
ARRGGH!
GRAAAAH!
ROOOAAAR!

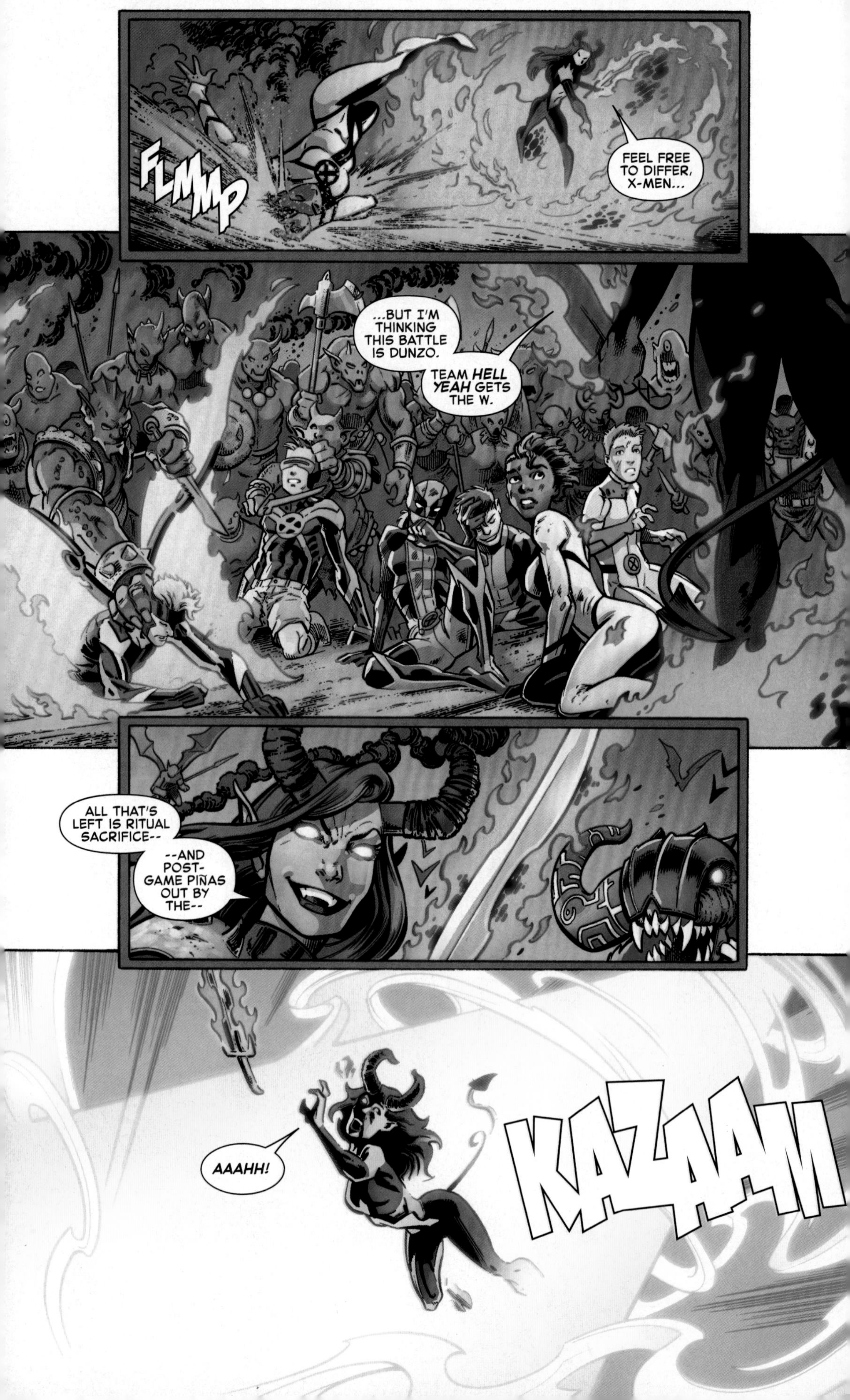
FLMMP
FEEL FREE TO DIFFER, X-MEN...
...BUT I'M THINKING THIS BATTLE IS DUNZO.
TEAM **HELL YEAH** GETS THE W.
ALL THAT'S LEFT IS RITUAL SACRIFICE--
--AND POST-GAME PIÑAS OUT BY THE--
AAAHH!
KAZAAAM

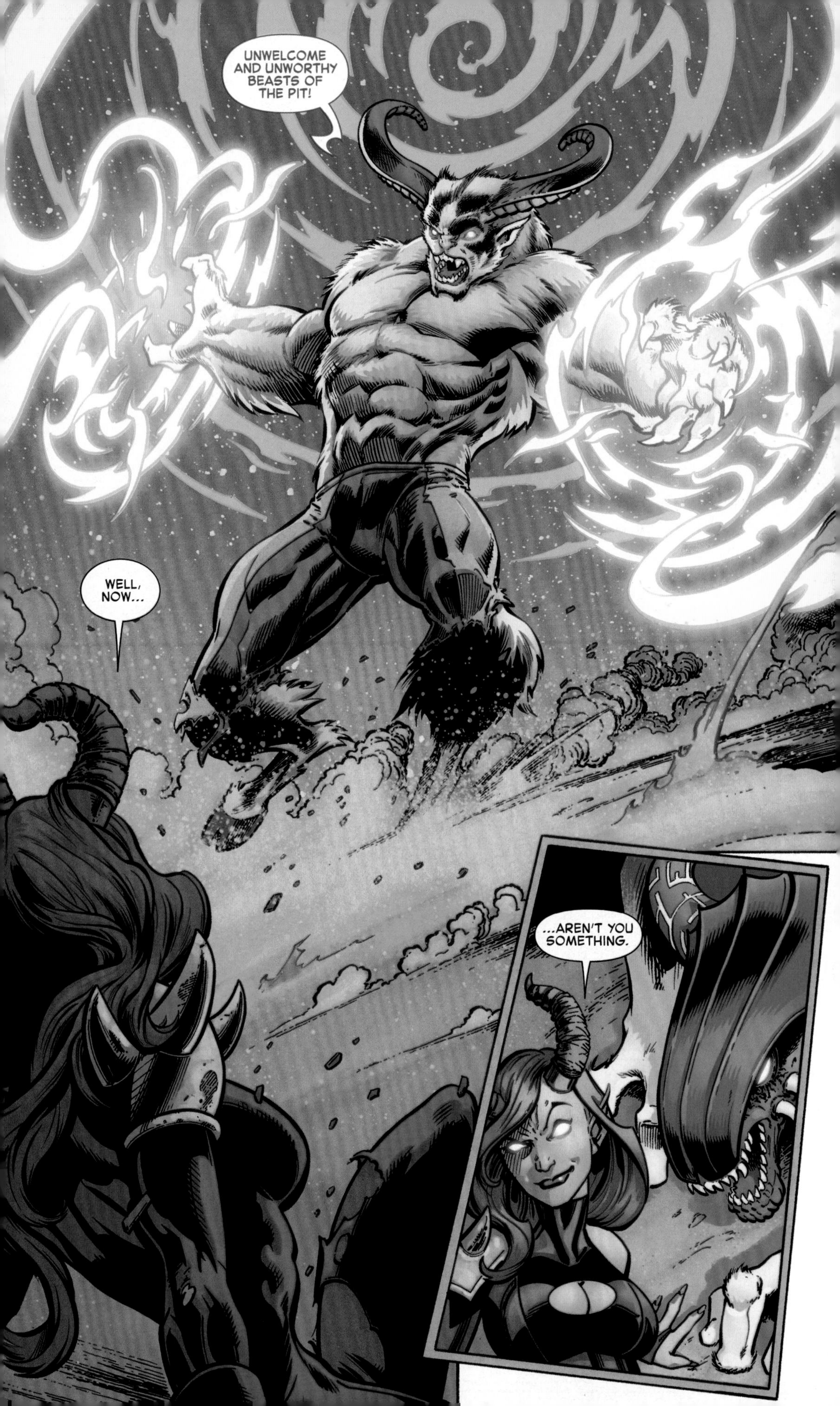
UNWELCOME AND UNWORTHY BEASTS OF THE PIT!
WELL, NOW...
...AREN'T YOU SOMETHING.

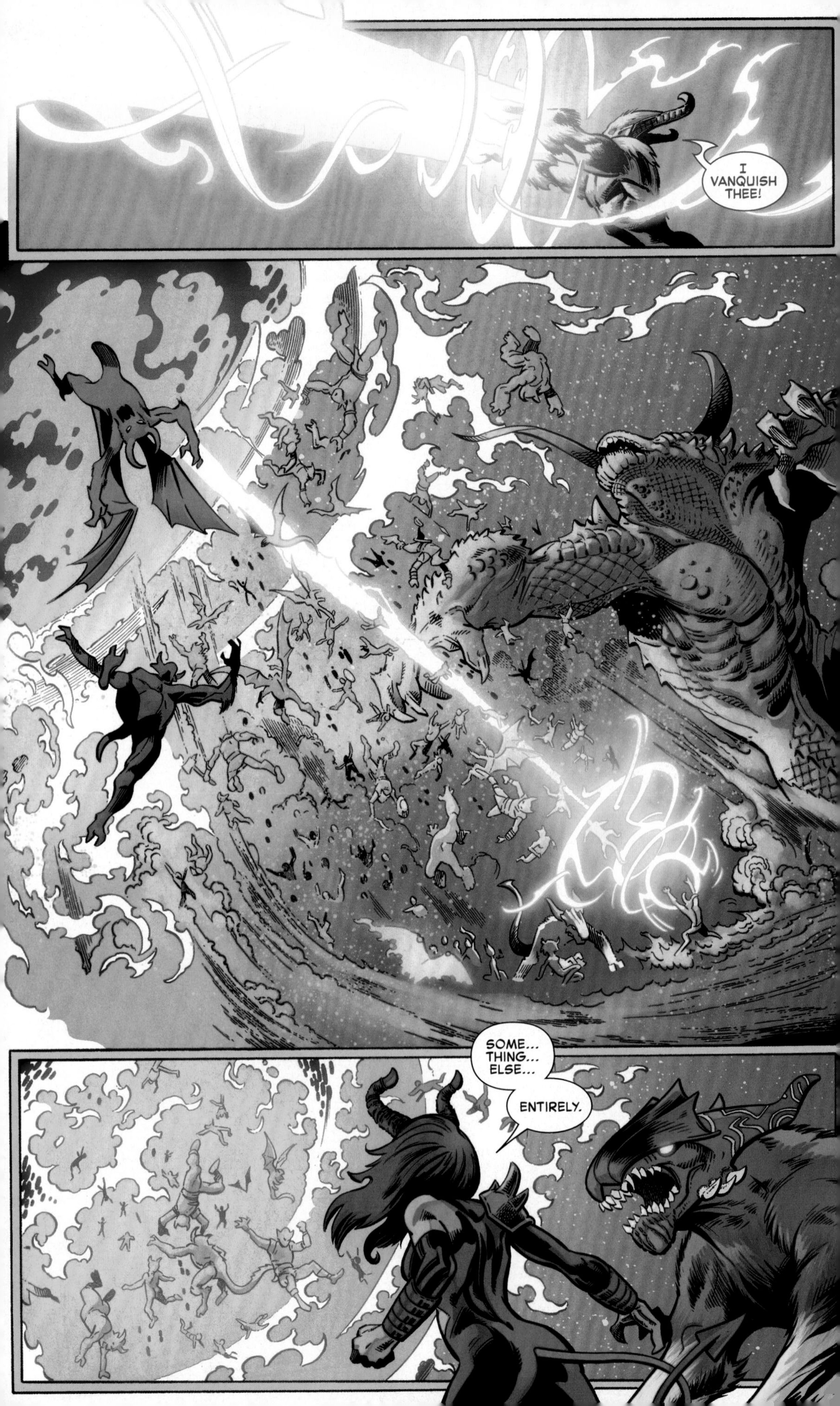
I VANQUISH THEE!
SOME... THING... ELSE...
ENTIRELY.

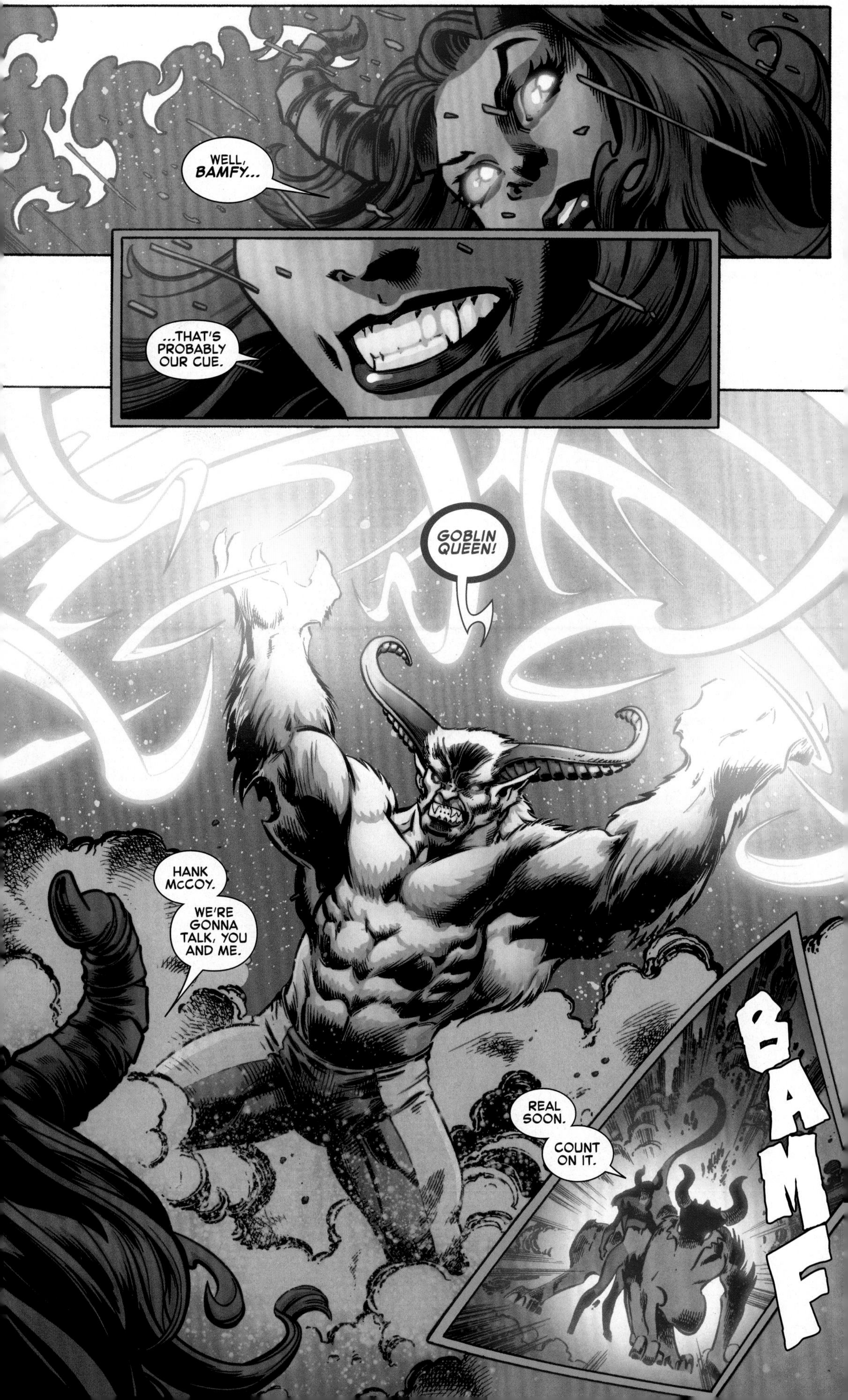
WELL, BAMFY...
...THAT'S PROBABLY OUR CUE.
GOBLIN QUEEN!
HANK McCOY.
WE'RE GONNA TALK, YOU AND ME.
REAL SOON.
COUNT ON IT.
BAMF

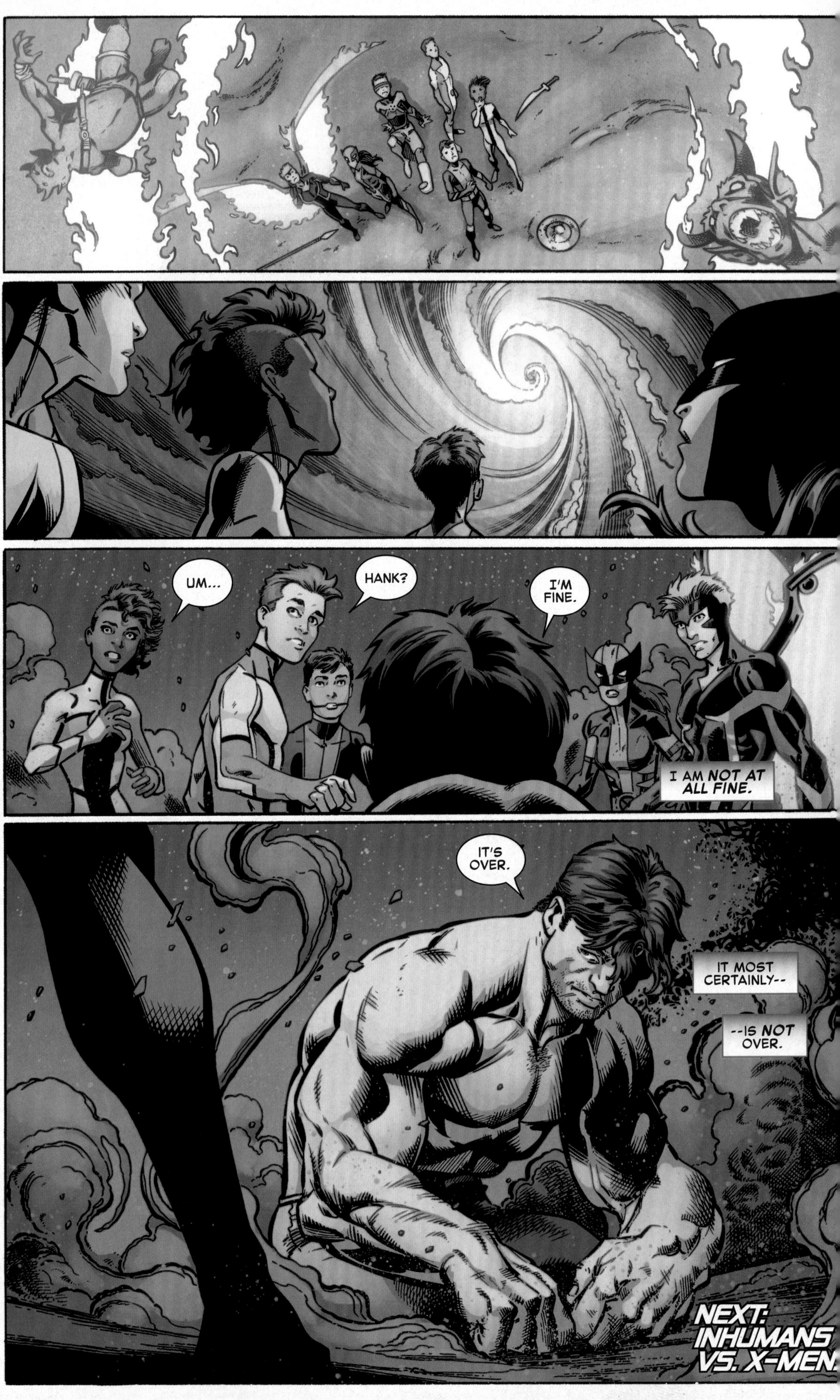
UM...
HANK?
I'M FINE.
I AM NOT AT ALL FINE.
IT'S OVER.
IT MOST CERTAINLY--
--IS NOT OVER.
NEXT: INHUMANS VS. X-MEN.

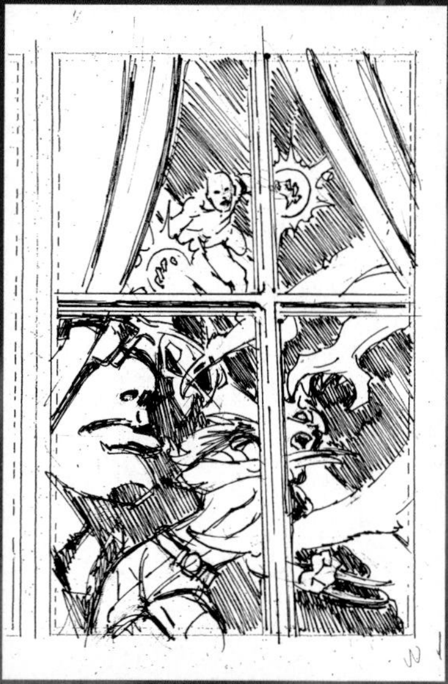

▲ LAYOUT

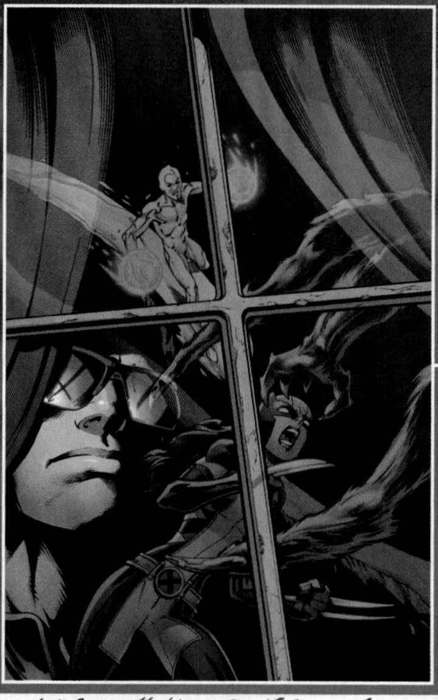

◀ COLORS

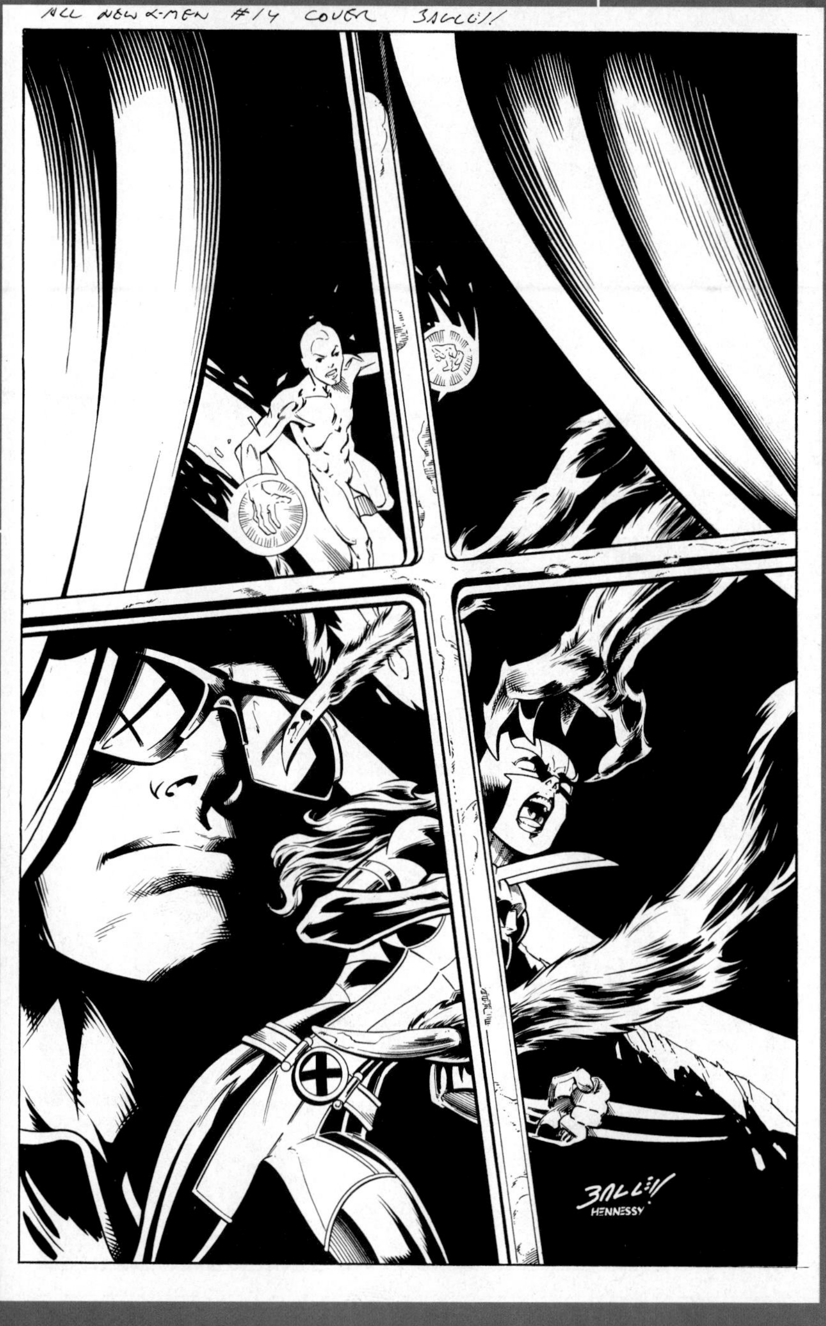
ALL NEW X-MEN #14 COVER BAGLEY!!
BAGLEY
HENNESSY

INKS ▶

#14 COVER PROCESS
BY **MARK BAGLEY, ANDREW HENNESSY** & **NOLAN WOODARD**

COLORS ▶

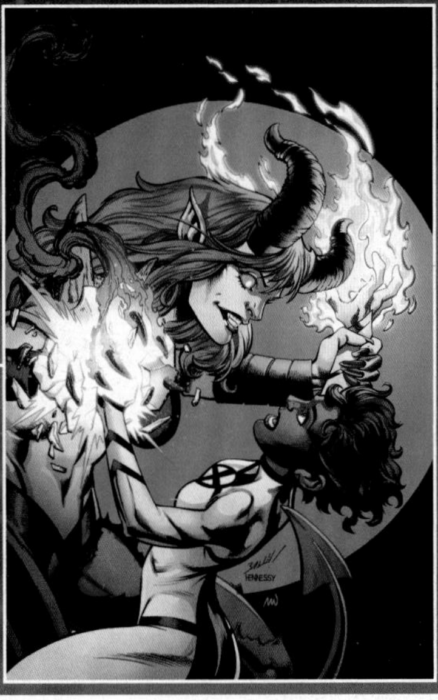

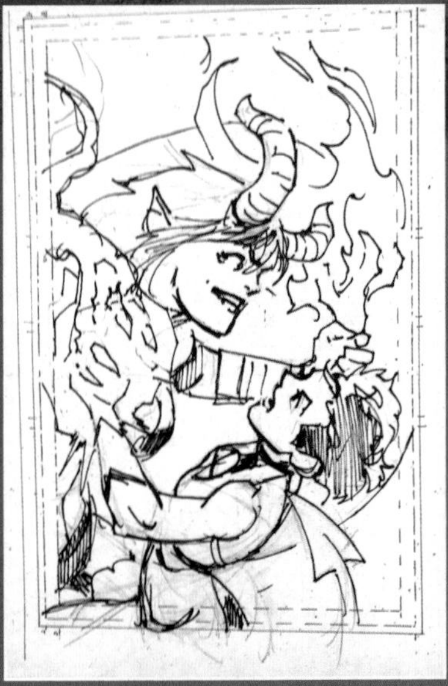

▲
LAYOUT

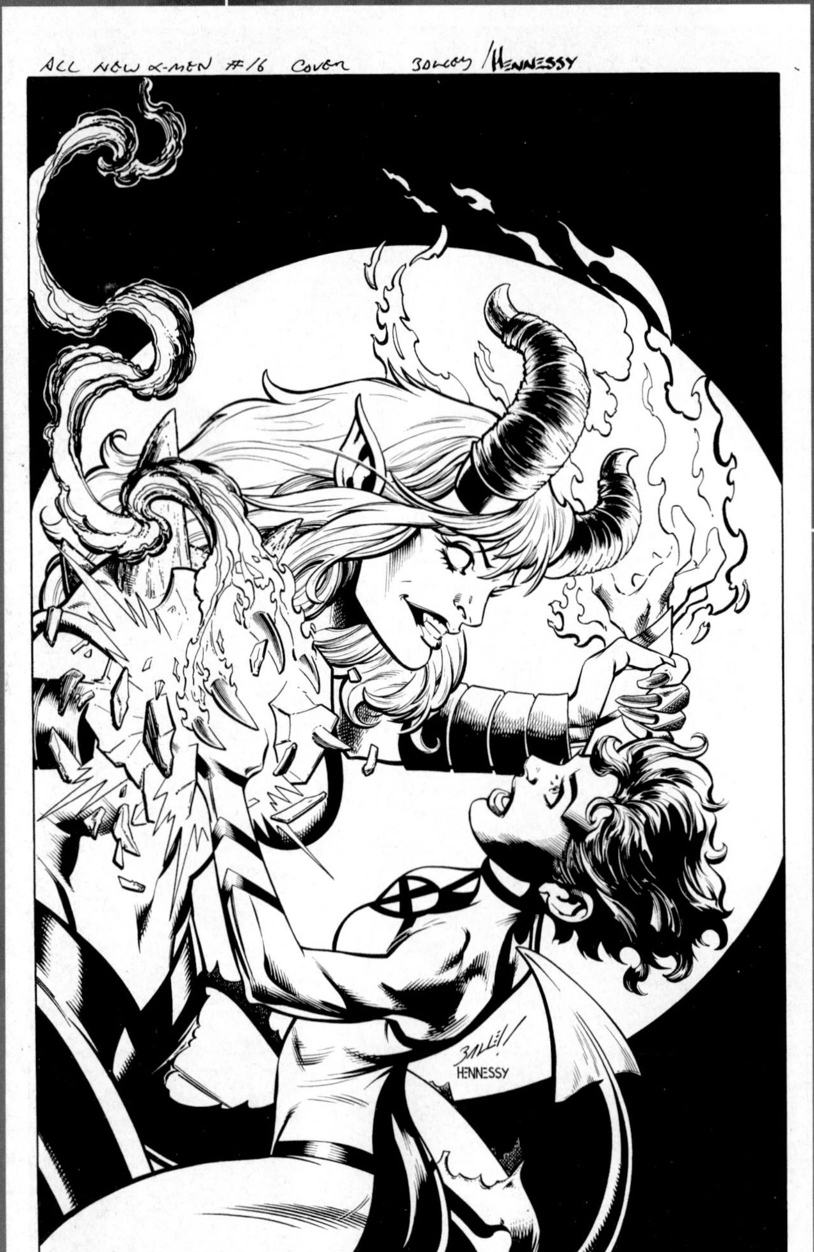
ALL NEW X-MEN #16 COVER
HENNESSY

◀ INKS

#16 COVER PROCESS
BY **MARK BAGLEY,**
ANDREW HENNESSY
& **NOLAN WOODARD**

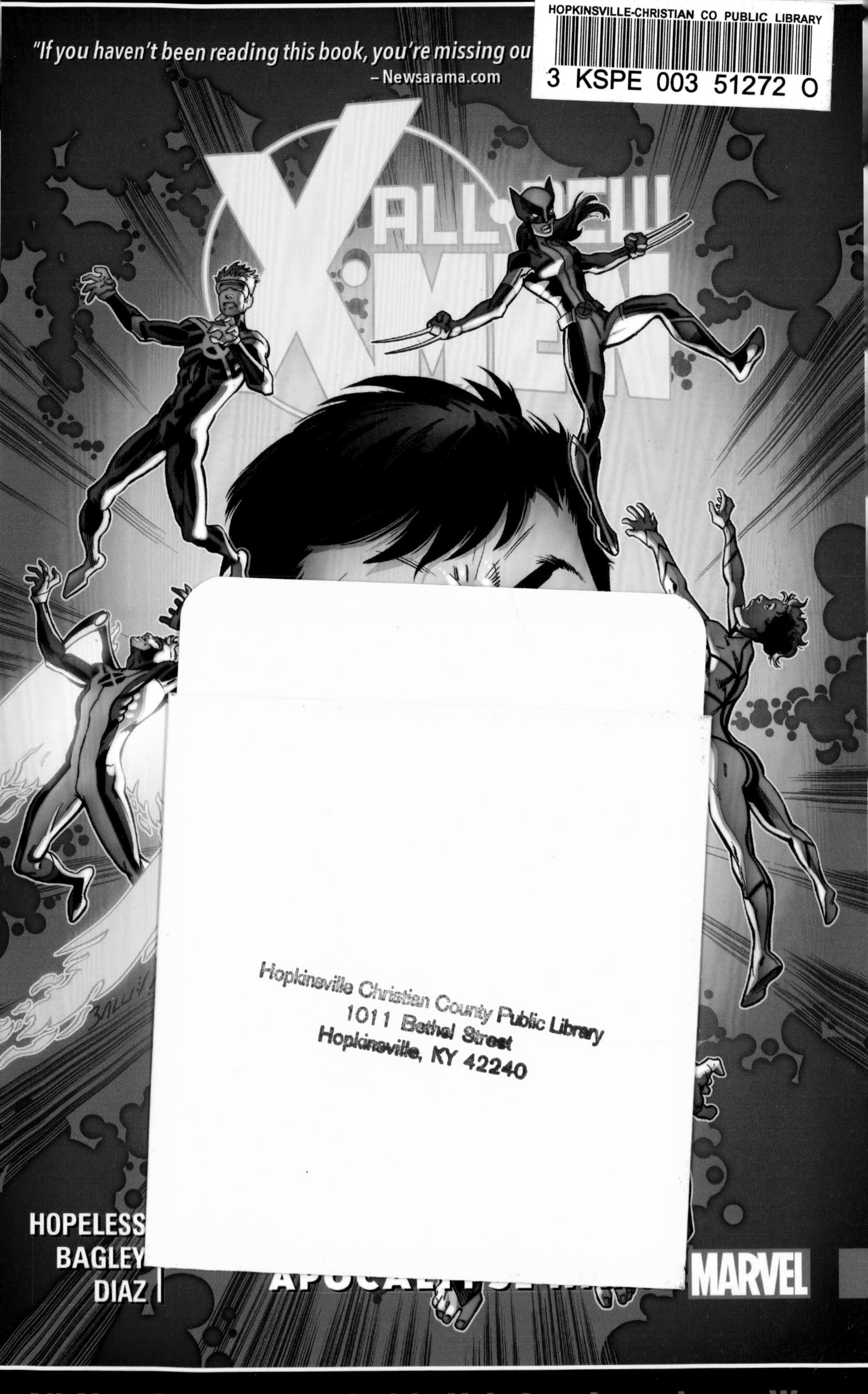
"If you haven't been reading this book, you're missing ou
– Newsarama.com
ALL-NEW X-MEN
HOPELESS
BAGLEY
DIAZ
MARVEL

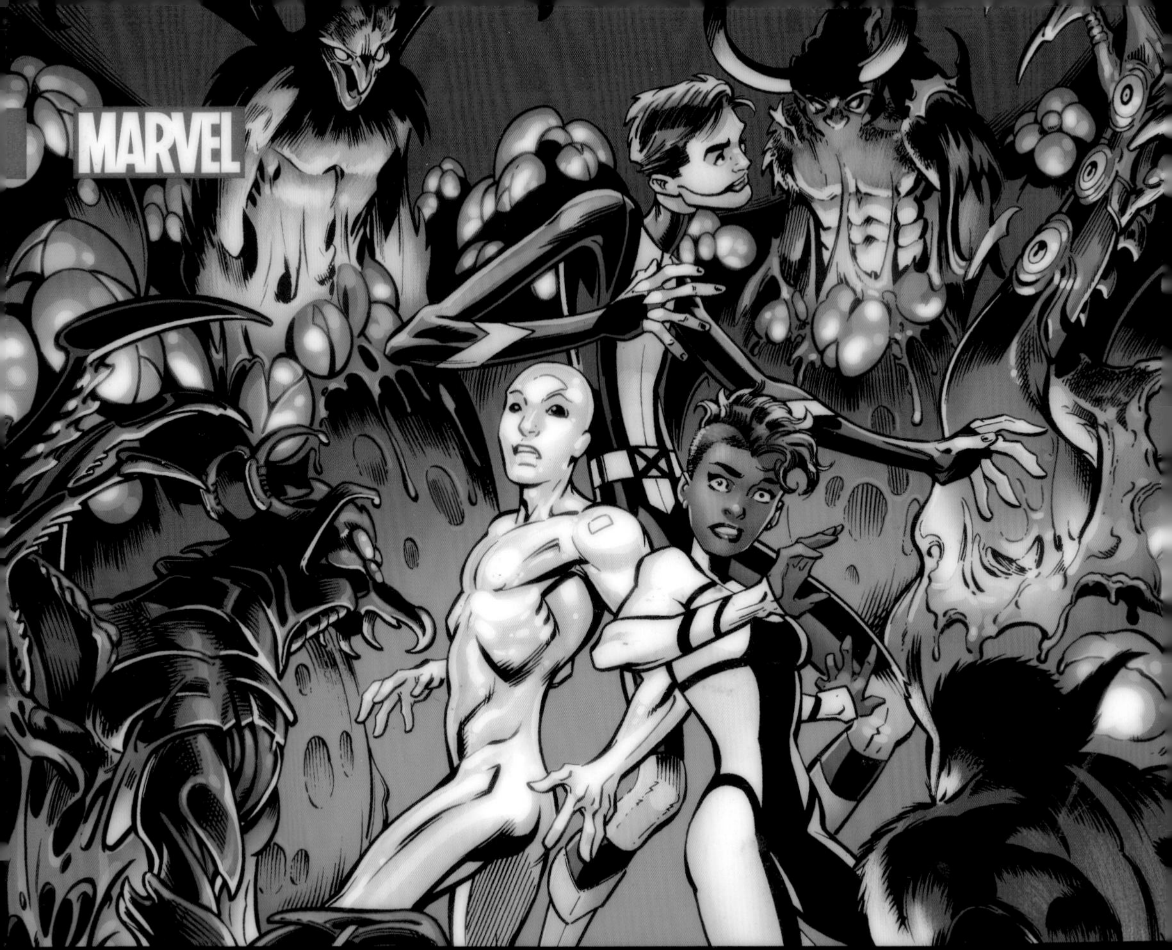
MARVEL

"A high point for Dennis Hopeless and Mark Bagley's run so far." – IGN.com

LOVE AND DEMONS –

THE X-MEN FACE NEW HELLISH DESTINIES!

ONE IS A TIME-DISPLACED, cosmically powered mutant. The other is a homicidal clone struggling to fulfill her dead mentor's legacy. But who says two crazy kids like Angel and Wolverine can't make their relationship work? Meanwhile, another romance will put one member at odds with the rest of the team! The X-Men spend so much time worrying about hate and fear — but love sure hurts, too! So does the Terrigen Mist — so much so that it spells doom for their entire species! But can the same be said for Genesis? Will he continue to fight his destiny as the maniacal villain Apocalypse — or surrender to it? Plus: A wheelchair-bound Cyclops plays out his own version of *Rear Window* with a suspicious-looking Beast, and the Goblin Queen's return forces the team members to confront their demons — literally!

COLLECTING ***ALL-NEW X-MEN (2015)*** **#12-16** – BY DENNIS HOPELESS, MARK BAGLEY, ANDREW HENNESSY AND NOLAN WOODARD.

T+

ISBN 978-1-302-90291-9
51599
9 781302 902919
$15.99 US $20.99 CAN
MARVEL.COM

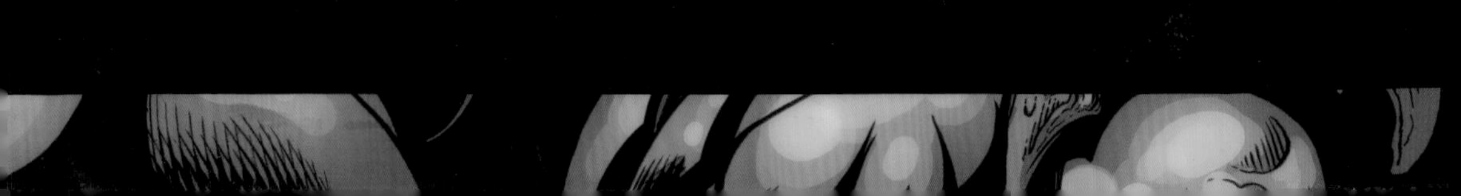

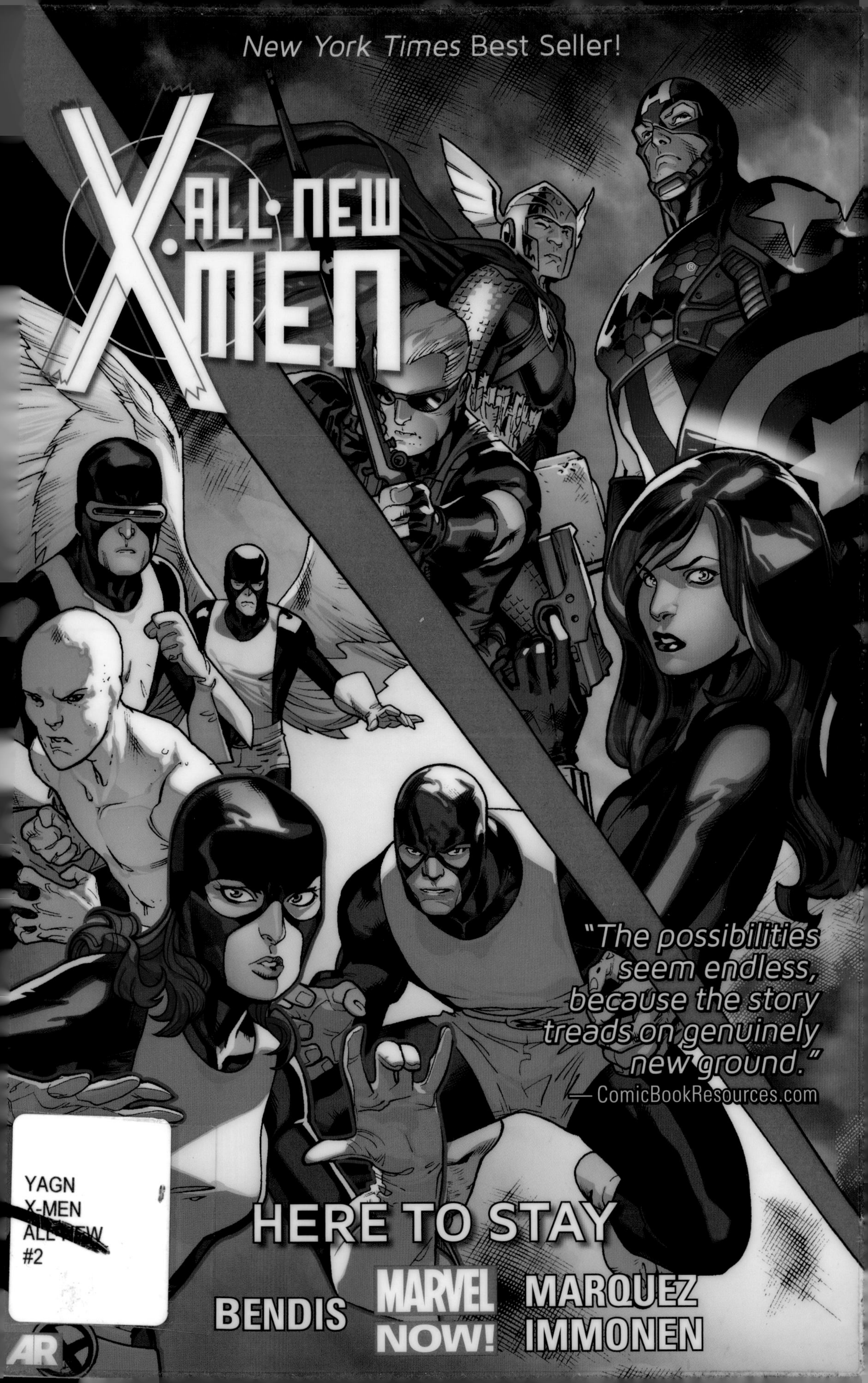

New York Times Best Seller!
ALL-NEW X-MEN
"The possibilities seem endless, because the story treads on genuinely new ground."
— ComicBookResources.com
HERE TO STAY
BENDIS
MARVEL NOW!
MARQUEZ
IMMONEN
AR

Collected Editions

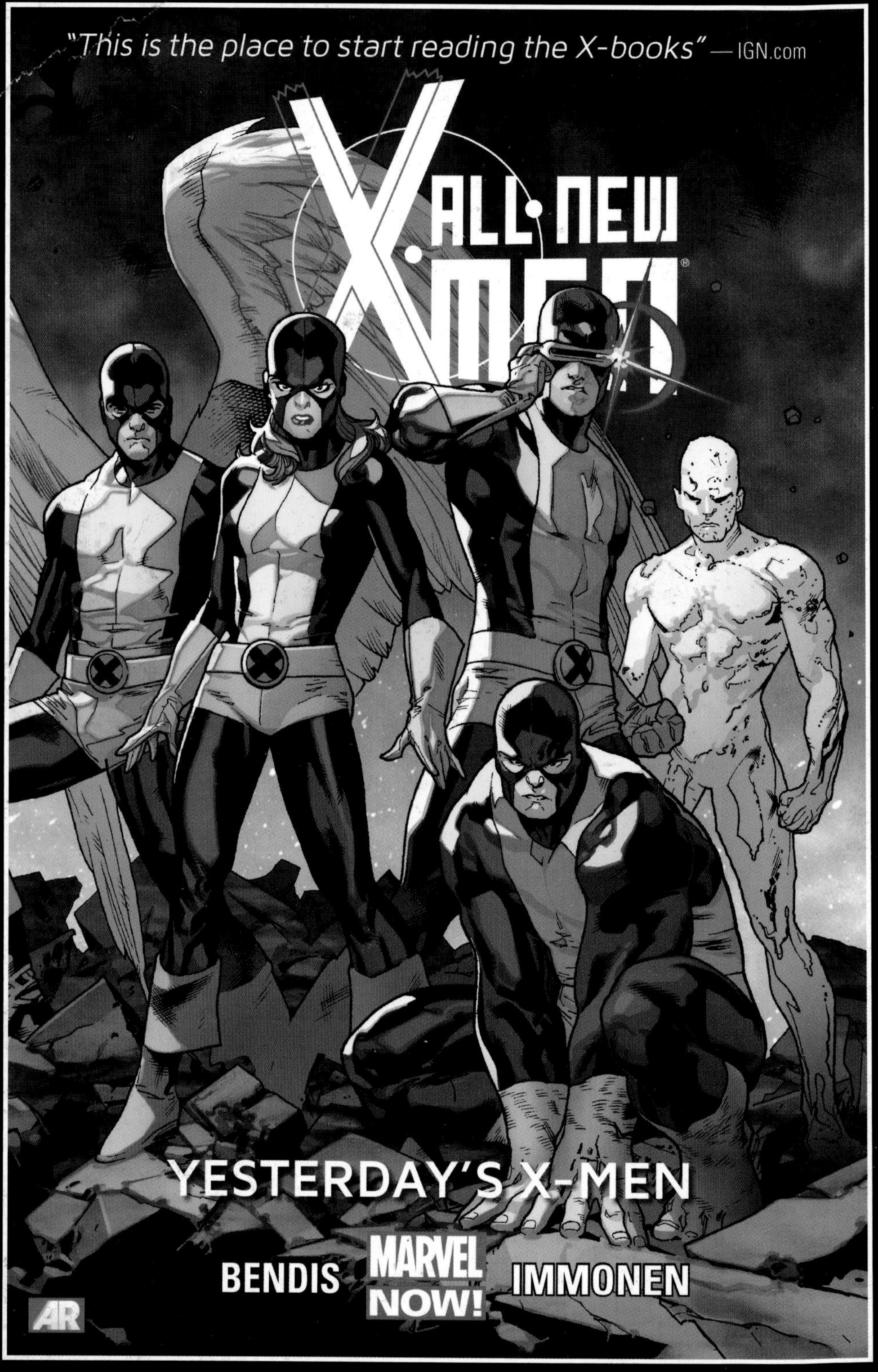
"This is the place to start reading the X-books" — IGN.com
ALL-NEW X-MEN
YESTERDAY'S X-MEN
BENDIS
MARVEL NOW!
IMMONEN
AR

All-New X-Men Vol. 1: Yesterday's X-Men

ISBN # 978-0-7851-6637-5